HOLLYWOOD AND EUROPE

HOLLYWOOD AND EUROPE

Economics, Culture, National Identity: 1945–95

Edited by Geoffrey Nowell-Smith
and Steven Ricci

 Publishing

UCLA Film and Television Archive Studies in History,
Criticism and Theory

First published in 1998 by the
British Film Institute
21 Stephen Street, London W1P 2LN

The British Film Institute is the UK national agency with responsibility for encouraging the
arts of film and television and conserving them in the national interest.

Published in association with the UCLA Film and Television Archive

British Library Cataloguing-in-Publication Data
A catalogue record for this book is available from the British Library

ISBN 0–85170–596–0 hardback
      0–85170–597–9 paperback

Cover designed by Swerlybird Art & Design

Typeset by Fakenham Photosetting Limited, Fakenham, Norfolk

Printed in Great Britain by St Edmundsbury Press, Bury St Edmunds, Suffolk

Contents

Acknowledgments

Many people were involved in planning, organising and participating in the con-ferences out of which this volume arose. We should like to acknowledge in par-ticular the roles of Colin MacCabe of the British Film Institute and Michael Friend of the Academy of Motion Picture Arts and Sciences, with whom the idea for the conferences originated. Besides the contributors to the book, valued con-tributions to the conferences were made by Gian Piero Brunetta, Michael Friend, Fritz Göttler, James Hay, Anne Jäckel, Colin MacCabe, Pierre Sorlin, Ginette Vincendeau and Paul Willemen. The presence of distinguished scholars from France and Germany at the London conference was made possible by the gen-erosity of the French Embassy and the Goethe Institute, London. At the British end we should also like to thank Kate Stables, Ed Buscombe and Roma Gibson at BFI Research, and Clyde Jeavons and Anne Fleming at the National Film Archive. And in Los Angeles: Luana Almares, Andrea Kalas, Lou Ellen Kramer, Robert Rosen and Geoffrey Stier, all of the UCLA Film and Television Archive, and Ed Carter and Bruce Davis of the Academy of Motion Picture Arts and Sciences.

Preface

In 1993 a complex set of issues regarding moving image culture became the chief stumbling block to the successful renegotiation of the General Agreement on Tariffs and Trade (GATT). The importance of film and television in this 'Uruguay round' of trade talks was also signalled by the dramatic extension of the negotiations into the public sphere. An international debate on the topic was played out in editorial exchanges between a wide range of culture ministers, industry leaders, intellectuals and film-makers. Well beyond the traditional confines of diplomatic missions and trade negotiation, heated discussions took place at numerous film festivals and at industry meetings. Moreover, the entire debate was marked by a remarkable mixing of concerns about culture on the one hand and disputes over economic policy and free trade on the other.

It was in this context that the British Film Institute and the UCLA Film and Television Archive organised a pair of study conferences on the relationship between Hollywood and European cinemas. Our meetings gathered together media scholars from around the world in an attempt to disentangle these issues by reviewing them from a broader historical perspective. The first conference was held in late 1993 at the British Film Institute in London. The second was held one year later in Los Angeles and was co-hosted by the UCLA Film and Television Archive and the Academy of Motion Picture Arts and Sciences. The chapters in this volume are a selection from papers presented at these two events.

There were, and are, other reasons for which media institutions and archives seek to engage in these issues which only apparently belong to the domain of trade representatives and the diplomatic corps. To begin with, one of our basic missions is to collect, preserve and exhibit our national cinematic heritages. But in a rapidly globalising media environment – populated as much by multinational media conglomerates as by multiple-nation feature film co-productions – the coherent identification of any single, stand-alone national heritage is becoming increasingly difficult. And when we consider that the experience of cinemagoers in most countries has almost always meant seeing more foreign films than those actually produced nationally, the notion of a hermetically sealed national cinema identity is virtually impossible to sustain.

The key exception to this condition is of course the United States, where the Hollywood film industry has long been able to control an extraordinary share of its internal marketplace. But here too, the exchanges between Hollywood and the international cinema scene are long-standing and deeply rooted. During the formation of classical Hollywood cinema, many of its key architects were in fact European émigrés – Lubitsch, Dieterle, Lang, Hitchcock, Sirk, to name but a few. More recently, many of Hollywood's finest contemporary directors – Scorsese,

Altman, Coppola and others – have often turned to Europe, to the French New Wave, Italian neo-realism and the New German Cinemas for a source of inspiration and influence. At least at the level of creative expression, the relationship between these two continents has always been, to say the very least, a two-way street.

The fluid relationship between creative communities and the shared experience of many national audiences are only a few of the circumstances that make discussions of cinema-related market issues so very complex. We haven't even begun to consider, for example, the fundamental differences between the European and the American conceptualisations of intellectual property – i.e. of artists' rights or *droit d'auteur* versus legal copyright. When we add into the mix the evolutionary changes which the arrival of digital technologies will bring to the international landscape of media production, distribution and exhibition, we can readily see how our first two study conferences only mark a modest beginning for the research and discussion which need to be pursued.

As befits its dual origin in conferences held in London and in Los Angeles, the present volume is, on the one hand, a BFI book but also, on the other hand, part of the UCLA Film and Television Archive Studies in History, Criticism and Theory. This series of scholarly publications grows out of archive-based research initiatives and also includes *Before the Nickelodeon: Edwin S. Porter and the Edison Manufacturing Company* (published by University of California Press) and *The Mexican Cinema Project* (published by University of Texas Press).

Steven Ricci
Los Angeles, April 1998

Introduction

Geoffrey Nowell-Smith

The theme of this book is the relationship of European cinema to Hollywood since 1945. This relationship is a dual one. On the one hand it is economic. The American film industry is a massive exporter, and at various times in the past fifty years the share of box-office acquired by Hollywood has ranged from 30 per cent to 80 per cent in the majority of European markets, while European exports to America have never captured more than an insignificant share of the market in the US. But on the other hand it is also cultural, and here the traffic has been two-way. European audiences have eagerly lapped up the imagery and values present in American movies and other culture goods (TV programmes, rock music, etc.) and European film-makers have taken many lessons from Hollywood in film style, content and narrative economy. But the American cinema also draws heavily on European cultural models. Many of the greatest Hollywood film-makers are émi-grés from Europe (Hitchcock, Lang, Curtiz, Preminger), as are stars from Greta Garbo and Bela Lugosi to Arnold Schwarzenegger and Jean-Claude van Damme. Recent film-makers, from Scorsese to Tarantino, owe and acknowledge a debt to European films seen on the campus circuit or late-night TV, ranging from the lush melodramas of Powell and Pressburger to the playful use of (American) genres in the early films of Godard.

Both aspects of the relationship are of great importance both in their own right and as part of a wider context. The American economy, its dominance in manu-facturing challenged by Far Eastern and other competitors, is increasingly dependent on its ability to sustain a leading role in a sphere of activities that range from bio-technology to computer software to telecommunications to the produc-tion and delivery of culture-goods such as TV programmes, movies and popular music. When the GATT negotiations were threatened with collapse at the end of 1993, the issues all had to do with America's insistence on maintaining its supremacy in these areas, and it was over the cinema that the battle took its most dramatic form, since cinema is the spearhead of American efforts to dominate the media and communications market in general. Europe's (and the world's) accep-tance of the Hollywood movie as the model for spectacular entertainment is the symbolic front for the acceptance of a slew of other products that ride upon its back. If the cinema on its own is no longer the economic force it was in the heyday of Hollywood between 1930 and 1960, it remains the central element in a much larger design.

The cultural aspect is also important. To watch an American movie is not like buying just any product that one discovers upon reading the label to have been

1

made in the USA. It is (or can be seen as) an act of buying into a distinct set of cultural values. Since the beginning of the century a host of voices have been raised in Europe deploring (though occasionally welcoming) the Americanisation of European culture. Particularly deplored have been American popular music (alternately loud and rhythmically insistent or slushy and harmonically insipid), clothing (alternately shapeless or shamefully body-accentuating), pulp fiction (monotonously crude and violent), and of course movies (violent, inartistic and alternately too reticent or too explicit about sex). It has also been suspected (not without cause) that the enjoyment of American culture-goods leads inexorably to the consumption of other American goods, or goods marketed by American companies, such as McDonald's hamburgers. (The latest expression of shock-horror came in a newspaper report in Britain in August 1995 that more school-children could identify the McDonald's M-shaped arches than the cross outside the local church.) American conquest of the cultural and related markets has been seen as a threat (though sometimes as a rejuvenation) to the native cultures of Europe, whether globally or in their regional peculiarities. Although other forms of culture-goods are similarly indicted, it is again the movies which, rightly or wrongly, are at the forefront of concern.

There is a lot of rhetoric surrounding these issues. There is a purely economic rhetoric, mainly on the American side, which presents the issue as solely one of free markets and consumer choice. And there is a culturalist rhetoric, mainly on the European side, which talks of cultural identities, of language as the soul of a nation, of the right to national self-expression, of resistance to alien cultural hegemony, and so on. These one-sided rhetorics are misleading in many ways: first because they can give the impression that the issue is only economic, or only cultural, when in fact the two are intimately inter-connected; second because they pose the issues antagonistically, as if the cultures and economies in question were always and exclusively locked into cut-throat competition and struggle, whereas there is and always has been a space for co-operation, exchange, plurality and symbiosis; and third because they reduce questions to do with modernity in general and of complex conflicting patterns of consumption, culture and lifestyle to an opposition between two continents, as if everything new and threatening emanated from America and everything old and traditional was a uniquely European heritage. Worst of all the rhetorics, perhaps, is the one replete with sexual metaphor, with its talk (on the one side) of market penetration and (on the other) of cultural rape. What this book hopes to show is that, however uneven the relationship has been or is becoming, it can also be seen as one of two (or more) economies and two (or more) cultures androgynously intertwined.

This is not to say that there is no cause for concern. There is indeed a case for arguing that the sometimes competitive, sometimes symbiotic relationship that has prevailed for the past fifty years is in danger of breaking down and that the state of affairs revealed during the GATT negotiations is one with serious – if not apocalyptic – implications for both industry and culture, both in Europe and in North America. First, however, the evidence must be reviewed.

I

Statistics vary, and in any case are not always reliable, but there is no doubt about their general drift. According to figures compiled by BIPE Conseil in Paris, the American share of the European (EU) film market has risen from just under 50 per cent in the early 1980s to over 70 per cent in the 1990s.[1] The shift is most dramatic in Europe's premier film-producing countries, France and Italy. In France the share of the market held by indigenous films has dropped from 47 per cent in 1980 to 32 per cent in 1994, while the American share has risen from 35 per cent to 58 per cent. Comparable figures for Italy show the indigenous share dropping from 43 per cent to a measly 15 per cent, the lowest figure since 1945, and the American share rising to 73 per cent. Of major countries, only Britain has to some extent bucked the general trend. Over the same period (again according to BIPE) the indigenous share has gone up (from 15 per cent to 20 per cent) while the American share has dropped from 80 per cent to a still massive 75 per cent. Meanwhile the share taken by films which are neither American nor indigenous but come from other European or non-European countries has also tended to fall: in France it stood at 18 per cent in 1980, rising fractionally to 20 per cent in 1994; in Italy it fell from 22 per cent to 11 per cent; in Britain it has remained more or less steady at something under 5 per cent, while in the EU as a whole it has dropped from an average of 27 per cent to 11 per cent over the same period.

Alarming though these figures are to defenders of Europe's film industries and European culture in general, it has to be said that there is nothing dramatically new about them. American films have dominated the European market since the end of the First World War. They have done so for a variety of reasons, ranging from more efficient business practices to sheer popular appeal. In the market free-for-all of the early 1920s (not exactly the same as a 'free market' and certainly not the 'level playing field' beloved of New Right ideologues), American films seized over 50 per cent of the market in a number of European countries and over 80 per cent in Britain and in Italy where a once flourishing industry was nearly destroyed by the competition.

If the European industries subsequently recovered some of their lost market share, this was due to a multiplicity of factors, most of which are unrepeatable. The coming of sound at the end of the 1920s created a demand for movies spoken in the audience's native language, which the American industry (until the institution of dubbing in the mid-1930s) could not easily supply. The introduction of protectionist measures, beginning in the mid-1920s, also helped to stem the tide of imports, while Fascism and then the Second World War were to close almost all European markets to Hollywood from the mid-1930s onwards. Germany was the first to bring down the barriers, followed by Italy which in 1938 provoked a trade war leading to the withdrawal of the Hollywood majors from the Italian market. Then, as Czechoslovakia, Poland, Belgium, the Netherlands, Denmark, Norway and France succumbed to the German blitzkrieg, after 1940 Britain became Hollywood's sole major market in Europe, a state of affairs which continued until 1945.

It is in fact with 1945 that the story traced in this book begins. It is the midway point in the first century of cinema in Europe (if we take the starting date to be the Skladanowskys' first film screenings in Berlin in the summer of 1895 and those of the Lumières in Paris later that year). It is also the year in which the liberation of Europe from Fascism and German occupation led to the division of the continent into its two Cold War components and the institution in the western half of a new democratic order one of whose pillars was the free-trade regime inaugurated by the first General Agreement on Tariffs and Trades (GATT) in 1947. For the cinema, as in other aspects of life, 1945 marks a new beginning. American films returned to European screens, under a new regime which in intention at least was far less protectionist than the old. After a shaky start, however, European cinema revived, profiting not only from such protection as was allowed under the dispensations put in place in the various countries in the late 1940s but also from confidence on the part of producers and rising popular demand. European films also found a place in the American market, beginning with the prodigious (and unexpected) success in 1945–6 of Rossellini's neo-realist classic *Rome Open City*, and their place in American cultural life was ratified by the institution after the war of an Academy Award for Best Foreign Film.

The conditions under which European cinemas were able to thrive were, however, precarious. Without exception, all governments, under pressure from industrial and cultural lobbies, negotiated some form of protection, to which the Americans (against whom the protection was aimed) reluctantly agreed. Before the war the most common form of protection had been the so-called contingent system, a numerical limitation on the number of imported (i.e. American) films allowed into the country in any given year. This being now outlawed, France and Italy argued for, and obtained, a system of screen quotas, by which exhibitors would be forced to allocate a certain number of weeks in each quarter-year to showing indigenous films. Originally introduced as a temporary measure to give time for the industries to rebuild after the war, screen quotas remained in force for many years and it was over the retention of a residue of the screen-quota system that the French and the Americans were to come to blows in 1993. In Britain, meanwhile, where the main protectionist measure in the pre-war period had been a quota system, the post-war Labour government opted instead for a levy on exhibition whose proceeds were recirculated to British producers – a system which lasted until the early 1980s.

The measures instituted in the post-war years were mainly economic in nature. They set out to protect jobs and capital investments in an industry which, it was felt, could not survive against unrestricted competition from an American product whose superiority in the marketplace was acknowledged, though never analysed. At the level at which they were designed to operate they were certainly useful, and in the early years possibly even necessary. They gave a breathing space for the revival of industries which – if the experience of what happened after the previous world war is any guide –would have been hard put to re-establish themselves. Depending on the system chosen, they gave room both for potentially unpopular experiment and for competition in the popular marketplace, for native comedy as opposed to American comedy, for home-produced inexpensive spectaculars as against the generally more lavish American ones, and (in the 1960s) for successful rivals to American Westerns and horror films. As such, it can be argued, they were both culturally and economically productive. In general, too, the greater the protection, the better the results.

But protectionism was not universally welcomed. It was not popular with exhibitors in France and Italy, who resented the loss of freedom to programme the films which, in their judgment, the public wanted to see. It was even less popular with exhibitors in Britain, who saw the levy (correctly) as a form of taxation imposed on them for the sake of a production sector which then failed to deliver the goods. It is also the case that neither screen quotas nor levies had any necessary cultural component. The criteria for what constituted an indigenous film were all economic; they had to do with the nature of the company producing the film and the proportion of labour input from indigenous sources. Undoubtedly, many producers saw themselves as being in business to make films which stood or fell by their national cultural content: Michael Balcon, with his aim to make films projecting Britain and the British character, is an obvious example. There is also a reasonable presumption to be made that, if (say) British actors had to be employed to make a film qualify as British, then British roles would be created for them to play and British settings devised to play them in (though the experience of the Italian and, even more, the German Western shows that such a presumption can be a risky one). With the exception of France, however, where the qualifying criteria included a specification that the film had to be a work of French expression (i.e. in the French language), cultural criteria were not normally written into the legislation, and there was no guarantee that protection would be used to promote national (or any other) cultural objectives. What the cinemas of Europe should be like (it is too early to speak of anything so grandiose as 'European cinema') was, as far as the post-war legislators were concerned, an open and – it would appear – unimportant question.

If there were a cultural issue around which, in 1945 itself, a large measure of agreement existed, it was that the new cinema in Europe should be democratic and the cinema should never again be allowed to be used, as it had been in Nazi Germany and to a lesser extent Fascist Italy, as an instrument of totalitarian ideology. Over this question it was the Americans who took the lead. Following the Allied combat troops into Italy and France came the spiritual crusaders of the Psychological Warfare Branch (PWB), armed not with guns but with movies, mostly documentaries but also a handful of features, designed to re-educate the peoples of formerly Fascist and occupied Europe about the virtues of democracy. These were in many cases the first recent American films to have been seen in Europe since 1940. Not only the invading British and Americans, but the continental Europeans themselves took part in this effort at re-education, which is the motivating force behind Jean Grémillon's *Le 6 juin, à l'aube* ('On June 6th, at dawn', 1945), about the Normandy landings, as well as Humphrey Jennings's *A Defeated People* (1946) and many other documentaries. The same impulse is present in the granting of American funds for the making of Rossellini's *Paisà* (1946) and in the Russians' encouragement of Wolfgang Staudte's *The Murderers are among Us*, made in the former Ufa studios in the same year.

When applied to industrial policy, however, this well-meaning anti-Fascism revealed a different, less attractive face. The 'expert' component on the Allied Control Commissions operating in the liberated countries was provided by film industry execs, often in military uniform and with military rank. It soon became clear that, for many on the American side, preventing the resurgence of antidemocratic film industries was simply a cover for obstructing the revival of any film industry at all. In Italy the chairman of the Film Commission, Admiral Stone, began a meeting by roundly declaring that Italy, as a rural and former Fascist country, did not need a film industry and should not be allowed to have one.[2] His fellow Americans concurred and it was left to the British representatives on the Commission, who included Alexander Mackendrick and Korda's close colleague Stephen Pallos, to denounce the manoeuvre for what it was.

The irony of the situation was that the immediate beneficiaries of the American attitude were the neo-realists, protagonists of an industrially minor but culturally significant cinema whose politics were at odds with the long-term aims of American policy towards Europe. Neo-realism signalled an affirmation by Italian film-makers that they could create a cinema whose aesthetic (and political) assumptions were opposed in equal measure to those of Hollywood and of Italy's own cinema in the Fascist period. But neo-realist films, although popular in aspiration, were not popular at the box-office. *Rome Open City* was a box-office success, but it was released in Italy before the Americans had been able to negotiate the return of Hollywood movies to Italian screens and when the Italian film industry was in disarray, with the Cinecittà studios disbanded and in use as a transit camp for refugees. Thereafter neo-realism had to compete first with a five-year backlog of American films being released on to the Italian market and then with a resurgent Italian commercial film industry.

Faced with this double-sided competition, neo-realism revealed its limitations as popular cinema. Although neo-realist films continued to win awards (De Sica and Zavattini's *Bicycle Thieves* was voted best film of all time by an international critics' poll in *Sight and Sound* in 1952) and carved out for themselves a market niche in export markets, they failed to find such a niche at home. Neo-realist films which did well at the box-office tended to be those which traded on the popularity of stars such as Anna Magnani or achieved a successful compromise with American genre models (as with De Santis's *Bitter Rice*, starring Raf Vallone and the young Silvana Mangano, in 1949). Meanwhile the Hollywood companies re-established the grip on distribution that they had lost in 1938, forcing the Italian industry to adopt entirely new strategies in order to maintain its share of the market. These new strategies were to prove harbingers of what was to become a crisis of the traditional notion of a national cinema.

II

André Malraux once described the cinema as *par ailleurs* ('also, moreover') an industry. He was wrong. The cinema is an industry through and through. The determining role of industrial factors has meant that national cinemas have always been principally defined economically, as the product of national industries, produced with national resources, and traded in a national currency. Unlike national literatures, which are defined in the first instance by language, their cultural nature has always been a secondary and derivative characteristic, which has varied in importance according to circumstances. Meanwhile, because of the over-determination of all issues concerning the cultural characteristics of cinema by economic considerations, the question of what the cinema should be like at any given place or time has almost always been cast in national terms. 'National cinemas' (that is, national cinema industries) have struggled for their place in the market against foreign (mostly American) competition, while 'new cinemas' (Free Cinema, the *nouvelle vague*, the *junges deutsches Kino*) have attempted to assert their place in relation to the national mainstream. With rare exceptions, the argument in favour of a cinema that would be different has been forced to take the direction of a correspondence with national needs, that is to say needs which can be construed as those of either a national economy or a national culture. Cultures which are international or sub-national (e.g. regional, ethnic, or class- or gender-specific) have not, on the whole, been part of the agenda.

But not everything can be crammed into the national agenda, whether economic ('our' balance of payments) or cultural ('our' culture). Cinema has also strained against the imposed boundaries of national economies and national cultures. In its first years the cinema operated across any frontiers that money could pass through. A stabilisation into national formations took place during the First World War, when the French companies lost control of the international market, and after it, when the European economies were reconstructing in the face of American competition. But throughout the 1920s numerous attempts were made at co-production between Britain and Holland, Germany and Britain (Hitchcock's *The Mountain Eagle*), Germany and France (Renoir's *Nana*), and other combinations. The coming of sound threatened to push the cinema back within national boundaries (at least to the extent that these coincided with linguistic ones), but the pressure to consolidate the market remained and the early sound years saw the emergence of multilingual films, produced by European consortia in competition (and sometimes collaboration) with those produced by Hollywood companies. The institution of dubbing around 1934 made multilingual production unnecessary, but co-production continued. Meanwhile the influx of European émigrés and exiles to Hollywood and the emigration within Europe of first Russian and then German artists helped to keep the medium international at a cultural level.

Behind these moves towards internationalisation there was, of course, always an economic rationale. But it tended to be the economics of producers, looking to increase their own share of the international market, rather than of governments. Politics entered at two levels. On the one hand much of the emigration of artists was involuntary, and was to become even more so in 1939 when Jewish artists throughout Europe had no choice but to escape or go into hiding. And on the other hand there is evidence of a concerted strategy between the American government and the Motion Picture Export Association of America to promote the export of American movies not only as earners of foreign currency but as bearers of the American flag. European governments, however, did not respond with a correspondingly aggressive strategy, preferring instead to protect themselves against all comers: that is to say, against Hollywood in particular but against other European countries as a side-effect.

The changes that took place after the war were of two kinds, corresponding to two different sets of economic, political and cultural priorities. On the one hand there were moves, tentative at first, then increasingly systematic, to turn (western) Europe into a single trading zone (with consequent effects on the notion of

'European' culture). And on the other hand there was the lure of America, the single most powerful nation in the world and in particular the world's largest film exporter with a massive, lucrative, and inwardly turned domestic market. Once again there was a move by producers to pool resources and bypass protectionism. This time, however, it received more active support in political circles, or at least among those politicians – mostly of a Christian Democrat and Atlanticist persuasion – who were interested in building a united Europe as both partner and competitor with the United States. Significantly – as Jean-Pierre Jeancolas relates in his chapter in this volume – it was Jean Monnet, the architect of what was to become the European Union, rather than Léon Blum, who actually formulated what became known as the Blum–Byrnes Agreement on the regulation of competition between the French and American film industries immediately after the war. Monnet's strategy envisaged not only protection for European industry but increasing co-operation among the European partners of the North Atlantic alliance, and it was in pursuance of this strategy that European governments began at the end of the 1940s to prospect co-production agreements for cinema, of which the first to be effective was that between France and Italy. These new agreements differed from previous, more ad hoc arrangements between producers in that they laid down conditions which, if fulfilled, enabled films to benefit from 'home market' protection in both or all the co-producing countries.

The new agreements coming into force from 1950 onwards had a dramatic effect on the pattern of production, initially in Italy and France, but then increasingly in other countries. In 1949 there were sixty-six Italian films released on the home market, out of which three were co-productions – one with France, one with Britain, and one with Spain. In addition there were four films in which Italian producers had a minority stake, the majority producer being variously American, British, Austrian and French. During the 1950s the proportion of co-productions steadily increased, while the choice of partners narrowed. At the end of the decade, in 1959, total Italian production had nearly doubled, and out of the 132 Italian films released that year twenty-nine were co-productions with France, while there were also thirty-seven films in which Italian producers had a minority stake, the majority producer of thirty-four of them being French. Needless to say, many of these so-called co-productions were so in name only, but quite a significant number are interesting attempts at cultural syncretism, the most famous perhaps being the 'Don Camillo' series in which the French comic Fernandel plays the eponymous priest opposite Gino Cervi in the role of the Communist village mayor Peppone. Other co-productions of the 1950s include two of Max Ophuls's late masterpieces, *Madame de . . .* (1953) in which a now silver-haired Vittorio De Sica reverts to the society charmer role of his 1930s comedies, and *Lola Montès* (1955), shot in Germany but with French majority participation, and starring Martine Carole, Oskar Werner and that most cosmopolitan of all actors, Peter Ustinov.

Contemporary with the move towards European co-production, however, producers in various European countries, notably Italy and Britain, began in the post-war years to explore various forms of co-operation and collaboration with American companies. How to break into the lucrative American market had always been a preoccupation of European film-makers. Korda had attempted it in the 1930s and scored a singular success with *The Private Life of Henry VIII*, a heritage movie *avant la lettre* released in the US by United Artists. It was Korda again who teamed up with Selznick in 1949 to make *The Third Man*. But even more it was the Rank organisation which after the war attempted by various means to make America, rather than Europe or even the Commonwealth, its main export target. Overall, Rank's efforts were a failure (and a major contributor to the crisis which was to engulf the organisation in the late 1950s), but they were not without individual successes, such as that of Powell and Pressburger's *The Red Shoes* (1948) which, after a slow start, went on to enthuse middle America with its distinctively European (rather than merely British) set of cultural values.

More prophetic from an industrial point of view was what happened in Italy. Parallel with the officially sponsored policy of European co-production, Italian entrepreneurs and producers in the 1950s not only attempted to export Italian films to the United States but opened up film-making facilities to American studios and independent producers. An early portent of what was to come was provided by Rossellini's ill-starred attempt with *Stromboli* in 1950 to use the popular and cosmopolitan Ingrid Bergman as a bait to interest RKO in the mainstream releasing of a decidedly un-American product. But more important industrially were the films aimed at worldwide markets made in Italy in the 1950s by both American and Italian companies, which briefly earned for Cinecittà and other Italian studios the title 'Hollywood on Tiber'. The crude reason behind this development was that it enabled the American companies to mop up profits earned in the Italian market and which they could not repatriate, by encouraging reinvestment in offshore production at low cost; but Italian producers also saw it as a chance to insert themselves into the world market by making films for release through the American majors. The careers of two of Italy's most flamboyant producers, Carlo Ponti and Dino De Laurentiis, were to take off from this propitious but precarious launchpad.

Underlying both intra-European and Euro-American co-operation from the 1950s onwards was a recognition that the individual markets of European countries were too small to support viable national film industries.[3] This was already the case in the early post-war years, when the markets were still expanding. But as first the British and then the various continental European markets began to contract under the impact of television and other leisure alternatives, the need for co-operative strategies became even more pressing. Faced with the challenge of television, the European film industries at first reacted more or less as Hollywood itself had done in the 1940s and early 1950s, by making films more spectacular and clearly differentiated from television. But whereas in America the Hollywood studios were able to adapt to the demand for television-oriented production by turning over facilities to the making of TV films and series for the networks, in Europe the publicly owned broadcasters were less open to offers of product from film companies and the relationship between cinema and television industries remained competitive throughout the 1950s, to the detriment of the former. Television grew inexorably and – with an equal inevitability, though the effect was slow to make itself felt – cinema shrank. For a while it maintained its rivalry with the new medium. Then, with some reluctance, it entered into co-operation. And it has now entered into a state of effective subordination.

III

Even in 1997, flags continue to be waved in support of the idea of European national cinemas, but they flutter feebly and look increasingly threadbare. Up to about 1970, indeed, the dream was not an impossible one. A number of strategies were pursued and met with a modest success. But any idea that Europe's cinemas could be independent of each other, boldly competitive with Hollywood, and resistant to the onset of television was always utopian. The current state of European cinema is one of a three-fold dependence. It is first of all dependent on television (and video) to the extent that virtually no film can be made nowadays without either a television participation or a guaranteed pre-sale to a TV network and/or a video distributor. Second, it is dependent on co-production between European countries, a practice which from its modest beginnings in the 1950s has now become an almost universal norm. And third, it is dependent on Hollywood. This third dependence is less obvious, since it is experienced not at the level of production but at that of distribution and competition for market share. TV and co-production deals are not enough to make European cinema a self-sufficient European entity. Many European films do enter the market without directly encountering the American-controlled sector of the industry. Production finance for them is raised from European sources, and there exist European-owned releasing mechanisms. But the market in which they find their slots is one which is shaped by the flow of product emanating from America and released by the American majors. This flow is reliable and consists of market-tested products, which are what exhibitors need. Although European producers can place films on the market, both in the mainstream and into the niche provided by *art et essai* circuits, what they can offer is single films, not the sort of body of work that can be properly called a cinema. By industrial standards, the cinemas even of major producing countries such as France or Italy lack the consistency necessary to hold a steady share of the market. Even where films are individually competitive, it is in a market geared in the first instance to American-led supply.

The area in which Europe has most seriously lost out over the past twenty or thirty years has been that of popular genre production. Until the mid-1960s the major European producing countries continued to produce genre films of various types – comedies, *policiers*, peplums, etc. – mainly for domestic consumption. But in the shrinking market of the 1970s this form of production went into decline. The spaghetti/paella Western survived for a few years and so did Italian horror, but throughout much of Europe the only type of genre production to flourish in the 1970s was the sex film, cheap to make and easy to export. Britain's great contribution to modern genre cinema, the Bond cycle, was from the outset American backed and has become progressively less 'British' as time goes on.

This decline in the European popular genre film coincided with a change in both official and unofficial government policy in a number of countries. In the post-war period legislation had been culturally indifferent, aimed at supporting film industries regardless of the nature of the product. But from the 1960s onwards France, Italy and Germany all moved in the direction of more targeted support mechanisms. The French began this move in the early 1960s with the introduction of the *avance sur recettes* system, a form of loan, some of which was payable to all producers but some of which (*aide sélective*) was reserved for projects thought particularly worthy of support. At first this *aide sélective* was given only to producers, but in 1968 it was made available to directors, thus providing an industrial boost to a number of otherwise unviable *films d'auteur*. Meanwhile in Italy and Germany state-controlled (and subsidised) television became a conduit for production monies for quality production, while popular films were left to sink or swim on the market.

The positive result of the change in emphasis in European government policy can be seen in the form of the New German Cinema of the 1970s, in the enduring legacy of the French New Wave, and in the continuing careers of directors like Francesco Rosi in Italy. The decline of traditional popular cinema, which was the counterpart of the rise of the directly or indirectly subsidised art film, cannot really be blamed on governments. It was a part of a cultural process (even more extreme in Britain than on the Continent) which saw the focus of popular national cultures in the 1960s and 1970s shifting towards television and then, in the 1980s and 1990s, beginning to dissolve altogether as the 'neo-television' of Murdoch, Bertelsmann, Hersant and Berlusconi took over from the 'paleo-television' of the state monopolies. Although the corporations that run the new private televisions do continue to invest in film production, their interest in cinema is marginal. Operating without infrastructure and with no brief other than corporate profit, they offer neither the basis for a revival of specifically cinematic genre production nor the promise of renewal of a culturally challenging art film movement.[4]

IV

Does this mean that the writing is on the wall for European cinema? Not necessarily. But it does mean that both industrially and culturally European films are on the defensive. Each film made in Europe has to carve out its own niche in the marketplace, either domestically or internationally. Despite the efforts of the European Union, a 'single market' for European film does not yet exist. The legal infrastructure has been established, support mechanisms are in place, but there is no product. Or rather, there *is* product, in the form of films made in the various countries of the European Union. But the product is not European. It is either obstinately local, able to capture audiences in its country of origin or within a culture zone where its local characteristics can be appreciated; or it is international, potentially appealing in a variety of markets but not necessarily able to conquer any of them. Meanwhile the situation of Hollywood in the mass marketplace seems impregnable.

The response in Europe to this apparent polarisation between a successful and united American industry and unsuccessful and divided European ones tends, as already mentioned, to be defensive. It is also, like the cinemas it purports to defend, disunited. Despite the front put on at the time of the GATT negotiations, the reasons put forward for defending European cinemas are different in different countries. The French (in particular) talk about the defence of national culture. The British (in particular) talk about reviving a national film industry. But whichever the objective, the measures proposed to achieve it tend to be the same:

economic incentives at either a European or a national level. Some of the proposals are eminently rational, but they always avoid the real question, which is who wants the intended product anyway. This is a cultural question, and has to be answered in cultural terms.

In the *Bioscope* of 8 January 1925, Joseph Schenck, then president of United Artists, commented brutally on British film productions: 'You have no personalities to put on the screen. Your stage actors and actresses are no good on the screen. Your effects are no good, and you do not spend nearly so much money.'[5] Similar remarks can be found about almost any European cinema in almost any decade. It is possible to question the aesthetic standards by which such complaints are made. It can be argued that slow rhythms, deliberate staginess, and lack of star presence or of visible production values are positive qualities which European film-makers have exploited in creative ways and which the Hollywood cinema is the poorer for not possessing. How Schenck would have hated *La Règle du jeu, Bicycle Thieves, The Bitter Tears of Petra von Kant* or *The Long Day Closes*! And how wrong he would have been. But at the level of mass perception Schenck was right. There are a lot of things he might also have said – about the resolute market orientation of the American cinema, about its efficiency and the cost control that accompanied higher budgets. All these features of American cinema were much admired in Europe and throughout the 1930s European industry moguls including Luigi Freddi from Italy and Boris Shumyatsky from the Soviet Union travelled to Hollywood to try to learn how the Americans did it.

None of this sedulous aping of what appeared to be the superior organisation of the American industry, however, enabled the European cinemas to challenge Hollywood's steady acquisition of cultural hegemony. When American films returned to European screens in 1946, public demand for them was enormous – as it indeed had been throughout the inter-war period. It was not just more efficient business practice (nor even the help provided by the now all-powerful American government) which restored American films to their dominant place in the market. Nor was it necessarily that the films were, in a sense that Schenck would have recognised, 'better' (though they usually were). The qualities that American films possessed were not simply quantifiable, but no less real for that.

Sometimes the banal truths are the valuable ones and the fact is that the much-mouthed banalities about Hollywood as dream factory are not only true but important. They are perhaps not all perfectly and unequivocally true, but they are true enough. Hollywood is the biggest fabricator of fantasy, and that is its enormous and unchallenged strength. It is a strength which arises partly from the system, from a market orientation which – initially for domestic consumption but increasingly for export as well – requires films to provide satisfaction across the board. But this market orientation, which is in principle copiable and has in some cases (notably in Hong Kong, India and Japan) been copied with some success, was necessary only to set things up. It created a momentum, a powerful force of inertia, which has swept up feeble attempts at imitation in its wake. It also produced a reaction which proved in the long term counterproductive. European cinemas, threatened by the power of Hollywood fantasy, responded in two ways. Sometimes they offered counter-fantasies – wish-fulfilment comedies, guilt-and-redemption dramas, or repatriated genres such as the English Gothic. But all too often they provided realism – a commodity deeply rooted in European culture and well adapted to the circumstances in which the industries found themselves. It could be inexpensively improvised. It suited a tradition in which artists were respected as individual purveyors of truth, and it offered a national–cultural distinctiveness, a mirror of everyday reality not provided by the fantasy factory.

In the event, realism was not the commodity audiences required of the cinema. It is not that realism is always unpopular. Huge quantities of quasi-realism, replete with local particularities, are lapped up every day by European audiences. But on television, not in the cinema. The cinema requires – or proves to have required – something else. And it was this something else that Hollywood has offered in profusion. If one looks at the comparative nature of American and European films today it is more and more the case that the American cinema scores with films with a heavy fantasy component, while in Europe films of this type are getting rarer and rarer. And it is not just overt fantasy or superspectaculars that are at issue here. The decline of the ordinary genre film has meant the loss of a main source of fantasy and of the mythic dimension which American films possess and European films, often, do not. What European cinema has tended to oppose to the Hollywood 'dream factory' has, besides realism, been an alternation between modernism and 'heritage' filtered through the classics of European literature.

Never mind the quality, taste the myth. European cinema has for too long been hung up on notions of quality – wrapped for preference in a national flag, like 'Belgian' chocolates. Hollywood, partly for reasons of sheer scale, has not had this problem. It can machine-produce quality when it needs to, but it can also shame-lessly produce trash. European cinema has lost the art of producing trash. But it is trashy films – whether 'good' trash or 'bad' trash makes no difference – that are the manure of film culture, the source of the modern mythologies through which the cinema speaks to its remaining audience. Europe's only mythology at the moment seems to be heritage. If it is to be viable as an industrial and cultural entity, European cinema needs to rediscover the present, forget rural idylls and plunge into urban nightmares, reconnecting with the mythologies of everyday fear and desire. If it can't do this – and it may well be too late – it will have to settle for a role of permanent understudy, bit-part player in the world game.

The case of *Fargo* can be taken as exemplary. For all its claim to be based on real events, *Fargo* is not a realistic movie. There would be no serious loss of authentic-ity if its story of a Walter-Mittyish salesman, a couple of backwoods psychopaths and an apparently slow-witted policewoman were to be placed somewhere else than in the mid-West. But if the film had been sited in Europe it would have lost something. It would have lost the mythic dimension which Hollywood has been able to endow on films about America and which European cinemas no longer seem able to give to films about Europe. *Fargo* is not a Hollywood film. Its writer-director-producers, Joel and Ethan Coen, are American. The production company, Working Title, is British.

European cinemas will certainly stay alive in some form. There are lots of bit parts to perform, and lots of ways in which they can be made bigger. European industries can help each other: Peter Greenaway now gets most of his production backing from Holland; Mike Leigh's *Secrets and Lies* was backed by a French company. European producers can make global films (*The Last Emperor*: Italian director, British producer; *The Piano*: New Zealand-born director, French and Australian finance). European directors can make American movies (*Twister* is one recent example). One thing, however, European cinemas cannot do is legislate themselves back into existence as national cinemas of the kind they were thirty or more years ago. This is both economically impossible and culturally retrograde. What they could perhaps do is put European films back into the cultural mainstream. This needs imagination, rather than money. It also means accepting that, just as the industry no longer divides along national lines, neither does culture. Over the half century since 1945 European culture has changed in many ways. It has lost a lot of its regional specificities, and it has also become Americanised. There is therefore a general problem for Europeans of redefining their culture and what they have that is specifically theirs. This is not a problem that can be solved by inveighing against coca-colonisation or deciding that what Europe has and America doesn't is heritage – that 'we' had Botticelli before 'they' were even discovered. What 'we' have are depopulated countrysides, burgeoning suburbia and multi-ethnic inner cities – at first glance not dissimilar to the United States. But behind the similarities lie deep differences, both of fact and of attitude. The parts of Europe remain different from each other, and different again from the United States. If European cinema could discover what these differences mean, and find a language in which they can be talked about, imaginatively as well as realistically, then perhaps . . . .

V

Hollywood is very important to Europe. Hollywood films dominate the European market and increasingly that of the rest of the world. Europe as a market is therefore very important to Hollywood. But how important is European cinema to America? The answer would appear to be: not very. European films occupy only a small niche market in the United States, and their place within that niche is controlled by the same companies as control the release of American films in Europe. Hollywood's strategy towards possible competition in the US market is much as it has always been. Successful European films are remade in English; successful directors and stars are offered contracts to work in America. Money is sometimes (though less often than in the 1960s and 1970s) invested in 'international' films – that is to say, foreign films thought to have potential in the US.

But movies that are too obviously 'foreign' are not popular in America. As European producers realised as far back as the 1950s, American audiences (and British, too) like films to be in English. Sub-titling and crude dubbing are acceptable only to audiences that have no choice in the matter. A Dutch or Danish audience is happy to watch American films with sub-titles, because that's the only way they will get to see them, while French and Italian audiences have the lifelong experience of watching American musicals with the songs in English and the dialogue dubbed, usually rather badly. But American audiences do not expect to have to deal with these things. The market for foreign-language films in the US has always been a minority market. Because the US is a large and pluralist country, minority markets are not insignificant. But because the American industry is inherently monopolistic, minority has always meant marginal. It is only if the minority swells to the point where it threatens to overspill into the mainstream – if Hong Kong martial arts films, or Italian Westerns or Scandinavian soft-core films become *too* popular – that the major players in the industry take an interest. And when they do take an interest this is not always good news for the audience.

If one looks at the current situation less from the point of view of the European producer, frustrated at not being able to make inroads into the American market, but rather from that of the American consumer, looking for a wider variety of films to sample, one fact is striking. The market for European (and Asian) films has moved to video. There may not be many new European films on theatrical release, but huge numbers of recent and 'classic' European films are available on cassette or laserdisc. The point about the video audience is that it is largely self-selecting. It consists of people who already have a reason to be interested in what they are seeking: it is an audience of film-buffs, students, gender and ethnic minorities and special interest groups. The video culture has greatly enriched the lives of these people, but it is a quiet culture, which only makes the headlines when, for example, as happened in Cincinnati a couple of years ago, a copy of Pasolini's *Salò* is seized from a gay bookstore and arraigned for obscenity. The high visibility culture remains that of mainstream releasing and the annual Academy Award jamboree. There is no sign (*English Patient* notwithstanding) that this culture is widening. While films by Jim Jarmusch, Todd Haynes or Richard Linklater are widely available and talked about in Europe, their European equivalents enjoy a relatively subterranean existence in the US.

VI

The story of Hollywood–European relations is a complex and ongoing one. To tell the entire story is impossible. What this book aims to do is to put the telling of the story more firmly on the cultural agenda. It aims to set the scene, and having done so, to probe various aspects of the complex relationship. It is divided into three parts. The first part looks at some of the larger strategies that have guided (or attempted to guide) the relationship over the past fifty to sixty years. The second and third parts are more in the nature of case studies. In the second part the stress is on economics and politics, the essential background (sometimes pushed into the foreground) of cinema. The third part examines more closely some of the films that have been shaped by the interaction between the great cinemas of Europe and the United States.

Notes

1 The main problem in dealing with statistics about films according to nationality is that figures are not always compiled in the same way in each country and there are not always unambiguous and generally agreed criteria for assigning films to one country rather than another. Figures given here should be regarded as indicative only.

2 Lorenzo Quaglietti, *Storia economico-politica del cinema italiano* (Rome: Editori Riuniti, 1980).

3 The key factor here is not just the size of the domestic market but the diffusion of the relevant language, and which country speaking that language is the most powerful. Of European languages, only English and Spanish have over 100 million speakers, though Portuguese and German are not far off, as is French if speakers of French as a second language are included. Italian comes next, with over 50 million speakers of Italian in Italy itself and several more millions scattered across the Americas. France has a good-sized natural market. So does Germany, though there was more exchange between Germany and Austria than the two parts of Germany in the years 1949–89. The market for Spanish-language films is enormous, and might have been supplied by Spain (rather than Mexico) had it not been for Franco. The English-language market is the biggest, but it is supplied mainly from Hollywood. Portuguese films never made any inroads in the largest Portuguese-speaking country, Brazil, though Brazilian soaps are now exported to Portugal. The natural market for films in other languages is much smaller. For Dutch-language films it is 18 million people (13 million in Holland, plus 5 million or so in northern Belgium), with the possible addition of a couple of million Dutch speakers in former colonies and 4 million or so speakers of Afrikaans. No other western European languages have more than 10 million speakers, which severely restricts the audience they can have without their films having to be sub-titled or dubbed.

4 An excellent survey of the current state of European cinemas, from a standpoint slightly different from the one adopted here, is provided by Angus Finney, *The State of European Cinema: A New Dose of Reality* (London: Cassell, 1996).

5 Quoted by John Hawkridge in his article in Geoffrey Nowell-Smith (ed.), *The Oxford History of World Cinema* (Oxford and New York: Oxford University Press, 1996), p. 134.

Part I

1
European cinema and the idea of Europe, 1925–95

Victoria de Grazia

I Cinema and European identity

In Europe, 1995 was commemorated as the centenary of the European cinema, the date to honour being the 1895 Paris premiere of the Lumière Brothers' Cinématographe, the first device patented to photograph, print and project film. Generally, commemorations afford a means to construct a lineage, to draw lines to include or exclude, and to mobilise a heritage, whose precise genetic make-up is open to doubt. They have become particularly resonant in an age of identity politics.[1] This act of commemoration is no exception. Though hardly as controversial as others recently (one thinks of the embattled bicentennial of the French Revolution or the Serbs' portentous celebration of the sixth centenary of the Battle of Kosovo) it too offers a genealogy and a message.[2] It should suffice to start our reflection to note that the Venice Film Festival, which celebrated the event with the selection and screening of one hundred European films, was Europe's first movie festival. When founded in 1934 with the Italian Fascist dictatorship's enthusiastic backing, its chief goal was to promote a renaissance of the European film industry as an alternative to the Hollywood cinema.

References to Europe or to belonging to European civilisation usually redouble when Europeans come under severe duress. These years which have seen rampant Euro-pessimism accompanied by denunciations of Eurocrats, together with the championing of a European cultural space – more specifically a Euro-audiovisual area and a Euro-cinema – are no exception. 'J'entends parler d'Europe, la guerre n'est pas loin.' That was the weary remark François Perroux heard from a friend in 1954, when the eminent French political economist told him that he had just finished writing about the unity of Europe. The book, the profound and still pertinent *L'Europe sans rivages* ('Europe without riverbanks') was dedicated to probing the industrial strengths and trade patterns of the great European nation-states, notably France and Germany, which, first under Napoleon, then under Hitler, had appealed to the idea of a unitary Europe in their doomed and catastrophic endeavours to legitimate the hegemony of a single power over the European continent.[3]

19

This latest revival of the idea of Europe, within the context of which the centenary of the European cinema is being celebrated, is, precisely, a counter to Europe's earlier catastrophic experiences of unification and disunity. Inevitably, then, the current debate over Europe suggests, much as it did in the first part of the century, the enormous stakes at play. Will Europe be little or large, closed or open, bureaucratic or decentralised, western or transcontinental? Will Europe be only an economic and political unity or a cultural unity as well? Defining whether there should be a European cinema, much less the characteristics that might define it, has always borne in some measure on these larger issues of definition. Should the label European apply only to products made on European territory and with European capital? Or should it refer to the products of European-born directors, even when made elsewhere or with foreign investments? Does it imply a quality of expression or creative tradition, expressing as it were the aesthetics of a culture? If there is a European cinema, is its other the American, or more specifically Hollywood? If the perspective is global, might not the European cinema be linked to some notion of a western as opposed to an eastern or colonial cinema; should it be juxtaposed against African, Latin American, Indian or Asian cinema? Finally, if there is a European cinema, what exactly is its relationship to 'national' cinemas; what qualities link together, say, art productions and outright commercial products, films of evasion and propaganda works, to group them with their equivalents in adjacent societies to form a distinctively European amalgam?[4]

The search for answers to the latter questions has a long history, starting in post-First World War Europe, as governments, political leaders, intellectuals, and in different measure cinemagoing publics responded to the vast economic and cultural potential of this new industry and to the challenge presented by the competition from Hollywood productions.[5] Though the competition from the United States affected European countries very differently and the domestic industries themselves were neither originally conceived as 'national' nor unified in their business strategies, intellectuals immediately categorised the shift in trade terms exemplified the influx of American movies as the opening of a life-and-death struggle between two competing civilisations.[6] In the inter-war years, trans-European alliances to confront this economic 'enemy', this cultural 'other', proved elusive. Those that eventually evolved under the leadership of Germany's powerful industry were ultimately subordinated to the German state's aggressive expansionism.

By contrast, during the post-Second World War period, the quest for unity was largely defined in economic terms. The search for a common cultural identity in western Europe was conceived as a secondary goal. The agreements founding the European Community in 1957 contained not a word about establishing a unified European culture nor about supporting the cinema as an industry (the first directive toward the latter goal dates to 1963).[7] Only recently, in the wake of the Maastricht Treaty and the further consolidation of the European Union, has the notion that Europe should be defined by a common cultural identity acquired a new resonance. This concern, born of the disputes about the extent and nature of unification but also in reaction to huge new pressures from American communications industries, has focused attention on the fate of a European 'audiovisual space'. This is the broad context within which the commemoration of 'one hundred years of European cinema' was invented.

My intention here is to trace the genealogy of the idea of a 'European cinema' by focusing on two earlier moments of European history when this term was invoked to respond not just to a crisis of the industries themselves but also to a broader crisis of cultural identities resulting from intra-national conflicts consequent upon the repositioning of the European region in global markets. First during the 1930s under the Nazi New Order, and then in the 1960s, in the context of building the so-called 'Europe of nations' under US hegemony, the problem of defending 'national' markets and culture was recast in terms of defending Europe, albeit in very different terms. Specifically, I am interested here in exploring the slippage between nationalism and Europeanism, as a consequence of which the notion of Europe or Europeanness operates like appeals to nationalist identity in order to uphold large-scale sectoral interests, reinforce ethnic and national solidarity, and curtail cultural diversity. To examine the definition of Europe emerging in these two moments of response to the US challenge – which itself changed significantly – highlights the difficulties European cultural and communications industries have had in reconciling local interests with national and transnational ones in pursuit of common strategies. This study also suggests the varying powers attributed to cinema culture in building national and European identities. During the 1930s for example, the cinema – aside from its obvious entertainment functions and profits as an industry – was regarded as a means of state propaganda and the main communicator on a mass scale of a national aesthetic. In the 1960s the cinema signalled the vigour of European recovery and western Europe's convergence around a common high standard of consumption. Today, the contribution to local economies of the movie industry in terms of employment and gross product is much less than it used to be and looks insignificant compared to the giant power and profits of the information industries. Nevertheless, the contribution of cinema to national culture has grown in esteem, such that arguments on behalf of protecting European cinemas end up treating the cinema not as a mere commercial product but as a veritable monument of high culture, akin to opera, symphony orchestras or great masters' paintings, or alternatively as the artefacts of popular subculture indispensable to nurturing a multicultural identity within a 'European homeland' that would extend from the Atlantic to the Urals.

To examine successive definitions of the Europeanness of European cinemas, then, we leapfrog from a region wracked by depression to an area basking in the capitalist Golden Age, before coming to rest on the Europe of today, stretched this way and that by processes of regional unification and newly intensified localisms, trans-global currents, and the pull eastward and southward toward Russia and the Balkans. In the 1930s, the European state-system, never fully restored after the Great War, was in crisis. The self-avowed champion of its rebirth was Nazi Germany: the organisation it proposed was a continent-wide, closed, German-dominated market (*Gross-wirtschaftsraum*); its cultural claim was to establish a 'spiritual' Europe by purifying the European geo-political space of Judaeo-Bolshevism. Within this context, the cinema was regarded as a central cultural device. In the 1960s, the claim to speak on behalf of Europe, now divided by the

Cold War, was advanced within the framework of the Europe of the Six by the leading states France and the Federal Republic of Germany. Policy-makers' quest for all-European policies was pragmatic, dictated by the desire to compete with the United States while remaining under American military protection and economic leadership. As idealistic visions of spiritual unity gave way in the 1950s to hard-nosed economic agreements, European policy-makers envisaged European identity as flowing naturally from the single states' convergence around a common course of modernisation. This idea was strongly supported by American social scientists' notion of processes of national cultural integration, according to which grass-roots organisations and civic values would be imbued with a sense of transcendent national civic purpose under the impact of mass communications.[8] Accordingly, governments foresaw a public-service function for audiovisual culture. By that time, this function was best performed by television; among this medium's qualities, in contrast with the cinema, it could be promoted under government monopolies. The loss of faith in this formerly pervasive view – that a unified economic market would yield a unified cultural identity, which in turn would yield a shared sense of citizenship – lies behind the 'identity' crisis prevalent today.

II The Europe of the New Order

In roughest terms, the incapacity of a cinema in Europe to respond to the US challenge in the early part of the century resulted from the inability of Europe's traditionally sovereign and warring nation-states to reconfigure themselves as a regional economic force. This scale of operation was imperative to devise common strategies to respond to the vast units of production and market increasingly required for success in the global economy. Some pragmatists – one thinks of John Maynard Keynes's eloquent writing of 1919 about the horrendous outcome of Versailles – forcefully argued that there could be no permanent European peace without widening domestic markets and establishing an international framework that could accommodate Germany, the continent's most powerful economy.[9] The powerful and visionary Erich Pommer, head of production at Ufa in the pre-Nazi period, could well envisage operating on this regional scale. Already in 1925, before his first period in Hollywood, Pommer advocated making 'European films, films that were no longer French, English, Italian or German, but continental', by which he intended 'works of rapid and wide European diffusion that would permit costs, which had become enormous everywhere, to be amortised'.[10] However, it was difficult for any European-based organisations to surmount deep inherited divisions, much less the raw new splits that resulted from the Allies' retribution against Germany, the virtual quarantine of Bolshevik Russia, the parcelling of the former multicultural empires of eastern Europe into vulnerable little nation-states, and the withdrawal of Britain and France within the protected confines of their vast overseas empires. The ambiguous American posture of economic involvement and political withdrawal only aggravated Europe's confusion.

Under these circumstances, European industries were faced with a troubling situation. On the one hand, American corporations boldly championed Europe's future as an economic region. At least they did so until the Great Depression, when many enterprises pulled back their investment from abroad. Manufacturers of consumer durables and office equipment, as well as film, conceived of a Europe that stretched from London and Rotterdam to Barcelona, Bucharest, and Alexandria in Egypt. With its far-flung network of commercial attachés, the Department of Commerce did likewise.[11] The proverbial US businessman was a visionary Dodsworth (as American writers portrayed him), or a rustic opportunist (as he was described by Europeans), brushing off observations about the peculiarities, say, of French culture, with an irritable 'don't bother me with the details'. On the other hand, some of the most competitive European industries sought alliances with US industry to try to break into the American market or latch on to its expansion abroad. Even the avowedly nationalist German media magnate Alfred Hugenberg followed this course. After his takeover of Ufa in 1927, this self-styled Weimar communications czar re-hired Pommer, hoping that he would transfer his Hollywood in making films for international consumption to making German films for international export markets and, most desirably of all, that he could use his American connections to break into the inhospitable and highly protected American markets.[12]

With the Depression US businessmen called off their imperious undertaking and European states raised tariff walls to protect shaky currencies and their shallow home markets. By the early 1930s, the quest among European entrepreneurs, notably in Germany, to develop a protected regional film market became more accentuated. It also acquired a distinctly culturalist twist with the spread of Fascist nationalism and economic protectionism, and as sound production afforded a new space for the operations of national-language cinemas.[13]

From the point of view of cultural influence as well as economic power, Germany remained the best situated to lead the way. Europe had a German-language population of about 80 million, spreading far into central and eastern Europe, where German culture and technology had great prestige. Germany alone, through the giant integrated Ufa firm, had a film industry capable of exercising European-wide influence. Moreover, German nationalists hailed the cinema not only for its propaganda and entertainment value, but also for its capacity to express creatively Germany's superiority as a *Kulturnation*. Beyond that, the German industry already performed a unifying role, Berlin being the pivot of a rich middle-European cinema culture, drawing in directors, actors and technicians from throughout central Europe. Starting in 1930, German-initiated cartel arrangements had also assisted faltering French distribution and equipment firms to compete once more in the European market.[14]

In the wake of Hitler's appointment as Chancellor in January 1933, as the Nazi leadership launched Germany's *revanche*, the German cinema industry took formal steps to consolidate its influence. The first move was to urge other national film lobbies to emulate its own vertically organised interest group structure – in the SPIO – to counter the influence of Hollywood's Motion Pictures Producers' and Distributors' Association (MPPDA). In 1935, at German instigation, the representatives of various European film establishments present at the Venice Film Festival signed accords to found the International Film Chamber (IFC), whose members, twenty-four in all, extended outside of Europe to include India and

Japan, the world's biggest film producers at the time. However, the IFC's major ambitions were clearly continental: its first president, Fritz Scheuemann, was also president of Germany's *Reichsfilmkammer*, its vice-president was Giuseppe Volpi di Misurata, founder of the Venice Film Festival and a behind-the-scenes promoter of an Italian 'vital space' in the Balkans. The IFC also wooed the French, by holding the subsequent meeting in Paris in 1937, during which a Frenchman was offered the next turn in the presidency of the organisation. The Italians naturally sought to play down the anti-US bias of the IFC since their cinema economy was so vulnerable. However, the US trade representatives, with their English allies, were keenly sensitive to the threat of competition posed by a German-led entente. Consequently, Anglo-American interests boycotted the Paris and subsequent meetings.[15]

Whether initially the IFC intended the so-called European film to embody a specific cultural message is unclear. In the 1920s, film-makers and critics had expressed considerable scepticism about whether any single European product could have the same visible brand quality as the Hollywood article. The effort to script plots to combine German leading men and French *chanteuses* with Austrian comics, American *ingénues* and Italian vamps was ridiculed as a contrived and specious cosmopolitanism.[16] But as bourgeois Europe veered sharply nationalist in the late 1930s, many men of culture acquiesced to the Fascists' vision of a 'third way' to revitalise European civilisation in the face of American and Bolshevik materialism. In this atmosphere, European film promoters, or at least those who regularly attended the Venice Film Festival and participated at awards ceremonies during which Germany and Italy carried off the top prizes, seemed to defer to the notion that European cinema had not only an economic dimension but a clear-cut cultural content as well.

But not until after the Second World War had started and German-style racial laws were being widely applied do we hear other national voices specifying the ethnic–political nature of this Europeanism. If the testimony of Vittorio Mussolini, son of the Duce and endowed with various film-industry and film-cultural responsibilities, is to be believed, European spectators were consummately grateful that the cinema had been 'snatched from the hands of Judaic finance and its masonic minions'. 'Once remoulded by European civility', it had been 'detoxified of Judaic poison, [which was] subtly falsifying of history, morally lax, licentious in habits, [and] deliberately confusing about interpreting bad and good'.[17]

Without the exclusion of US films from Europe, it is hard to imagine the success of this German-dominated European bloc. Purely in terms of numbers, the combined Hollywood production for 1939 was 527, whereas Germany and Italy together produced only about 160 films.[18] However, very rapidly after 1940, as Germany extended its control by conquest and alliance over the entire European continent, the German industry, under orders from Goebbels, set about revamping local film industries under German control. During the war years, racial-ideological dictates, combined with economic and military factors, caused some national movie industries to be extinguished and others to flourish. In the wake of the conquest of Poland, the German occupation government virtually obliterated the Polish cinema. After 1938, in retaliation for the anti-German quotas of the 1930s' Czech governments, the Nazi occupiers reduced Czech production to 20 per cent of its pre-war level. Nazi racial extermination policies extinguished the ebullient film culture of eastern European Jewry. At the same time, the German New Order encouraged the birth of the Croatian, Slovenian, Slovakian, Bulgarian and Romanian national cinemas, and greatly boosted the vitality of the Italian, Hungarian and French.

The French case, analysed by Evelyn Ehrlich, is paradigmatic.[19] Reorganised according to the centralised Italian model, under the protection of UFI (the giant trust that combined Ufa with other German and foreign concerns) and with massive infusions of German capital, French movie production during the four years of occupation yielded 220 feature films. Moreover, many observers argued that the French cinema also experienced a 'cultural blossoming'. Initially, the German overseers equivocated as to whether French film-makers should be confined to producing only mediocre, as Goebbels put it, 'light, frothy and if possible corny pictures' for home consumption.[20] Eventually, business as well as political considerations prompted a wiser use of French resources and talent. After all Vichy was the Third Reich's ally. The decision was made to turn the French industry into a source of high-quality productions for export through UFI's distribution systems. That this strategy eventually proved successful depended a lot on the complete exclusion of US films. It also presumed the expropriation of Jewish-owned distribution systems which, in turn, facilitated the establishment of an oligopolistic business structure that reduced production units from 410 in 1939 to forty-two in 1942. This structure, together with cheap labour, the banning of double features, the lack of alternative amusements which sent movie attendance soaring, and a lax German-run censorship system, created ideal conditions for building what local supporters of the French industry regarded as a genuine 'national cinema'.

Critics of the European organisation of the cinema under the Nazi New Order (which deserves a more thorough study using newly available German documents) might argue that it was a wholly artificial system, coerced into existence by the Nazis and incapable of enduring US competition. True, it could not have operated without the exclusion of the United States. However, managers of UFI, together with their overseer, the Minister of Public Enlightenment and Propaganda, Goebbels, well understood that publics could not be forced to go to movies. Movie operations were generally conducted according to business principles, with an eye to the crowd. By far the greatest portion of movies were escapist. It is true that business under the Nazi warlords was hardly business as usual. The confiscations of Jewish property might be characterised as unfair business practice, to say the least. But if the search is for a genealogy for their national cinema, such circumstances seem irrelevant, or so it would appear from those who have crowed over the French cinema's renaissance under Vichy.

Whether Nazi rule would have long tolerated the tension within itself, between producing a widely marketable commodity and promoting a 'nationalistic' – as opposed simply to a 'national' cinema – to legitimate the Third Reich, is unlikely, just as it proved impossible, as the war was clearly lost, to avoid despoiling its satellites and former allies. In the United States, the problem in effect of 'denationalising' domestic cultural products to facilitate export had been resolved more or less automatically; the industry absorbed its personnel and themes from

25

a vast emigrant population and the national audience to whom they appealed was ethnically as diverse and socially less stratified than that of Europe. Moreover, Hollywood was without the pretension to being *Kultur*, in the deep German sense, the test of the value of the product being unabashedly measured by its popularity on the markets as calculated by business balance sheets.

Indeed, the Allied war against Europe's closed imperialist systems only validated this vision. In the inter-war period, American movie industrialists, together with federal government promoters of foreign commerce, argued that trade followed the film, playing on the idea of trade following the flag. In other words, US-made films would promote the American way of life by promoting trade in the very goods that were shown in American films.[21] In the course of winning the war, Hollywood seems to have won the right to treat American communications products as having an inherent cultural value; the Hollywood 'mission' now became something more than promoting a material 'way of life'. Hollywood had done battle against the cinema of a closed economic system. This enemy cinema was by definition an inferior culture, not so much because it was tainted by totalitarian propaganda, but because it was untested by the market of public opinion. The hallmark of the free world won by Allied arms was the free movement of goods, cultural and otherwise. Whatever the commodity's nature – and there was no fine distinction between Coca-Cola, expressionist art exhibits and *Readers' Digest* – movements of goods not only facilitated communications among people, but indeed fostered a real form of cultural progress by exposing stagnant localisms to the fresh main currents of contemporary mass culture. Henceforth, the US industry regarded it as legitimate on cultural as well as economic grounds to muster its vast power (which included US government agencies) to challenge states which denied access to their markets.[22]

III Europe of the nation-states

Two decades after European societies had been divided and reconstructed under the rule of the superpowers, the 1960s presents an altogether different scenario. In the west, the US model, with its emphasis on wide markets, mass consumption and conservative democracy, was still dominant. But its grip was weakening in the face of the declining productivity of its domestic economy, the Vietnam War and the rise of European projects for greater autonomy, alternatively expressed in President de Gaulle's Grand Design and the opening to eastern Europe or in the Ostpolitik of West German Chancellor Willy Brandt. The 1960s was a time of promise and perils for the cinema in western Europe. Attendance was under increasing pressure from television, though still relatively high, especially in southern Europe. At the same time, cinematic culture was being enlivened by the great talent of a younger generation of film-makers. And Hollywood itself was in bad straits, its inflexible structures ill responding to competition from television, high production costs and changing tastes. It was thought that these circumstances would create an opening for European production, and the 1960s were indeed years in which output picked up in France and Italy. Yet this trend was hard to sustain by any concerted European strategy, nor was it turned to developing a lasting new European cultural identity.

One major obstacle lay in the very nature of post-war western European unity. This involved both the greater intervention of national governments domestically and greater convergence across European societies. It used to be argued that the single European states, France and the Federal Republic of Germany in the lead, had renounced nation-state rights, or sovereignty, to establish a basis for sustained co-operation. Now the premier historian of European unity, Alan Milward, argues that they only delegated certain decision-making processes over resources and trade to the European Community in order to strengthen their sovereignty.[23] This would explain the persistence of protectionist and particularised legislation, the much greater inner cohesiveness of European states, and the divergences in policies in the 1970s as the international economy soured in the wake of the oil crises. But to stress only sovereignty, with its implication of autonomy and distinctiveness, is to forget growing commonalities. By the 1960s, European societies were more densely linked internationally and government regulatory powers were far more pervasive. In that sense they were stronger nation-states. At the same time, these changes took place at a common tempo as the outcome of more or less shared responses to the broadening of markets under the US aegis, Cold War divisions and economic growth moved European societies closer together.

If we emphasise *sovereignty* and *convergence* we can better explain the significance of the cultural politics of that era, toward the cinema in particular. Notoriously, the EEC (European Economic Community) states pursued no common cultural policy. And that is altogether understandable historically – *pace* those who now allege that Jean Monnet wished that he 'had started [unification] with culture', for that forgets that European states had to be prostrate from total war and practically under foreign occupation before they took the first steps in the direction of unity. That said, the EEC states carried forward policies that had ample cultural implications. Those related to the cinema were fourfold. First, to facilitate trade among the Six, the European Community stipulated rules defining what 'national' meant in terms of each industry. In the case of the cinema, 'national' had to be broad enough to accommodate co-productions, which meant recognising any company established under the prevailing incorporation laws. Inevitably, national firms included the proliferating numbers of US subsidiaries. Second, the EEC states tacitly recognised that the local movie industries were girded with protections and subsidies, all the while equivocating as to whether these favours were being offered on purely economic grounds such as sustaining employment or building up a strategic industry, or on cultural grounds. Third, all treated television as a public service, as a form of public education and as an agency by which to control information. European governments thus tacitly concurred on dividing the audiovisual sector according to two models: the movie industry following a market model while television remained a state monopoly. This division deterred them from conceiving of any overall national or transnational audiovisual politics. Finally, all shared the assumption that a modernised economy would yield a common national and cross-European value system.

This system, if it can be called that, had its logic: open yet covertly protected, it integrated Europe on a societal level around a common material culture, yet supported governmental efforts to claim more autonomy on behalf of European states in the face of faltering US hegemony. Developments in the world of cinema fit within this bigger picture. By the mid-1960s, the then nine members of the European Community comprised an audience and a productive capacity larger than that existing in the US. Output experienced a big growth, following major investments in the industries and, at least in the case of Italy and France, some significant restructuring along the lines of US manufacturing. Business growth was accompanied by great artistic vitality, the output, in brief, of a new generation, schooled in European and US film culture, its audience the giant cohort born after the war, often close to the left-wing parties and new social movements of the 1960s and 1970s and influenced by the sea change in sexual, social and cultural values of those years.

The trouble was that this 'European' development was hardly European, either in some of its major sources of investment or in the eyes of some of its major protagonists, much less in the mind of the audience, if we can presume to know that.

Indeed, the European cinema boom of the 1960s was bound up with US decline. American investment dollars, overvalued on global markets, their returns diminishing in the United States, went abroad, encouraged by tax incentives on overseas investment. By contrast with the decrepit studio system in Hollywood, the European cinema, with its cheap labour, pools of talent, and still significant local markets, proved an investor's paradise. Best of all, if US investors went native, incorporating themselves as local businesses in Europe, they benefited from the same tax breaks and quota protections extended to national industries. At the same time, the US industries' presence skewed local development. Typically American firms operated to raise production costs; they also sought to evade local unions. Finally, as European cinema attendance declined, inflation mounted and the dollar was devalued, the Americans withdrew their investment, sinking local markets.[24]

Those who sought to define a common European culture under these circumstances faced a real challenge. With respect to Europe's old claim to offer a universalistic and unifying culture, only the French cultural establishment persisted in this endeavour. Under the leadership of de Gaulle, with André Malraux as his first appointment to the newly established Ministry of Culture, French intellectuals spoke on behalf of European 'civilisation'. Unlike the German concept of a *Kulturnation*, which was racialist, exclusivist and irrational, the French vision was universalist and rational, foreseeing enlightened state bureaucracy interacting with the market to protect and promote cinema and other undertakings of high culture. Then there was the left, which was also Eurocentric in its presuppositions. But its intention was to establish an internationalist culture, one that would ally American popular culture, Marxism and Third World populism to take on the hierarchical, authoritarian and racialist culture of the old Europe. Perhaps the one really unifying cultural force, if it can be called European, was international youth culture, originating in the US, but galvanised by local pop and rock groups in 1960s Europe.[25] Fed by the common consumer-driven way of life emerging from the boom years, it traversed all of Europe, from Liverpool to Leningrad, undermining conventional notions of national boundary and allegiance, and may even have generated a new Euro-American identity, though surely not one that fitted within any existing political configuration.

Coming out of the 1960s, then, there was no unitary vision of a European culture, except as it was filtered through national economic interest. Significantly, the appeal to respond to the American challenge that resonated most widely in those years was advanced by Jean-Jacques Servan Schreiber in his call for European states to confront the United States' technological lead, signally in the upcoming communications field, with a generalised reform of the educational system and state investment in research and design.[26]

IV Towards a multicultural Europe?

Recent studies recognise that the current push to unify Europe derives not from the success of earlier efforts, but from the failure of projects on behalf of economic unification to confront the new challenges posed to the region by a new phase in globalisation of the world economy. To counter the centrifugal tendencies among the western European states as each tried to respond more or less separately to the oil crises of the 1970s, convergence required fuller economic union. But for economic union to succeed, policy-makers had to recognise the need to promote integration at all levels, including the cultural.[27] Indeed, in the face of resurgent localisms accompanying the restructuring of international capitalism, the break-up of the Soviet bloc which yielded a proliferation of nation-states and ethno-minorities, the surge of emigration from outside of the traditional confines of Europe, and, finally, the vast resistance within Europe itself, the cultural dimension of European unification has acquired far greater salience and urgency.

Under these circumstances, the linkages provided by a European-based audio-visual industry would appear as central, with communication, culture and information reinforcing identity across the common territory. This recognition has been accompanied by two woeful discoveries: first, that the very processes of market reorganisation have enacted tremendous human costs (cutbacks on welfare, vast migrations, unemployment, segmented labour force), which in turn have multiplied and fragmented identities; and, second, that not even a unified Europe can easily control this audiovisual space because it is dominated from without. Thus one line of argument goes that the Europeans are being deprived of the very agencies that they need to rein in this identity crisis and reorient loyalties to European institutions.[28]

The European cinema today, though a relatively minor player economically in the vast audiovisual industry, has come to symbolise this dilemma. Demands to protect it as 'European' have thereby become the bellwether of broader demands for the protection of identities.[29] That the French cultural establishment and cinema industry have become leading voices is also comprehensible on several grounds: because France's elite has a long tradition of thinking in Europeanist terms, because French cinema is relatively strong, in part because of strong state support, because France taps into east-central European cultural movements that strongly endorse the idea of Europe (usually as a weapon against Russian hegemony), and last but not least, because French communications enterprises are especially vulnerable to the encroachments of multinational enterprises, being dwarfs compared to the German Bertelsmann or the United States' Time Warner, Disney, Newscorp or ICI.

As the competitive pressures mount and the identity of Europe is more and more disputed, we can expect ever more argument over what Europe should be culturally. The past raises its head in proposals for French leadership or for a Franco-German axis that would recognise Germany's new sphere of influence in east-central Europe and combine the two nations' corporate power ('to stiffen the backbone of the vulnerable European mollusc', as one French commentator put it).[30]

The dilemma of European identity is not only of Europe's making, not today or in the past. Currently, US-led audiovisual interests, backed by US government policy, stand for a vision of the free market that radically challenges the cultural viability and social value of local identities. True, there is an economic reason for American negotiators' pressure to lift protections on the cinema, since US export balances to Europe from movies are second in value only to aerospace technologies and agricultural products. Overcoming resistance to free trade in film, American negotiators also aim to break down resistances in the vast market that American firms anticipate in cable, digital television, information, and other areas of the audiovisual economy which are opening up with immense rapidity.

Specific economic interests aside, the stage has been set for a new counterposition between American and European models of market society. According to the script, the United States, in the interests of global capitalist growth, has reproposed a pure model of market, whereas the Europeans, their so-called 'Rhineland model' of capitalism self-servingly pivoting around a relatively protected regional economy, still advance a social vision of the market and the purposes of state intervention.[31]

These two models stipulate very different relationships between market and culture: the US's neo-economicism is the very caricature of Karl Polanyi's bleak portrayal of the market's utter desolation of society in early nineteenth-century Britain.[32] Its operations are similar to that of the New Poor Law against aristocratic *noblesse oblige*: the market will only be truly free for global investment when cleared of the debris of all past institutions, from Fordist plants and inefficient distribution chains, to national pension systems and health care. This was not always the position of US business elites. In the past, they grasped that in the name of social cohesion, major transformations of an economic nature had to go hand in hand with a major mobilisation of identities. Hence every reordering of the market was accompanied by a burst of social inventivity and campaigns on behalf of American 'values' in the form of nativism, anti-vice campaigns (prohibitionism) and religious fundamentalism.

From the vantage point of 'levelling the playing field', it is implicitly being proposed for Europe (but also for Mexico and Russia) what American elites never tolerated on their home territory: that there be a *tabula rasa* from the perspective of institutions and identity.[33] Historical memory has become too short to recall that every time there has been a major reordering of capitalism, there has been a major unsettling of cultural identities, bringing with it destabilising ideologies, new social moments and unpredicted realignments in politics with disastrous consequences for Europe.

For now, however, unlike the 1930s and in new ways with respect to the 1960s, the definition of what is intended by European identity and European culture remains blessedly open and inventive. There is reason to debate that there is such a thing as a European cinema, much less a European culture in any canonical sense. There is reason to denounce the dangers of invoking these legacies in the name of identity politics. But movements to cultivate a vast cultural space in Europe in which to experiment with cultural diversity and innovation are sound, intriguing and worthy of respect.

Notes

1 See John Gillis (ed.), *Commemoration and the Politics of National Identity* (Princeton: Princeton University Press, 1994).
2 The decision about what cinema anniversary to commemorate was itself a struggle, reflecting not scholarly difficulty at establishing the sequence of events, but competing claims for primacy on the part of Europeans and Americans. The rush to commemorate the 'first' hundred years of film-making actually started in 1989 when Eastman Kodak proclaimed the centenary of cinema film (no matter that there was no cinema to show it off in) and was followed by celebration of various stages of Edison's progress, to which various dates could be given – first patent lodged, first working Kinetograph, first Kinetoscope for peep-show viewing in New York – but all prior to 1895. The European interpretation (which many American scholars agree with) is that nothing Edison or anybody else did before 1895 was actually *cinema* because cinema means not just moving pictures but projection to an audience.
3 François Perroux, *L'Europe sans rivages* (Paris: Presses Universitaires de France, 1955), p. 15.
4 European analysts of popular culture and media have made signally important contributions to the debate over Americanisation and the relationship among the local, national, trans-European and global. See the publications edited by Rob Kroes et al., in particular *Cultural Transmissions and Receptions: American Mass Culture in Europe* (Amsterdam: VU Press, 1993). The handbook for the recent conference in October 1994, 'GATT, the Arts, and Cultural Exchange between the United States and Europe', edited by Annemoon van Hemel, offers important materials. One may also signal the writing of Philip Schlesinger, especially 'On National Identity: Some Conceptions and Misconceptions Criticized', in *Social Science Information,* vol. 26 no. 2, pp. 219–64. Gilbert Rochu's 'Marché commun contre Hollywood', *Libération*, 12 May 1992 offers a clear-eyed assessment of the difficulties of employing the term 'European' as counterposed to 'American'; he notes that films such as De Broca's *Le Diable par la queue* or Truffaut's *The History of Adèle H.* were made with American capital. On the idea of the 'national', as in 'national cinema', see Thomas Elsaesser, 'Holland to Hollywood and Back: or Do We Need a National Cinema?', in J.C.H. Blom, J.Th. Leerssen, P. de Rooy (eds), *De onmacht van het grote: cultuur in Europa* (Amsterdam: Amsterdam University Press, 1993), pp. 81–95.
5 The broad lines of this expansion abroad are traced in Ian Jarvie, *Hollywood's Overseas Campaign: The North Atlantic Movie Trade, 1920–1950* (Cambridge: Cambridge University Press, 1992) and Kristin Thompson, *Exporting Entertainment* (London: British Film Institute, 1985). Studies on the local impact include Victoria de Grazia, 'Sovereignty and the Star System: the American Challenge to the European Cinemas, 1920–1960', *Journal of Modern History* vol. 61 no. 1, March 1989, pp. 53–87, and the excellent recent study by Thomas Saunders, *Hollywood in Berlin: American Cinema and Weimar* (Berkeley: University of California Press, 1994).
6 The first International Motion Picture Congress, held in Paris between 27 September and 2 October 1926, was under the auspices of the International Institute of Intellectual Co-operation. The goal was to develop transnational standards, under the leadership of a 'European bloc'. The Institute was a League of Nations organisation, of which the

United States was not a member. There was therefore no official US participation and the American trade was entirely absent (at least partly for the reason, politely expressed by Ufa's general director, that no businessman could afford to take off the four weeks needed for a European trip without good reason). The leading European trade magazines were dismissive, on the ground that the Congress was dominated by intellectuals (the *London Renter and Moving and Moving Picture News* reported that 'speeches were all in the vaguest terms about what they would like to do with the cinema and the usual nonsense about raising the moral and intellectual standard of films') and that, given US prominence in the industry, no effective gathering could occur without American participation. See: National Archives, Department of Commerce, Bureau of Foreign and Domestic Trade, F. 151, France, 4, October–December 1926. Report G. Canty, 12 October 1926.

7 Thomas H. Guback, 'Cultural Identity and Film in the European Economic Community', *Cinema Journal* vol. XIV no. 1, Fall 1974, pp. 2–17.

8 On civic culture and communications and social integration, see Gabriel Almond and Sidney Verba, *The Civic Culture* (Princeton: Princeton University Press, 1963). See also Reinhard Bendix (ed.), *National Building and Citizenship* (New York: John Wiley and Sons, 1964) and Karl Deutsch, *Nationalism and Social Communication,* 2nd edn (Cambridge: MIT Press, 1966).

9 *The Economic Consequences of the Peace*, 1st edition 1920 (New York: Harper and Row, 1971). Perroux too makes this point very strongly.

10 Cited in Mino Argentieri, *L'asse cinematografico Roma–Berlino* (Naples: Libreria Sapere, 1986), pp. 30 ff. On Pommer, see Ursula Hardt, *Erich Pommer: Film Producer for Germany* (Berkeley and Los Angeles: University of California Press, 1993).

11 See in particular Mira Wilkins and Frank Ernest Hill, *American Business Abroad: Ford on Six Continents* (Detroit: Wayne State University Press, 1964). State strategies are clearly revealed in myriad documents from the commercial attachés of the Department of Commerce stationed in Europe from 1921 to 1941 located in the National Archives, Department of Commerce, Bureau of Foreign and Domestic Trade F. 151. On the strategies of a major advertiser, J. Walter Thompson, see Victoria de Grazia, 'The Arts of Purchase: How American Publicity Subverted the European Poster, 1920–1940', in *Remaking History* (DIA Art Foundation: Discussions in Contemporary Culture, no. 4. Seattle: Bay Press, 1989), pp. 221–57).

12 Saunders, *Hollywood in Berlin*, pp. 89 ff., esp. p. 90.

13 Richard Maltby and Ruth Vasey, 'The International Language Problem: European Reactions to Hollywood Conversion to Sound', in David Ellwood and Rob Kroes (eds), *Hollywood in Europe: Experiences of a Cultural Hegemony* (Amsterdam: VU Press, 1994).

14 Recent works on German cinema during the inter-war years, especially the 1930s, include: Klaus Kreimeier, *Die Ufa-Story: Geschichte eines Filmkonzern* (Munich/Vienna: Hanser, 1992); Arthur Maria Rabenalt, *Joseph Goebbels und der 'Grossdeutsche' Film* (Munich: Herbig, 1985); and Eric Rentschler, 'German Feature Films, 1933–1945', *Monatshefte* vol. 82 no. 3, 1990, pp. 257–66.

15 Argentieri, *L'asse cinematografico*, pp. 30–6.

16 de Grazia, 'Cinema and Sovereignty', pp. 74–5.

17 Argentieri, *L'asse cinematografico*, p. 16.

18 Ibid., pp. 20–1.

19 Evelyn Ehrlich, *Cinema of Paradox: French Filmmaking under the German Occupation* (New York: Columbia University Press, 1985).

20 Ibid., p. 80.

21 This position is clearly presented in US Bureau of Foreign and Domestic Commerce, *Review of Foreign Film Markets during 1938* (Washington, DC: 1939).

22 To back up its free-market principles, the US was massively institutionally involved in cultural organising during the Cold War. To start with, it put the J. Walter Thompson Agency in charge of advertising the Marshall Plan, but there was a discreet quasi-official presence across the board in cultural (or semi-cultural) endeavours aimed at persuading Europeans of the values of the American way of life, from the Congress on Cultural

Freedom to self-service supermarkets. In practice, political considerations forced the US industry to back down on its purist perspective on free markets. In France, the Blum–Byrnes Agreements, once viewed as a sell-out to American interests, have been reinterpreted to highlight the concessions the United States was willing to make in the name of social pacification, in particular to ward off Communist-instigated protests against the end of protectionist measures. See Jean-Pierre Jeancolas's chapter later in this book and Jacques Portes, 'Les Origines de la légende noire des accords Blum–Byrnes sur le cinéma', *Revue d'Histoire Moderne et Contemporaine* vol. XVIII, April–June 1986, pp. 314–29. In other words, the US government was willing to accept that pure market ideology could be politically self-defeating if it so undermined local identities and local industries as to feed indigenous Communist movements.

23 Alan Milward, *The European Rescue of the Nation-State* (Berkeley: University of California Press, 1992).
24 Thomas H. Guback, 'Cultural Identity and Film in the European Economic Community', *Cinema Journal* vol. XIV no. 1, Fall 1974 – a very important article. See also his *The International Film Industry* (Bloomington: Indiana University Press, 1969). In a personal communication, Heide Fehrenbach argues that the West German industry followed a somewhat different trajectory. See also Fehrenbach's *Cinema in Democratizing Germany: Reconstructing National Identity after Hitler* (Chapel Hill: University of North Carolina Press, 1995). On financing generally, see Eitel Monaco, 'The Financing of Film Production in Europe', *Cinema Journal* vol. XIV no. 1, Fall 1974, pp. 18–25. On stylistic as well as economic convergences between US and European film-making, see Peter Lev, *The Euro-American Cinema* (Austin: University of Texas Press, 1993).
25 On the internationalism of youth culture, spearheaded by American trends, see the contributions of Alessandro Portelli, Franco Minganti, Kaspar Maase, Mel van Elteren, Steve Fox and Rob Kroes from Rob Kroes et al., *Cultural Transmissions and Receptions*; also Timothy Ryback, *Rock around the Bloc: A History of Rock Music in Eastern Europe and the Soviet Union* (New York: Oxford University Press, 1990).
26 *The American Challenge*, 1st edition 1967 (New York: Atheneum, 1968).
27 George Ross, 'Confronting the New Europe', *New Left Review* vol. 191, 1992, pp. 49–68; Alain Minc, *The Great European Illusion* (London: Blackwell, 1987) offers a prescient analysis of the importance of the cultural dimension of European unity.
28 The debates around this issue are fully summed up in *Médiaspouvoirs*, January–June 1994 (*Les Médias face á l'Europe*), pp. 3–34.
29 Christophe Adriani, 'Pour le cinéma français et le cinéma en France', *La Pensée* vol. 296, November–December 1993, offers a typical example of this viewpoint. Dominique Wolton, 'L'Europe aux risques de la communication', *Médiaspouvoirs*, January–June 1994, pp. 63–70 makes the important point that, whereas in the past identity seemed to be an obstacle to communication, in contemporary societies it seems indispensable. An overview of the state of the cinema is provided by David Hancock, 'Cinema in Europe: A Panorama', *Communications et Stratégies* no. 6, 2me Trimestre 1992, pp. 139–53.
30 Jean-Michel Frodon, 'Le Cinéma en panne', *Le Monde*, 11 June 1994.
31 The term 'Rhineland model' is developed in Michel Albert, *Capitalism vs. Capitalism* ('Capitalisme contre capitalisme') (London: Whurr Publishers Ltd, 1993).
32 Karl Polanyi, *The Great Transformation*, first edition 1944 (Boston: Beacon Press, 1985).
33 The antagonistic poles of this debate are represented in the exchange between Régis Debray and free-marketeer Mario Vargas Llosa, who suggests that the free market promotes values; thus he counterposes the open market to tribalism, neutral to partisan, hospitable to bellicose, open to closed, in 'Quelles tribus? Cher Mario', *Libération*, 5 December 1994.

2
Free trade as cultural threat: American film and TV exports in the post-war period[1]

Ian Jarvie

Until comparatively recently, most discussion of the impact of American motion picture exports on Europe has been written by Europeans, using European sources, and controlled, inevitably, by European points of view.[2] Lacking has been the view from the United States, using its primary sources and taking account of its points of view.[3] This paper moves in that direction, dealing with a period that is relatively well-documented, while gesturing towards the understanding of what was to come, and acknowledging that trying to pin down American points of view is no straightforward matter.

Another feature of the discussion has been more stable: it was produced largely by and for members of various elites. Intellectual, business and political elites were talking among themselves, patronising the masses at whom mass media are primarily directed. No doubt this is inevitable, since it is one function of the classes in question to articulate social concerns, hence to claim to think for others. Everyone agrees that it is hard to find the voice of the mass audience in box-office figures, preview lobby cards, Nielsen ratings, focus groups, direct observation, questionnaires, letters to the press, and such like. Intriguingly, however, the intellectual elite displays little concern with its own partiality.

Unlike those articulate elites who acted as voices of the political *status quo*, the tradition in film studies has always been enriched by an element of oppositionalism. The political persuasion of many influential writers on film was radical. The effort to legitimate film as a fine art, however, drove them to adopt the elitist discourse of traditional aesthetics. The populist aspects of mass culture could scarcely be appreciated in such terms. These demotic materials were threatening to elites – even progressive ones – because they challenged the *status quo* which elitist aesthetics presupposed. Overseas audiences saw displayed in American movies mores, values and attitudes they took to be subversive of local custom and political arrangement. American films were marked by an aggressive egalitarianism in dress, speech, action, relations between the sexes, and access to the basic necessities of the good life, as well as by an attitude implicit in their mode of address to the audience that they were out to please. This was and continues to be part of their attraction and of their threat.[4]

I Historical background

Kristin Thompson has provided us with the nearest thing to a definitive account of the emergence of the United States film industry as a leading exporter.[5] Primarily, this was an effect of the First World War, which disrupted production in the then leading exporting countries of Germany and France, as well as affecting the transportation and communications upon which international commerce relied. The United States film industry, alone among major film exporters, experienced no disruption of production and was, from its base in a neutral country (until 1917), able to navigate the hazards confronting international commerce more freely than the industries of the belligerents. With the return of peace United States film exports might have been expected to retrench as its business rivals reconstructed. Both the French and the German film industries did rebuild after the war and sought out export markets, especially in Europe.[6] Despite these efforts, in the eight years between the Armistice and the introduction of sound, American pre-eminence in the film export trade was not usurped.

By the mid-1920s the Germans and French had established schemes to promote and subsidise their own films and had enacted discriminatory measures directed against American imports. The British followed suit in legislation of 1927. These were not merely the disgruntled reactions of former market leaders. State Department files report European feeling that there was something contingent, even unnatural, about American export success. This comes through in the praise lavished on domestic films while discussing measures to protect them from competition or to give incentives to production.

Those who, in the 1920s, hoped that Germany or France could resume their pre-war place in the international trade in films were comforted by the thought that Hollywood's domination was neither natural nor inevitable. Various kinds of European co-production and consortia challenged American domination, sometimes including Britain.

Why did the challenges fail to dislodge American dominance? Was the world export success of the United States film industry simply opportunistic and contingent in the first place, and an exercise in hegemonic power afterwards?

Two obvious considerations first. The United States, the biggest and most developed movie market, had of necessity become self-sufficient during the First World War. This has changed little in seventy years. The separate issue of whether the American market is closed to imports will come up later. The other consideration also crystallised during the First World War, namely the marketing attraction of the movie star. By 1918 the economic importance of American stars was apparent not only in the immense salaries paid to those at the top of the system, but by the way four of them discussed founding their own company, United Artists, and three of them eventually did so (William S. Hart thought better of it).[7]

Equally important, and stressed by Thompson as relevant both at home and abroad, was the consolidation of power in the mechanism of distribution. Distribution had emerged as the locus of power in the United States film industry, which attempted to reorganise the export market on the same principle. Films were no longer sold, nor were they entrusted to foreign agents. United States distributors sought to set up exclusive arrangements for their films to be looked after by local subsidiaries of the home firm. This ensured that American films got the same special promotion and attention as they received at home; marketing could exploit the glamorous images of stars, location and production values, and insinuate these as qualities the best films ought to have. Local films could seldom match these qualities.

The uncertainties surrounding the advent of sound were a potential threat to American hegemony. Would the rest of the world follow the United States in converting to sound? Would the star system not now favour those who spoke in local languages and accents? Would foreign films not seem much more 'foreign'?

If any answer is to be ventured to these questions it has, I believe, to focus on distribution. The self-sufficient American market was in the hands of a small number of integrated firms fully confident of finding formulas and mixtures to keep the turnstiles clicking.[8] Many films were guaranteed distribution before they were completed. The industry invested heavily in public relations and in publicity for particular films, selling the mixtures, formulas, stars and company images to the public as guarantees of satisfying entertainment. Only in rare circumstances did investing in the selling of a foreign film, or in its extensive distribution, offer advantages. During and immediately after the Second World War some effort was made widely to distribute selected British films. The overall results were disappointing.[9]

II The situation at the end of the Second World War

The Second World War further strengthened the export position of the American industry, film production having proceeded without interruption (although in smaller aggregate) or significant loss of the qualities which worldwide audiences had come to expect – production values, locations and, especially, stars. Despite being driven by war conditions from many European and Asian markets, American film-making remained profitable and was poised at war's end with a backlog of films to release to liberated countries.

The American industry began planning in the middle of the war for the campaign it would mount to recoup its lost markets. The hope was not just to regain what had been lost to Fascism and occupation, but also to roll back the unsatisfactory pre-war situation in friendly countries. An all-out effort was planned to dismantle all pre-war restrictions. United States industry spokesmen claimed that foreign films were free to compete for time on American screens, and occasionally achieved success. The fact that integrated production and distribution companies made almost enough product to fill the nation's theatres, and that they operated *de facto* as an impenetrable oligopoly, was fudged. Or, to be more precise, the operations of that oligopoly were justified as the exercise of entrepreneurial knowledge of what would and what would not sell with the American audience.[10] Europeans wondered whether it was less a matter of what would sell and more a matter of what the integrated companies would try to sell. To test this would involve taking control of their own distribution in the United States. Most foreign firms could not afford this.

The American government bureaucracy, especially the Departments of

Commerce and of State, had been co-operating with the organised motion picture industry for twenty years, and saw it as their obligation to advise and help with the post-war export campaign. A major achievement was the circular letter, 'American Motion Pictures in the Post-War World', sent by A.A. Berle, Assistant Secretary of State, to all diplomatic posts on 22 February 1944.[11] This document, developed after discussion 'for some time past' with the Motion Picture Producers' and Distributors' Association (MPPDA), directed diplomatic officers to bear in mind the importance of the film industry for the economic, intellectual and advertising welfare of the United States. Officers were to report efforts of foreign governments to restrict or burden US motion pictures; to give feedback on what type of pictures attracted audiences in places they were posted; and to make suggestions at their discretion. The stated overall aim was 'the unrestricted distribution of American motion pictures abroad, especially in the post-war period'. The dominant partner among the western allies had bold aims.

Film personnel were favourably placed in the United States armed forces, including General Marshall's military secretary (later secretary to the General Staff), Frank McCarthy, eventually a Motion Picture Export Association officer in Paris and a 20th Century-Fox producer. There is clear evidence in the files that these men monitored US industry interests.[12]

Yet the industry was thwarted in its wider aims, not just by the newly established governments of the formerly occupied countries, but by other United States officials who advanced two clear reasons to constrain American film exports. One was that, in its devastated condition, Europe could ill afford the dollars for film remittances. This argument from currency shortage would persist into the 1960s.[13] Second, some State Department officials, and some of the military officers concerned with de-Nazifying Germany and other places, held that much Hollywood output depicted the United States in a light that would not impress Europeans favourably, and projected values different from those that the United States and its allies believed should inform reconstruction of Europe and prosecution of the Cold War. Thus there was no question of permitting Marshall Aid monies to be used to import more American films. Only if Marshall Aid and other factors stimulated economic development would Europe be able to afford more film imports. When the International Media Guaranty scheme was introduced, films seeking compensation were vetted within the European Co-operation Administration bureaucracy.[14]

In this last argument we find ideological and cultural considerations foregrounded for the first time. Present notions of 'culture' were not common in American official documents of the time. 'Culture' was mostly used in reports on the positions of European officials, and was regularly decoded as a subterfuge for protectionism. This makes a lot of sense.[15] Most European government measures concerning motion picture imports were overtly discriminatory: carefully designed to target American films, rarely other foreign films. There was clear intent to burden the American product, seen as the greatest threat to any indigenous industry.[16]

Weaknesses in the thinking of British governing elites were exposed by the seven-month MPEAA (Motion Picture Export Association of America) boycott on shipping new films to the United Kingdom in 1947–8; they tended to oversimplify opinion in American official circles and to underestimate the political influence of the American film industry. British official assessments of their own industry's strengths and the likely reactions of the parties proved unfounded, and Ernest Bevin had personally to mediate for the sake of larger foreign policy considerations.[17] Yet in the settlement the United States film industry had to settle for an ad hoc bilateral arrangement that acknowledged the right of the importing country to enact such measures. To this day the organised American film industry longs for an international trade regime that would make such discrimination illegal.

III GATT

Part of American grand strategy for economic reconstruction of the post-war world was the idea of a General Agreement on Tariffs and Trade (GATT) and an International Trade Organisation (ITO) that would create a new legal framework for trade, under which the contracting parties would commit themselves to phasing out discrimination towards co-signatory nations, and engage in a series of tariff-cutting measures with the aims of boosting levels of world trade, thus creating a complex global interdependency. Such an international trade regime would be a legal instrument for fostering concrete interests in peace – commerce flourishing best in peaceful conditions.

During negotiations at Geneva and Havana the United States conceded that cinematographic films were a special case that could not be left to the general provisions of the Agreement. Failing agreement on total free trade in films, attention was turned to simplifying the many protectionist schemes proposed or implemented by different member nations attending the conferences. The United States film industry saw interim advantage in such simplification and unification of the market. Britain was in many ways a crucial case, being one of the victor nations and also the largest export market for American films. It was thought by American officials that Britain's decision would have great symbolic effect for other nations. The British operated both a screen quota and a distributors' ('renters' in British film industry parlance) quota. With some persuasion they eventually decided they could accomplish all goals with only a screen quota. Screen quotas were enshrined in Article IV of the GATT as the sole legal constraint on international trade in films. Tariffs, distribution quotas, contingents, visas, import licences and other pre-war measures were disallowed. The record of the GATT talks at Geneva reveals clearly that the United States wanted a free trade regime, despite the economic giantism of its film industry. Other countries were hoping to place a cordon sanitaire around movies as part of national culture, not subject to all the provisions of tariff-cutting towards free trade. No country represented at the GATT talks agreed with the United States position (most wanted to tighten their pre-war regimes), yet by conceding that quotas rather than tariffs were the only legal regime, they isolated the film trade. Quota-imposing countries thus placed themselves in a vulnerable position: forced to negotiate bilaterally with the main exporter, the United States, over a single trade item, with the MPEA able to get the full attention and weight of the State Department apparatus behind its cause at a time when the quota-imposing country was likely to be deeply dependent on United States economic and political support.

In 1947 and 1948 there may have been the will to appease the United States at Geneva, or there may have been shrewd awareness that the concessions to the US position over the GATT article on films by no means exhausted the possibilities for discrimination, provided the emphasis was shifted from overt measures against American films to measures in favour of domestic films. Subsequent to the signing of the GATT, in all the film-producing countries of western Europe, various kinds of what the GATT literature now calls 'non-border' discriminatory measures were devised and implemented. The United Kingdom had its Eady levy and National Film Finance Corporation, other countries their prizes, incentives, tax breaks and other forms of favourable treatment that constituted domestic measures not subject to the GATT obligation of 'national' treatment of imports, since they were not directed at imports. Thus did the Europeans succeed in protecting their industries using non-border measures. Unlike the alleged closed-market situation in the United States, these protectionist measures were state actions and subject to government-to-government protest as well as to direct MPEAA lobbying. Where popular and creative film industries revived under such protection sooner or later their ambition turned towards the supposed rewards of the American market.

The British film industry, for example, suffered through the ambitions of Korda and Rank, both of whom copied the American strategy by buying into the American industry: Korda into United Artists, Rank into Universal. Neither purchase was into a fully integrated company, so results were meagre. Furthermore, British production costs inflated staggeringly in the full-employment conditions of the post-war period, so that many British films could not possibly cover their costs at home, and became dependent on export success. Failure was thus catastrophic.

The Americans were by no means complacent. Industry representatives always took foreign challenges seriously, perhaps too seriously. Every foreign scheme was fought as though the health of the industry turned on it. Any argument that came to hand was used. J. Arthur Rank seemed to have the financial resources to mount a major challenge. The United States market glittered before European exporters. It was an illusion. Aside from being locked up by the integrated American majors, it was an insular market, fragmented in complex ways and inward-looking. Like other peoples, Americans took delight in seeing their own country on the screen, and seeing foreign locations through the imaginations and distortions of American film-makers. After the divorcement decrees of the Paramount decision broke up the integrated majors after 1949 there was no change in this preference schedule. Change came only with the later restructuring of the audience and of the industry wrought by television. There was an asymmetry: non-Americans seeming far more ready to see films from exotic Hollywood than were Americans to see films from or about the old countries, especially if they were not in English.[18] How was this parochialism to be overcome? Is it even now overcome? Does not Europe *still* represent the exotic other to American normality?

American strategies for marketing films (and now television programmes) abroad, co-ordinated by the MPEAA, a cartel legalised under the Webb–Pomerane

Act, carried out by subsidiaries of the integrated producing-distributing companies, and focused on trade fairs in the United States and abroad, remain unchanged in 1995. Limited screening rights for packages of materials are negotiated for national markets, which revert to the copyright-owning firms. These firms monitor carefully the use of their properties and demand strict adherence to contracts, sanctioned by refusal of further supply. In many importing countries demand is more managed in television than in films because broadcasting systems are so often organs of the state. United States success in selling their product in such a managed market may be a measure of demand rather than of managed supply.[19]

In the fifty years since the GATT was negotiated, film and television issues have not made it beyond the agenda of the various 'rounds' of renegotiations (e.g. the Torquay round, the Kennedy round, the Dillon round, the Tokyo round). The United States holds firmly to the view that film and television screen quotas are a form of discrimination and aims to eliminate them by negotiation. Their case rests on paragraph 4 of Article III of the GATT, which prescribes that goods imported from signatory countries will be accorded so-called 'national' treatment, meaning that imported goods will be treated the same as domestic products. The 'special provisions for cinematographic films' are an obstacle to such national treatment.

Various devices have been used to regulate television programming imports, including broadcasting time quotas, which resemble screen quotas for films, and other non-border measures such as dubbing rules and state and private monopolies. In the final stages of the 1994 Uruguay round the United States, sensing a momentum to complete the round and further free up trade, pressed very hard on those countries that discriminate against American films, television programmes and popular music.[20] The Americans wanted the national treatment clause to cover even non-border measures, and the Article IV exception to be ended. Non-border measures are outside the scope of the GATT, but the United States wants them brought in, along with trade-related aspects of intellectual property (TRIPS). Keen though many nations were for a success, stubborn resistance and brinkmanship came from EC countries, especially France. Going on the offensive, France argued both that the American market was effectively closed to their films and television programming and that indigenous production was in the national cultural interest. In the event, film and television issues were taken off the table.

IV   Is the American market closed?

Our market is totally open, absolutely free. There are no restrictions, no barriers, no quotas of any kind. What IS in our marketplace, however, is the most fierce kind of competition to win the eyes and ears of those who go [to] the cinema and/or watch TV.

Jack Valenti[21]

Before the Paramount case divorcement decrees, the anti-Communist purge and the rise of television made the American film industry radically restructure itself in the early 1950s, the domestic market was organised to be self-sufficient and thus, effectively, closed.[22] As restructured, the market for film became complicated and diverse, as is now also true of television. Whether this diverse film and television market is still closed needs to be addressed as several sub-questions. Is the market closed to other English-speaking product? Is the market closed to the product of foreign-language countries? Also, the market for films has to be distinguished from the market for television programming.

It is hard to be definite about the film market. Some foreign films, English-speaking or not, do get shown extensively in the United States, and not only in the art house ghetto; witness such diverse examples as the Hercules/Maciste films, spaghetti Westerns, Bruce Lee and other kung fu films, *Mad Max*, *Das Boot*, *La Cage aux folles*, *Nikita*, *Crocodile Dundee*. Complicating the picture, foreign directors and stars make films in the States and appear in co-productions shot abroad. The television market would appear more closed than the film market to foreign-language product than to English-language product. As far as I know, no foreign-language programmes appear in dubbed or sub-titled form on primetime network television. Programming imported from English-speaking countries is mostly found on independent stations and the Public Broadcasting System, where it is showcased as a quality alternative to mass-marketed shows. The situation is changing rapidly as industry restructuring increases diversity and may create windows of opportunity for foreign-language imports. Wholly foreign-language stations serving ethnic audiences, which import much of their programme material, have existed for some time. But of course the money to be made from these segments of the market is not such as to mollify those who complain about closure.

Was the closure of the film market for so long and the continuing closure of network primetime a matter of policy? It was certainly not a matter of government policy. There is plentiful evidence that both the State and Commerce Departments urged the majors, through the MPPDA, to see that reciprocity is good business practice. Extensive experiments with the distribution of British films in the 1940s represented a partial result. How government officials view imported television programming will be revealed only when the archives are opened.

Market closure also does not seem to have been a matter of industry policy, if by policy we mean a written or spoken agreement between the industry's firms to keep out foreign films. Self-sufficiency was not a result of some kind of cultural insularity. Its foundation was economic. Effectively forced to be self-sufficient in supply during the period of rapid growth of the industry during the First World War, it was hardly to be expected that the industry would voluntarily down-size itself afterwards. To distributors and exhibitors the key strategic consideration was to have a steady supply of reliable product. Once self-sufficiency was achieved only those imports likely to be super-profitable would be attractive. Since the popularity of all films is unknown until they are exhibited,[23] and since hits abroad may not be hits at home and vice versa, substituting imports would be a high-risk policy for integrated firms. This explains why only the occasional foreign film got distributed and why the American film industry had always dabbled in co-productions abroad as one way to diversify offerings while still having some flexibility in the management of supply.[24] From James Bond to Superman this seems to have been the way the market was opened up.[25]

The remake phenomenon throws some light on both film and television. In the movies *3 Men and a Baby*, *Cousins* or *The Vanishing*, or in 'All in the Family', 'Absolutely Fabulous' and similar versions of British shows on American television, we see clear evidence that the Americans judge the European original to need modification to suit American tastes. We could argue endlessly as to whether there is any way to test this judgment. American executives think they understand the American market best. Dubbing or sub-titling is judged out of the question. More important, the informed guess of the responsible company officer is the last word. The fact that successful executives usually only have short strings of luck, like gamblers, may seem an irrationality of the system. But in an industry catering to an unknown and possibly fickle public, the one irrationality may be an unavoidable mirror of the other.[26]

While not legally closed by state action, then, the American television market was and is very hard to break into because of self-sufficiency built up when other countries did not have much television. Changes in market structure presently unfolding might open it up.

V   The question of cultural invasion

Why this EC quota? Its defenders, those who would build the siege wall, claim 'Our culture is at stake!' Can this be true? Is a thousand, two thousand, years of an individual nation's culture to collapse because of the exhibition of American TV programs? Is the culture of any European country so flimsily anchored, so shakily rooted, that European viewers must be caged and blinded else their links with their honored and distinguished past suddenly vanish like an exploding star in the heavens?[27]

Jack Valenti[28]

I drew attention above to how the rhetoric of cultural nationalism is usually deployed by members of elites, intellectuals, businessmen and politicians. Intellectuals are often suspicious of the discourse of businessmen and politicians; they might be encouraged to extend suspicion to their own discourse. The attraction of American demotic art is first of all the attraction of the demotic. Second, it is the job-threatening attraction of the foreign. The attractiveness of the demotic threatens the hegemony of cultural mandarins, from film critics to schoolteachers, and it also poses a threat to the political influence of intellectuals.

In *Hollywood's Overseas Campaign* I was critical of the use of the 'cultural defence' card in Anglo-American film talks of the 1940s, and tried to show that British official use of it was rhetorical disguise for straight commercial considerations. I also noted that 'culture' was an unfamiliar term in the vocabularies of American officials, who sensed protectionism behind it. When business invokes 'culture' most of us would treat it as self-serving. For intellectuals having an even closer relation to culture, their discourse deserves at least equal sceptical treatment.

The underlying puzzle is why mass culture should attract the cultural defence argument, when products of high culture do not. By most accounts, high culture has real and lasting influence, popular culture is ephemeral and superficial. British elites feared that American films would teach American manners, mores, morals and, horror of horrors, American accents. Countries speaking other tongues had no linguistic fears, especially if the films were dubbed. Diffusion of manners, mores and morals were, however, a concern.

The small high-culture audience was not accused of complicity in cultural invasion, even though much high culture is imported. Intellectual elites, which generate the rhetoric of cultural invasion, tend to use high culture as their reference. Confident of their own immunity to cultural pollution, they patronise the mass audience. Why? Suppose the media had taught British schoolchildren to speak with American accents. It would be no more than an interesting historical phenomenon, similar to the way the American accent owes much to the seventeenth-century English of the West Country.

The conception of cultural defence, then, is very confused. There are deep problems with conceiving of culture as a distinct entity having some specifiable relation to state boundaries, thus inviting state governments to manage these matters. Some elements of culture, especially those related to language, are results of influence and drift that make the effort to assert control, by the state or the guardians of culture,[29] seem ahistorical and futile, like the much-ridiculed French language legislation of 1994. A culture, like a language, is a historical tradition that did not need the nation-state to crystallise it, and no doubt will develop in ways that will confound the nation-state that tries to control it. Why should this cause concern? What is so deplorable about the worldwide enjoyment of *Jurassic Park*, with its multinational cast, or of that great Austrian Arnold Schwarzenegger, or of that great Belgian Jean-Claude Van Damme, or of Clint Eastwood? The answer is, I believe, a political one.[30]

Something sinister and reactionary underlies the rhetoric of cultural invasion and cultural sovereignty. The question turns on what the United States and its society signifies in the conceptual economy of the critic of American cultural invasion. That vast unknown land to the west of Europe often functions as a *tabula rasa* on which Europeans can project their hopes and fears.[31] In the nineteenth century, generally speaking, progressive and leftist elements looked to America as a beacon of hope; reactionaries feared it as the land of the common man. This polarity reversed in the twentieth century when America became identified with advanced industrialisation and robber baron capitalism, and its social problems became a dire warning for progressives – the more vociferous the more powerful it appeared – and a refuge for reactionaries.[32] America was a radical ideological state and both its economic policies and its egalitarianism were threatening to European elites. Its commitment to consumerism and competition is not comforting to businesses seeking to operate behind risk- and competition-reducing trade barriers; its egalitarian demotic gives no special place or weight to intellectuals and their values. In so far as politicians defer to both business and intellectual elites, they find America a double threat. American popular media unself-consciously espouse the virtues of Americanness and Americanisation, make propaganda for what Nataša Durovičová calls Americanness 'as the very signifier of universal human evolution, subsuming under it all the local currencies of cultural exchange, a limitless melting pot of mores, nations and classes'.[33]

VI   Conclusion: American advantages

At the end of the Second World War the American film industry had at least five distinct advantages over all potential rivals in international trade:

1. It had extensive investments in Europe and intended to resume control of those properties.
2. Some local exhibitors and distributors were favourably disposed towards American films because their supply was reliable and their public appeal relatively constant, and they came with certain pre-sold and pricing advantages.
3. Blocked currencies gave the Americans incentive to diversify their output by spending on European location shooting and by investing further in overseas industries and overseas talent.
4. America, as the dominant military, political and economic power of the west, had clear plans for freer international trade in the post-war world.
5. America displayed exemplary skills in the manufacture of popular entertainment.[34]

These factors show that American export success was no simple contingency that could be reversed. European dreams of usurping the American position overlooked these factors. It was reasoned that, were the audience given the choice they would choose the local product or, failing that, given no choice but the local product they would content themselves and keep up their rate of attendance. Underneath this lay a hidden premiss, namely that, when you have seen one film you have seen them all.

On the contrary, films are not perfect substitutes one for another and American films deliver unique forms of audience satisfaction. Consider how many countries would like to compete with American and British popular music, and consider the difficulty the French, Germans, Russians and Japanese have. What they produce is successful domestically but almost never back in the United States. American films had stars, distinct genres and diffuse qualities that connect to the positive image of America in the minds of so many, pinpointed by John Grierson as their 'Optimism'.[35] These ideological uses and gratifications of American films had as much to do with their export success as the trading strategy and tactics of their industry, their direct control of distribution, and their partial ownership of theatres. We might say control of distribution was a necessary but not sufficient condition of their success, as was their content, but the two together were both necessary and sufficient.

With appropriate modifications for the greater direct role of European states in broadcasting, I believe much of the above analysis applies, *mutatis mutandis*, to the American export of television programmes.

Notes

1 The argument of this paper relies upon results documented in Ian Jarvie, *Hollywood's Overseas Campaign: The North Atlantic Movie Trade, 1920–1950* (Cambridge: Cambridge University Press, 1992). See also Jarvie, 'Dollars and Ideology: Will Hays' Economic Foreign Policy 1922–1945', *Film History* vol. 2, 1988, pp. 207–21; and 'The Postwar Economic Foreign Policy of the American Film Industry: Europe 1945–1950', *Film History* vol. 4, 1990, pp. 277–88.

2 The American Thomas Guback is the exception that proves this rule, since his *The International Film Industry* (Bloomington: University of Indiana Press, 1969) takes on from time to time an unsympathetic and even anti-American tone, viewing countries that import American films primarily as victims of rapacious capitalism.

3 Various historians, including Paul Swann, Richard Maltby, Toby Miller and others are beginning to change that.

4 Much of this analysis stems from John Grierson. See Ian Jarvie and Robert Macmillan, 'Grierson on Hollywood's Success', *Historical Journal of Film, Radio and Television* vol. 9, 1989, pp. 309–26.

5 Kristin Thompson, *Exporting Entertainment* (London: BFI, 1985).

6 The German industry suffered from the additional barrier of strong anti-German sentiments among the victorious powers, with some localities, like my home base of Ontario, not permitting the public screening of German films until the late 1920s.

7 Tino Balio, *United Artists: The Company Built by the Stars* (Madison: University of Wisconsin Press, 1976).

8 See the analysis in Keith Acheson and Christopher Maule, 'Understanding Hollywood's Organization and Continuing Success', *Journal of Cultural Economics* vol. 18, 1994, pp. 271–300.

9 See Jarvie, *Hollywood's Overseas Campaign*, ch. 8.

10 In a superb paper, De Vany and Eckert challenge the received view of the integrated industry as monopolistic. See Arthur De Vany and Ross D. Eckert, 'Motion Picture Antitrust: The Paramount Case Revisited', in Richard O. Zerbe, Jr. and Victor P. Goldberg (eds), *Research in Law and Economics* vol. 14 (Greenwich, CT: JAI Press, 1991), pp. 51–112.

11 The text is in Jarvie, *Hollywood's Overseas Campaign*, pp. 379–81.

12 See ibid., ch. 12.

13 An interesting research topic would be the nexus between blocked currencies, runaway production and government encouragement of tourism to assist with the dollar shortage. Europe was attractively showcased in quite a few American films of the 1950s and 1960s, the protagonists frequently being tourists.

14 See Paul Swann, 'The Little State Department: Washington and Hollywood's Rhetoric of the Post-War Audience', in David W. Ellwood and Ron Kroes (eds), *Hollywood in Europe: Experiences of a Cultural Hegemony* (Amsterdam: VU Press, 1994), pp. 184–5.

15 See the argument in Jarvie, *Hollywood's Overseas Campaign* about the underlying economic concerns of Britain which were regularly dressed up in the rhetoric of culture.

16 An exception was France, where the Blum–Byrnes Agreement of 1946 left the British film industry with few import licences, a situation not alleviated when it was renegotiated in 1948. See Jean-Pierre Jeancolas, 'L'Arrangement. Blum–Byrnes à l'épreuve des faits. Les relations (cinématographiques) franco-américaines de 1944 à 1948', *1895* no. 13, December 1993, pp. 1–49 and its sequel, 'From the Blum–Byrnes Agreement to the GATT Affair' in this book.

17 For further discussion see Ian Jarvie, 'British Trade Policy *versus* Hollywood: "Food before flicks"?', *Historical Journal of Film, Radio and Television* vol. 6, pp. 19–41, and the relevant chapters in Jarvie, *Hollywood's Overseas Campaign*; Margaret Dickinson and Sarah Street, *Cinema and State: The Film Industry and the British Government 1927–1984* (London: BFI, 1985); and PEP, *The British Film Industry* (London: PEP, 1952).

18 For an interesting discussion see Richard Maltby and Ruth Vasey, 'The International

Language Problem: European Reactions to Hollywood's Conversion to Sound', in Ellwood and Kroes, *Hollywood in Europe.*

19 Instructive in this regard was the monopsony pricing imposed in the British market by the refusal of the BBC and ITV companies to bid against each other, which was revealed by the scandal over *Dallas*. See Richard Collins, 'Wall-to-Wall Dallas?', in his *Television: Policy and Culture* (London: Unwin Hyman, 1990).

20 See the urgings of Jack Valenti, president of the MPEAA, in *Hearings Before the Committee on Finance, U.S. Senate, 102nd Congress, 1st Session, 17–18 April 1991* (Washington: USGPO 1991), pp. 60–2 and 149–51.

21 Ibid., p. 151.

22 For an analysis from the simplest of premisses of why it was organised as it was see De Vany and Eckert, 'Motion Picture Antitrust'.

23 See Keith Acheson and Christopher Maule, 'The Business of Films: Making the Right Films and Making Films Right', forthcoming.

24 De Vany and Eckert's Paramount analysis could be fruitfully applied here.

25 It should not be forgotten that imports have often proved a disappointment, as with the British 'Prestige Experiment' and the similar disaster over swinging sixties' imports. Cf. John Gregory Dunne, *The Studio* (New York: Farrar, Straus and Giroux, 1969).

26 See Harold Vogel, *Entertainment Industry Economics* (New York: Cambridge University Press, 1986).

27 Another conundrum is that, unlike their French cousins, Québec nationalists are reported as feeling far less threatened by American media than are English Canadians. See 'Yoked in Twin Solitudes: Canada's Two Cultures', *New York Times*, 18 September 1994, section 4, p. 4; and Richard Collins, *Culture, Communication and National Identity: The Case of Canadian Television* (Toronto: University of Toronto Press, 1990).

28 Valenti, *Hearings Before the Committee*, p. 150.

29 Robert Sklar's apt phrase: see *Movie-Made America* (New York: Random House, 1975).

30 For another view see Victoria de Grazia, 'Mass Culture and Sovereignty: The American Challenge to European Cinemas, 1920–1960', *Journal of Modern History* vol. 61, 1989, pp. 53–87.

31 Heidegger's loathing of America, which he had never visited, is a striking example.

32 See Henry Pelham, *America and the British Left* (London: Adam and Charles Black, 1956), and the burgeoning literature on the attitudes towards America of French intellectuals.

33 Nataša Durovičová, 'Translating American: The Hollywood Multilinguals 1929–1933', in Rick Altman (ed), *Sound Theory, Sound Practice* (London: Routledge, 1992), p. 141.

34 As to TV, 2, 4 and 5 were directly applicable, 1 was inhibited and 3 was not important.

35 See Jarvie and Macmillan, 'Grierson on Hollywood's Success'.

3
From the Blum–Byrnes Agreement to the GATT affair

Jean-Pierre Jeancolas

On 26 May 1946, an agreement was signed in Washington between on the one side Léon Blum, former head of the Popular Front Government, deportee in Germany during the latter half of the war and now special envoy of the French Provisional government, and on the other James F. Byrnes, American Secretary of State. The agreement was wide ranging, obtaining for France coal, wheat and dollars, settling questions outstanding since the end of the First World War, and laying the foundation of what was to become the western bloc in the years of the Cold War. Attached to this agreement were two brief typed pages concerning the cinema. These two little pages are now referred to as the Blum–Byrnes Agreement, while the main document goes by the name Washington Agreement.

Our story begins with these two little pages – that is to say a particular moment in what we might call the Franco-American cinema war, dating back to the times of Pathé and Edison and continuing to the recent fracas over GATT and authors' rights which briefly filled the newspapers in 1993. The episode of the Blum–Byrnes Agreement, which dealt with the reopening of contact between the French and American cinemas after the break imposed by the Second World War and the Occupation, is a particularly tense moment of this 'war', setting the French against the Americans but also a war among themselves, an episode of civil war against the background of the Cold War.

I

To explain this, a brief flashback is necessary. Between the Armistice of June 1940 and Liberation in summer 1944, American films were banished from Parisian screens. The Armistice divided France into two zones. There was an occupied zone, comprising two-thirds of French territory, including Paris; and a non-occupied zone covering the centre and south-west and governed by the puppet regime at Vichy. In the non-occupied zone American films imported before 1940 continued to be screened until 1942.

Fighting continued in France throughout 1944 and into 1945. The country was in a terrible state, affecting the cinema as well as other aspects of life. Studios and cinemas had been destroyed; there was no heating, no film stock. But for de

Gaulle's Provisional government, the cinema was not a priority: priorities were to recreate an army, feed the population, restore communications.

The invading Americans had plans for the installation of an occupying administration, staffed by specially trained American officers, to act as a temporary replacement for the collaborationist structure of prefects and sub-prefects. This was to be called Allied Military Government for Occupied Territories (AMGOT). De Gaulle resisted this, and it was never activated. But as part of their plans the Americans brought with them, on the backs of army lorries, between forty and fifty dubbed movies, which the Office of War Information (OWI) gradually handed over to French distributors.

Meanwhile a number of films had been hidden away in Paris and elsewhere (some of them, according to Cinémathèque legend, in the Palais de Chaillot). In Limoges, liberated by the Maquis in August 1944, four American films appeared on local screens in September. These would have been old films, not the new ones brought by the OWI. Between the Liberation and July 1946 these two groups of films – those from the OWI, including some war documentaries, and those that had been hidden away – were the only ones available to cinemas as they gradually reopened.

For the Americans, the war was a parenthesis, and they expected a rapid return to the situation that had existed up to 1939. This situation was regulated by a trading agreement known as the Accord Marchandeau, signed in 1936. This was to become a source of conflict between French and American negotiators.

For the cinema, the Accord Marchandeau made official a policy practised since the early 1930s, that of the 'contingent', according to which the French government granted import licences to 188 dubbed foreign films per year, of which 150 could be American. The French opposed renewal of this agreement, arguing that the market could not support such a high level of imports. They pointed out that the earlier figure had been based on double-bills. The Vichy government had banned this practice and the Provisional government had retained the ban. Up to 400 cinemas had also been destroyed or damaged during the war, and these two factors combined meant that the market could not absorb as many films as before the war. Estimates differed, but it was thought that the total capacity of the market was less than 200 films per year. A government memo prepared for the Washington negotiations suggested between 150 and 180. Under the circumstances a return to the figure of 150 American films was out of the question.

On the other hand the demand for American films was enormous, covering all strata of society and all political tendencies. To be able to watch American films was seen as a sign that the country was free again. People wanted to see colour films like *Gone with the Wind*, still not released. For cinephiles there was *Citizen Kane*, also not released, but which Jean-Paul Sartre, among others, had seen in America. In the left-wing weekly *Action* in July 1945, Nicole Vedrès called for a return of what she called 'our American film, our little Saturday night god', while Edgar Morin, then a brilliant up-and-coming Communist intellectual, declared in November 1944: 'We need the American cinema like an old friend back from afar.'

The 'profession' – a somewhat mysterious term which designates, even today, the circle of influential producers, directors, financiers, etc. – was divided. The Comité de Libération du Cinéma Français, a resistance organisation dominated by the Communist Party (PCF), spoke in military terms in September 1944 about the need to release French films on to the market 'to engage battle with the American cinema'. In May 1945 the veteran film-maker Raymond Bernard called for the French cinema not to become the slave of the American or any other cinema. Julien Duvivier, returning from exile in Hollywood, said: 'If we let ourselves be invaded by American production without a countervailing place for French films, in two years there will be no more French cinema.' Producers, concerned at the difficulty of creating enough good films to release on to the market, were afraid of the backlog of American films – 1500 to 2000 movies already released in America and Britain and ready to be dumped on the French market. But the distributors and exhibitors were more restrained in their patriotism, and on the whole looked for the release of these films, which they knew the public wanted.

So negotiations began. On the American side, the MPPDA vigorously lobbied the French Foreign Office to restore the system of import licences. The Provisional government hesitated. In the October 1945 elections the left had gained 50 per cent of the vote – Communists 26 per cent, Socialists and their allies 24 per cent – and there was talk of nationalising the cinema. The climate was heavy with suspicion. Meanwhile the demand to see American films grew more insistent on all sides.

February 1946 brought an impasse. The Americans wanted a return to the contingent system, possibly lowering the ceiling from 150 to 108 films per year. The French negotiators preferred a screen quota system, whereby each cinema would be obliged to devote a certain number of weeks per quarter to showing French films only, possibly as many as seven weeks out of thirteen.

Meanwhile the country was in crisis. Industrial production stood at 70 per cent of pre-war levels, inflation was at 5 per cent per month, cold and hunger reigned. American aid was essential. In February 1946, after the resignation of de Gaulle, the new head of the Provisional government, Félix Goin, sent Léon Blum on an extraordinary mission to Washington to obtain urgent loans but also to negotiate a solution to more long-standing problems of debt. The irritating question of the return of American films to the market was added to the list.

Blum and his team arrived in Washington on 15 March. The Agreements were signed on 28 May, with the cinema part in an appendix, to which was added a letter from the French Ambassador on the repatriation of earnings made by American companies in France.

The contingent system was abolished and replaced by quotas, initially set at four weeks per quarter beginning on 1 July 1946. There was to be no restriction on imports, so thirty-six weeks per year were open to 'free competition'. No one was under any illusion as to what this meant: the door was now open to the entire backlog of American films waiting to be released.

On 14 June a press conference was called bringing together the 'profession', trade unions and individuals such as the historian Georges Sadoul and the Communist deputy Fernand Grenier. There was widespread and shared concern. Four weeks per quarter were not felt to be enough; there was a danger of American companies buying up most of the exhibition sector. And fear was expressed of the French public being 'intoxicated' by the 'American mentality'.

To calm things down, Eric Johnston, head of the MPEAA, sent a telegram to

Paris offering on behalf of the eight majors to restrict the import of dubbed films to 124 in the first year of the Agreement.

When the Agreement was debated in Parliament, speakers stressed the fragile state of the French cinema and called for state intervention to protect it. The Agreement was then ratified unanimously, with 550 deputies (including the Communists) voting in favour.

The Hollywood companies promptly reopened their Paris offices and started advertising in the trade press. The quotas were widely disregarded both in Paris and in the provinces, as exhibitors fell over each other to satisfy popular demand.

The cinema Agreement had not been negotiated personally by Blum, but by Pierre Baraduc, a colleague of Jean Monnet. But Blum assumed full responsibility in defending the Agreement against attack. Rather tactlessly, he declared: 'If, in the higher interests of France, I had had to sacrifice the cinema profession, I would have done so.' With more justification he also expressed his belief that the Agreement placed the French cinema 'in a far better situation than it had been previously'.

Forty-five years later it is possible to make two different readings of the consequences of the Agreement and the place it has assumed in the history of the cinema and the 'black legend' (in the words of Jean Portes) which surrounds it.

1. *The technical approach.* 'Blum has sold out the French cinema to the Americans'; 'The French cinema will die'; and (Pierre Kast in January 1948): 'French production dropped from 140 films in 1936 to 80 in 1946, and has undoubtedly dropped to less than 40 in 1947.' Kast was wrong. The French cinema did not die in 1947. Study of the trade press and official figures of the Centre National de la Cinématographie (CNC) give the following figures:

1946	80 films
1947	92 films
1948	94 films

In 1947 the French cinema not only still produced films (often cheaply, and many of them terrible) but it also found screens on which to show them.

American films were released on to the market not only by the majors, through their offices in Paris, but also by small French distributors, who bought a number of films (often old ones) from the independents, and had them dubbed in Paris. By 1949, there were forty-four such distributors, with a portfolio of 117 dubbed films, sold to exhibitors not over-concerned with quality.

In the second half of 1946 many cinemas did not respect the four-week quota for French films. Then in 1947 the CNC began to threaten exhibitors with sanctions for exceeding the maximum of American films.

It was during these first few quarters that the American offensive, assisted by the fifth column of small French distributors, seriously threatened the national cinema. During the last quarter of 1946 and the first two quarters of 1947, when supply and demand for American films were at their highest, the quota offered a breathing space, enabling the French cinema to survive.

The Washington negotiators were not as foolish as they have been portrayed.

They gave way on the number of weeks for the quota (their instructions were to go for six), but they held firm on the principle, which the Americans were opposed to. It was the quota, and its application on a quarterly basis, which was the effective umbrella protecting French films from the Hollywood deluge. By the end of 1947 the mania for American films had more or less subsided.

The Washington Agreement should also be placed in the wider context of reconstruction of French cinema, which itself is part of the wider context of reconstruction practised by the Fourth Republic. Jean Monnet was involved in the negotiation, and a telegram sent by him to Paris on 27 April 1946 proposing a 'reflection' on the cinema suggests to me that the Franco-American Agreement was part of a coherent political move, including the creation of the CNC in October 1946 and the appointment of Michel Fourré-Cormeray as its first director general in January 1947. It was the CNC that was made responsible for the application of the Agreement, and Fourré-Cormeray who was to negotiate the Paris Agreement, more favourable to the French, and with an extension of the quota to five weeks, which replaced the Washington Agreement on 16 September 1948.

On that same day, moreover, the National Assembly passed its first Aid Law to the film industry, devised by Fourré-Cormeray. And it was again the CNC which negotiated and signed the first Franco-Italian co-production agreements, broadening the basis of the market to resist the trans-Atlantic invasion.

It was the new French mode of production, put in place in the two years following the Blum–Byrnes Agreement, which was able to render its provisions obsolete.

2. *The political approach.* On 18 April 1948, Maurice Thorez, general secretary of the PCF, addressed the assembled party militants as follows:

> The American films which, thanks to Léon Blum, are invading our screens, do not merely deprive our artists, musicians, workers and technicians of their daily bread. They literally poison the souls of our children, young people, young girls, who are to be turned into the docile slaves of the American multi-millionaires, and not into French men and women attached to the moral and intellectual values which have been the grandeur and glory of our fatherland.

One year earlier, on 5 May 1947, a decree by the head of the government, the Socialist Paul Ramadier, had removed the Communist ministers from office, bringing to an end the three-party coalition that had emerged from the Resistance and marking the consolidation, in France, of the Cold War. As another Socialist put it: 'The Communists are no longer to the left, they are to the east.'

The Communist Party thus marginalised was, in the post-war period, an extremely powerful force. Up until the 1950s it had a consistent 25 per cent of the popular vote. In 1946 it had maybe 400,000 members. It had its own press, which it controlled either directly or through frontist associations often emerging from the Resistance. It had great intellectual prestige. Aragon and Picasso were among its members, and there were many fellow-travellers. It held power in many towns and rural areas where its existing base had been strengthened during the Resistance.

After the Liberation, the PCF was active and influential in film culture at many levels. Léon Moussinac and Georges Sadoul were important party voices. Sadoul was an internationally renowned historian, influential critic of the party magazine, *Les Lettres Françaises*, professor at the IDHEC film school, vice-president of the Cinémathèque Française, president of the association of critics. The PCF was influential in the film societies, organisationally and through the magazine *L'Ecran Français*, which from 1948 came under the control of the *Lettres Françaises*. It also had influence in the trade unions.

Its initial response to the Washington Agreements had been reserved, though – as mentioned previously – it had voted for them in Parliament. But after their eviction from government, the party's leaders found in the Blum–Byrnes Agreement an ideal point of attack – both against the Socialists in the person of Léon Blum, and against the Americans as instigators of the Cold War.

Thus there arose the Committees for the Defence of French Cinema, which brought together party militants and valued fellow-travellers to fight and demonstrate for the revision of the Agreements. (In 1993 one of these, Claude Autant Lara, was still, aged 92, fighting the same cause but from a different angle: against the Americans and the 'Jew' Blum, under the banner of the Front National.) The Committees and the massive demonstrations they organised undoubtedly strengthened the hand of the French side during the negotiation of the Paris Agreement of 1948.

The same situation also gave rise to a perversion of critical values on the part of the Communist and pro-Communist press, especially in the years 1947 to 1955. Everything American was bad – except the film-makers blacklisted by McCarthy. To like John Ford was to support German rearmament, the war economy, extended military service, American aggression in Korea, and so on.

Let me conclude this section by quoting the peroration of a brochure published in 1954 under the title *Menaces sur le cinéma français* (it has Joan of Arc on the cover: the last resort of all French nationalism):

> To let American films become masters of our screens would not only mean the death of an industry. It would mean giving way to the incessant pressure to 'think American', to think like Senator McCarthy. This we do not want. We cannot support a cinema inspired by a policy which preaches hatred of all those who do not think like President Eisenhower, a cinema whose content is a constant incitement to war, brutality, racism, pessimism, not to mention eroticism.

II

The mobilisation for the defence of the French cinema, which reached its peak in the last years of the 1940s, was, therefore, more a political than an economic or artistic matter.

The Paris Agreements of 1948, which had extended to five weeks the three-monthly quota reserved for French films, were due for renegotiation in 1952. The two sides were unable to reach agreement, and the French government decided unilaterally to maintain the five-week quota, while also imposing a 'contingent' on dubbed foreign films.

This decision did not provoke a strong reaction. Passions had cooled. Since

1949, the French cinema had more or less achieved parity with Hollywood on the home market. Out of 387 million spectators in that year, 42.4 per cent had been for French films, against 44.5 per cent for American.

In the 1950s and 1960s, protected by its Aid Laws and by co-production agreements, the reconquest of the market continued. Some examples: in 1956, out of 399 million spectators, the proportions were 48.6 per cent for French films as against 33.4 per cent for American. In 1967, when the number of spectators had dropped to 211 million, the proportions were 52.2 per cent for French films, and only 29.6 per cent for American.

Finally, for the 1970s the proportions were as follows:

	French films	American films
1970	49.03%	25.98%
1971	52.99	24.79
1972	53.51	24.32
1973	58.32	19.72
1974	53.87	21.28
1975	50.64	26.94
1976	51.12	27.71
1977	46.53	30.38
1978	46.02	32.55
1979	50.11	29.25

Source: CNC. info. no. 182/183.

In May and June 1953, Colette Audry published two articles in Jean-Paul Sartre's magazine *Les Temps Modernes* under the title 'Où en est le cinéma français?' ('What's the state of French cinema?'). During the Goin government, she had been Secretary of State for Information in Gaston Defferre's office and was thus a privileged witness at the time of the Blum–Byrnes Agreement, and she remained an acute observer of the reconstruction of the French cinema.

Writing in 1953 she observed, on the subject of the reconstruction then going on: 'There is no doubt that protection has been advantageous to the cinema as a whole and to workers in the industry in particular.' She then referred to the abortive renegotiation of the Paris Agreements in 1952 and expressed concern at a quasi-official agreement between Jacques Flaud, director general of the CNC, and Eric Johnston, president of the MPAA.

Her anxieties were misplaced. Either that or they were forty years ahead of their time, since she concluded in terms which prefigure those of the GATT 'battle' of 1993:

> Cinema is something very different from an industry. It is a means of expression through the image, a means of expression for a collectivity. The image which a country, a society, offer of themselves. That is why a politico-economic offensive which seeks to stifle this means of expression in a given country can only be compared to the forcible means which conquerors sometimes use to deprive the vanquished of their language.

François Mitterand was to say the same thing, on 21 September 1993, in his Gdansk speech.

The dossier of the Blum–Byrnes Agreement, the analysis of the difficult relations between the French and American cinemas in the immediately post-war period, was made in a historically classical way: the composition of a body of sources which were available, more than forty years afterwards, a collection of evidence and analyses, put in the form of a dossier which could lay claims to being a scientific document. The years that followed had more or less calmed the feelings that had been so strong, so *franco-françaises* (to adopt the term used by the French to designate differences between Frenchmen), and also the disputes between left and right during the late 1940s.

The GATT affair (or as it is often called, the GATT battle), such as occurred during the last months of 1993, is a less solid affair altogether than the Blum–Byrnes dossier. If there really was a battle, it was only a moment in a war that has not yet ended; observers are still in place and the sound of battle can be heard in the professional press on both sides of the Atlantic. The calm which accompanies historical research is not there, since the protagonists are aware of the fact that the Agreement, or more precisely the non-agreement, of 15 December 1993 has established only a truce: nothing has been resolved.

What I shall call the crisis of 1993 (historians will no doubt give it another name, in the light of events to come over the next decade) is a new episode in the unequal competition – which Pierre Kast in 1946 called 'the fight between the clay pot and iron pot' – between the French cinema and Hollywood, then as now a matter of sharing the French market between national cinema and American cinema.

Already in 1918 Charles Pathé had proposed, in his famous letter to the journalist Nozière, that there should be a law imposing on French exhibitors a quota of 25 per cent French films in their programmes. In 1946 the Blum–Byrnes Agreement set a screen quota of four weeks in every quarter to be reserved for French films. In the 1950s, the French cinema was rebuilt, under conditions we shall discuss later, and was able to reconquer a sufficiently large part of the market to flourish and to resist the crisis of the 1980s better than other European cinemas such as the German, the Italian or the British.

The Paris Agreement, signed on 16 September 1948 by two French Ministers, Robert Schumann and Robert Lacoste, and by the American Ambassador Jefferson Caffery, revised the Agreement of 1946 in a way favourable to French interests. This new Agreement took the form of a common declaration of both governments, stating in particular that the French decision to enlarge the quota to five weeks in each quarter was compatible with Article IV of the General Agreement on Tariffs and Trades signed on 30 October 1947. This Agreement of 1947 was the foundation of GATT.

The 1947 GATT Agreement provided for the possibility of making regular adjustments to its provisions. It was the eighth renegotiation of GATT, the so-called Uruguay round, begun in 1986, which provoked the crisis of 1993. It was during 1992–3 that what we call the profession – hundreds of people, such as producers and directors, journalists and financiers, sophisticated persons and some high-ranking government officials, who supported the cinema in France or believed that they did – awoke. These people became aware of the danger in the American insistence on opening the cinema and audiovisual markets to the unrestricted circulation of goods, in the production of which the United States had an overwhelming superiority. In January and February 1993, an anguished debate shook the French press, concerning the identity of some French films made in English, at the time of the annual César awards, which are to the French cinema what the Oscars are to the American. Director Robert Enrico, vice-president of the Society of Film Directors (Société des Réalisateurs de Films), spoke in a number of interviews about the danger which threatened 'the European cinema, a reflection of our cultures and our differences'. He reminded his listeners that 'the American film industry is omnipresent in all European film markets' and drew attention to a fact at that time largely unnoticed in the media: 'At the present moment we are engaged in a real battle inside the European Community and in international commercial negotiations to defend a pluralistic European cinema.' On 11 March *Le Monde* published an interview with Jack Valenti. The tone was particularly strong:

> I think that the United States will not sign a GATT agreement which makes culture an area of exception. We will not sign it. We will not be partners to such an agreement. ... There would be a commercial war about it if we don't set up competition and free access to the markets.

Two weeks later, producer Alain Tarzian answered him in the name of the UPF (Union des Producteurs de Films, or Film Producers' Union) in the columns of the 26 March issue of the most important film trade paper *Le Film Français*:

> The UPF is not indifferent to the threatening statement of Jack Valenti. Jack Valenti said in substance: 'We will make war on the Europeans if they don't give up their laws protecting the audiovisual media.' If Mr Valenti is disturbed by the word 'culture', we are ready to answer him; for culture cannot be sold, and it is not a question of eliminating it with a stroke of a pen. If he wants war, he will get it.

Two days earlier, on 24 March, *Le Monde* had published a full page of replies to Jack Valenti, including one from Jack Lang, at that time Minister of Culture, in which he declared: 'As far as culture is concerned, free exchange is synonymous with the death of pluralism.' It also included a response from Dominique Vallon, General Director of the CNC, and one from Jean-Claude Carrière, a writer and scriptwriter of the last films of Luis Buñuel, who said:

> Yes, it's true, we are at war. ... European authors and producers, at first incredulous, have had some difficulties in reacting and in defending themselves. But now they have done it. Almost everywhere, week after week, we have been organising ourselves. Mr Valenti's anger is perhaps a result of this resistance.

The rattle of swords and shields was almost audible. The moment has come to try to understand what was, for the French protagonists, at stake in the battle they were preparing themselves for.

In 1993, the French cinema existed, and not only as purely French cinema. The state-supported CNC, which since 1946 has supervised the administration and finances of the French cinema, publishes in its bulletin *CNC Infos* statistics on French production. In its 1993 bulletin French production of feature films was given as 152 (showing a slight variation from previous years: there were 155 in 1992, 156 in 1991, and 146 in 1990). These 152 films were divided into two categories:

1. There were 101 films *d'initiative française*, themselves divided into two sub-categories:
   a. sixty-seven films completely financed in France;
   b. thirty-four co-productions with a French majority stake.
2. There were then fifty-one films which were either co-productions with minority French participation (of which there were thirty-six) or films supported by the so-called ECO fund for aid to co-production with central and eastern Europe (of which there were fifteen).

In reality the majority of this production was supported by a variety of means which can be specified as the 'French method of film production' (*mode de production français*). This method originated in the reconstruction of French national cinema after the Second World War.

In 1948 the French Parliament approved a law to aid the film industry. Originally this was a temporary measure only, but it was reviewed and strengthened in 1953 and again in 1959, and has been continually readopted since that date. In simple terms, the principle of this law is based on a sum of money, now called the support fund or *compte de soutien*, which comes from two principal sources: a tax called TSA (*taxe spéciale additionelle*), taken from theatrical box-office receipts; and (since 1984) a tax on the profits of television networks. In 1993 the support fund amounted to FF953 million, of which 457 million came from the TSA and 458 million from tax on television.

The word tax here may be misunderstood. In fact the support fund is more like a levy, raised from exhibitors on both the large and the small screen. This money comes from the business but goes back into it.

It is this support fund which provides a range of assistance which has contributed to the survival (or the prosperity) of various branches of French national cinema over four decades, including the New Wave of the early 1960s and the *cinéma d'auteur* of the 1980s. It has also supported the activities of a number of European and African film-makers. It is divided into automatic support (*aide automatique*) for the production and distribution of French films in general, and selective support (*aide sélective*) given to certain projects only. The main selective mechanism is the *avance sur recettes*, an advance given against the expectation of future profit and repayable only if the project is sufficiently profitable. The amount of FF107 million was granted in *avance sur recettes* in 1993, divided among fifty-five film projects chosen by a commission. There was also some specific selective aid for a number of co-productions, for films chosen by the ECO fund (in 1993 for four Russian films, three Czech, two Hungarian, etc.) and for some films made in developing countries, mostly in Africa.

Confining oneself to films *d'initiative française*, a further original characteristic can be noted. The number of first films has been rising steadily: thirty-four film-makers directed their first film in 1991, thirty-nine in 1992, and thirty-nine again in 1993. Of those making their first films in 1993, twenty-one benefited from an *avance sur recettes*. Also in 1993, twenty-two other film-makers directed their second film. The French cinema of the 1990s is a cinema of debutants. This phenomenon can in part be explained by the fact that they are eligible for, and receive, the advance, which encourages private producers to have confidence in them; but it is also a feature of a specific cultural moment which has roots in cinephilia and in the New Wave of the early 1960s.

In fact money from this support fund represents only a small part of the financing of French film production. The largest contribution to production comes from private finance and from both public and private television networks.

The system appears to function very well. It has benefited from years of experience, and the co-operation between public and private sectors has been achieved without major conflicts. The French cinema produces its own films, among which are a large number of *films d'auteur*: personal works, often fragile and individual. The French cinema remains a creative art, of which one can also observe that it is a cinema of prototypes.

But films of this kind have a small market. The export earnings of French films are low and the share of box-office taken by French films on the domestic market has declined considerably in the last ten years, as shown on Bar chart 1.

In ten years, the French cinema has lost 15 per cent of its share of the market, while the American cinema has gained 20 per cent (see Bar chart 2 and Table 1). The *cinéma d'auteur* cannot compete with the dinosaurs of *Jurassic Park*.

Two other features of the 1993 figures deserve comment, one positive and the other negative. The positive one is that the total cinema audience, which had been in decline throughout the 1980s, has suddenly taken a sharp upturn, rising from an annual figure of 116 million to 133 million, an increase of 15.6 per cent.

The negative feature is this: the favourable results of 1993 (34.6 per cent of a growing market) derive almost exclusively from the exceptional success of a single film, Jean-Marie Poiré's comedy *Les Visiteurs*, which attracted 12,513,000 spectators between 26 January and the end of the year, and was one of France's greatest blockbusters ever.

The French cinema is economically fragile, and it knows it. But – and this is where the gap emerges between the unanimous French conception and the MPAA view as expressed by Jack Valenti – the French cinema is not just an economic fact. For French film-makers (and for film-makers working in the European Union, in central and eastern Europe, or in Africa where films derive sometimes more than half their budget from the CNC), and for French opinion as displayed in the last months of 1993, film is a cultural fact, a creation of the spirit.

French film is part of a continuity of artistic creation that has for centuries been expressed by, and cements, a community which was a kingdom before becoming a nation, and extends today to be a part of Europe still searching for its political unity and identity. The President of the Republic, François Mitterand, expressed this in his speech at Gdansk in Poland on 21 September 1993, defining the official French position in the battle of GATT:

> Creations of the spirit are not just commodities; the elements of culture are not pure business. Defending the pluralism of works of art and the freedom of the public to

Bar chart 1   Comparative share of French and American films in the French market

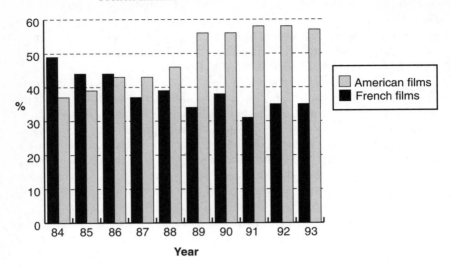

Source: J. Lubczanski.

Bar chart 2   Cumulative share of French and American films in the French market

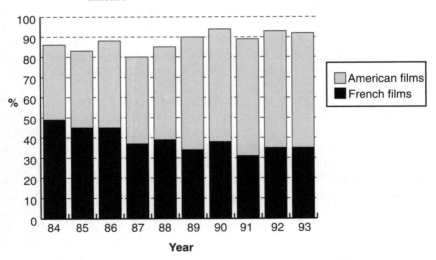

Source: J. Lubczanski.

Table 1   Percentage share of French and American films in the French market

Year	84	85	86	87	88	89	90	91	92	93
French films	49.3	44.5	43.7	36.2	39.1	34.2	37.6	30.6	34.9	34.6
American films	36.9	39.2	43.3	43.7	45.7	55.5	55.9	58	58.2	57.1

choose is a duty. What is at stake is the cultural identity of all our nations. It is the right of all peoples to their own culture. It is the freedom to create and choose our own images. A society which abandons to others the way of showing itself, that is to say the way of presenting itself to itself, is a society enslaved.

It is unusual, and indeed unprecedented, to see the President of the Republic engaged in an economic debate and at the same time clearly advancing a cultural argument. The battle of GATT succeeded in creating a unanimity of opinion, binding together the political parties, from the traditionally anti-American Communist left to the liberal right which is generally hostile to state intervention. Because it was a question of culture, the right made an exception, citing Louis XIV's Finance Minister Colbert at the time of the construction of Versailles and a partisan of state intervention. ... Two successive Ministers of Culture, Jack Lang from the left, and Jacques Toubon from the right, who took over after the March 1993 elections, adopted the same aggressive stance. The film profession also spoke with a single voice, learning how to lobby the political parties and the European Commission in Brussels. Bertrand Tavernier, a well-known left-wing film director, stood side by side in the European Parliament in Strasbourg with Nicolas Seydoux, president of Gaumont, which is Buena Vista's French partner and by that token one of the main distributors of American films in France. In Strasbourg Tavernier evoked the following metaphor, much quoted in the French press:

> The Americans want to treat us like they treated the Indians! If we are good, they will give us a reservation, they will give us the Dakota hills. And if we stay quiet, they will give us another hill.

There was a *franco-française* unanimity, which in itself is a rare event. There was also, around the French nucleus, an impressive mobilisation of the European professionals, with the association of auteurs at the head. The message was passed from the film-makers and the world of culture to the politicians. The European Community had to defend its positions, even with the unenthusiastic support of Sir Leon Brittan, its representative in the final round of negotiation at Geneva. The victory of 15 December was the result of this concerted effort.

My conclusion can, obviously, only be provisional. To paraphrase the famous saying of de Gaulle in 1940: 'France has lost a battle, but not the war.' Today, France has won a battle, but not the war: 15 December was only a respite.

Agreement will be reached, if it is reached, on three levels: first, that of the economy; and second, that of law, and in particular the law of *droit d'auteur*, the authors' rights that are recognised in most European countries in conformity with the Berne convention, but not subscribed to by the United States. And finally, the agreement that will be hardest to attain, that of the mentalities involved.

The final word should go to a film-maker, not a Frenchman, but the Spanish director Juan Antonio Bardem, who declared recently, in a European perspective: 'The present problem of the European cinema is not so much production as distribution.' If the Europeans do not use the reprieve they got in December 1993 in order to organise their distribution, their victory will have been no more than a rearguard action, glorious but ineffective.

Part II

4
The art film market in the new Hollywood

Tino Balio

According to French filmmaker Bertrand Tavernier, a mere two per cent of all screen time in the United States is allotted to foreign films. 'We are kept on reservations like the Cherokee or the Navajo,' said the creator of *Round Midnight*, a 1986 hit exploring the 1920s Paris jazz scene. 'Our films are shown only in a few places – New York City, Los Angeles, a few other big cities.'[1]

Moribund throughout the studio system era, the art film market in the United States was revived by successive waves of imports from different national cinemas after the Second World War. The number of theatres that regularly played art films (defined as foreign-language films and English-language films produced abroad without American financing) increased from around one hundred in 1950 to close to 700 by the 1960s. Foreign film distribution in the United States was originally handled by dozens of small independent outfits, but when Brigitte Bardot's *And God Created … Woman* broke box-office records in 1956, Hollywood took over. In search of foreign pictures with commercial ingredients, the majors absorbed the most talented foreign film-makers with offers of total financing and promises of distribution in the lucrative US market.

With Hollywood's help, the work of famous auteurs such as Federico Fellini, Ingmar Bergman, Akira Kurosawa, Michelangelo Antonioni, François Truffaut, Alain Resnais, Bernardo Bertolucci and Tony Richardson enriched American film culture during the 1960s. But the heyday was short-lived. The demise of the Production Code, liberal Supreme Court rulings on censorship, and profound changes in American social mores ushered in a period of unexpected frankness in the American cinema beginning in 1967 and, as *Variety* put it, 'knocked the bottom out of what once was an art house market'.[2] The majors, as a result, curtailed investment in overseas production and disbanded their art film distribution subsidiaries, making it more difficult than ever for foreign films to penetrate the American market.

I shall argue here that, after 1970, the art film market functioned as a niche business and was nourished mainly by foreign-language films and English-language films produced abroad without any US backing.[3] Independent distributors and so-called 'mini-majors' such as Orion Pictures and Dino De Laurentiis Entertainment serviced the market and demonstrated that speciality films with proper handling could occasionally fragment the theatrical audience

63

and acquire residual value in ancillary markets, particularly the emerging home video market. The art film business was small and only the hardiest firms had the staying power to survive. During the consolidation of the American film industry in the 1990s, the art film market was taken over by the Hollywood majors who either created classics divisions or acquired the leading independent art film distributors. Although such moves were reminiscent of the companies' behaviour during the 1960s, the renewed interest in speciality film in the 1990s did not spur the new Hollywood to invest in indigenous foreign film production. Like the 1960s, however, Hollywood absorbed promising foreign film-makers, thereby depriving 'other national cinemas of their major talents and thus reducing competition for its own products'.[4]

I The shrunken art film market

Variety's figures differ slightly from Tavernier's given above. According to the trade paper, foreign- and English-language imports captured between 1 per cent and 9 per cent of US theatrical box-office and on average earned around 5 per cent of the revenues annually.[5] Every year one or two foreign hits would do most of the business. Vilgot Sjöman's *I Am Curious (Yellow)* set a record as the highest-grossing foreign-language film in the US by grossing $19 million at the box-office in 1969 – a record not surpassed until Alfonso Arau's *Like Water for Chocolate* surpassed the $20 million mark in 1993. Other foreign-language hits during the period included Edouard Molinaro's *La Cage aux folles* ($17 million in 1979), Wolfgang Petersen's *Das Boot* ($11.2 million in 1982), Pedro Almodóvar's *Women on the Verge of a Nervous Breakdown* ($7.5 million in 1988), and Giuseppe Tornatore's *Cinema Paradiso* ($13 million in 1990).

English-language imports fared better. Bernardo Bertolucci's *Last Tango in Paris* grossed over $40 million in 1973, Hugh Hudson's *Chariots of Fire* $62 million in 1981, Richard Attenborough's *Gandhi* $52 million in 1982, and Bertolucci's *The Last Emperor* $43.5 million in 1987. However, these films do not qualify as true imports, since they were either US co-productions, American films produced abroad by foreign production companies, or foreign films made with US backing.

The demand for art films, either foreign- or English-language, has changed little since 1970. 'In an industry that routinely makes calculations in tens of millions of dollars,' said *Premiere* magazine,[6] 'the distribution and marketing of small, independent American films and foreign art films count as small potatoes, perhaps only an order of fries.' It took Miramax's Mexican acquisition *Like Water for Chocolate* more than a year to become the all-time foreign-language box-office champ; in contrast it took Paramount's *Forrest Gump* just four days to surpass that record.[7] A new release from a major studio is routinely given a national launch of between 1500 and 3000 simultaneous bookings but even the most promising art film seldom plays in more than one hundred screens at a time. Art films have to be distributed slowly to allow word of mouth and critical praise to build up interest. Because of the volatility and unpredictability of the market, a foreign film is considered a hit if it achieves a $5 million US gross. And a foreign film producer is fortunate to receive a $500,000 advance from an American distributor for the rights to a picture.[8]

The Oscar for the best foreign-language picture confers prestige on the winners and translates into longer runs and greater takes at the box-office. Surveying the winners from 1986 to 1993, *Variety* reported that the post-award percentage jump in box-office performance of the winner could in certain cases be as high as 2000 per cent. But in terms of the actual dollar take, the grosses ranged from a low of $260,000 for the 1991 Swiss winner, Xavier Koller's *Journey of Hope*, to a high of over $13 million for Italy's *Cinema Paradiso* in 1989. Five of the eight winners in this period grossed less than $5 million.[9] *Variety* again:

> For most of Europe's art-house distribs, Oscar's added-value b.o. clout is questionable. Most film execs believe a pic will make it on its own worth, and will often have played most territories before the Academy bestows its favors. And if a film is a downer in subject matter or flops first time around, Oscar won't get it back on its feet.[10]

Foreign films confront formidable barriers to entry. New York is the launching pad for the art film market. The city is the home of most of the national press and contains a large part of the art film audience; but, as the *New York Times* put it, 'New York is both the dream and the nightmare.' Advertising costs are exorbitant and, although good reviews can propel a film to a successful nationwide release, a bad review or an unfavourable notice by the *New York Times* can kill it. Outside New York, a picture without a famous director or recognisable stars has little chance of garnering any media attention. Distributors have complained that 'even newspapers in major cities have abandoned their commitment to art films, seduced by the glamour and the money of Hollywood. It's almost impossible, they say, to lure critics to screenings.'[11]

Even with favourable media attention, foreign films have difficulty reaching an audience. At the exhibition level, the number of specialised theatres in the US declined steadily during the 1980s, succumbing to real estate pressures, home video, and the trend of large theatre chains to convert single-screen 'art' or 'revival' houses into more profitable multiplexes showing new Hollywood fare. In New York City, for example, such venerable art houses as the Cinema Studio near Lincoln Center, and the Embassy, Regency, Metro, Thalia and New Yorker theatres on the Upper West Side all either closed or were converted into first-run theatres. In Boston, a 'bedrock of the art-house circuit', nearly every independent theatre in the city was acquired by a major Hollywood company.[12] In recent years only one chain of any size has catered exclusively to the art film market – the 125-screen Landmark circuit belonging to the Samuel Goldwyn Co.[13]

At the distribution level, the number of companies handling foreign films and independent American films actually rose during the 1980s, stimulated by the easy money of pre-sales to video and cable. But a shake-out occurred at the end of the decade as hundreds of pictures of dubious quality glutted the market. Dozens of companies collapsed or dissolved into bankruptcy. The casualty list included Aries, New World Pictures, New Century, Cinecom, Island Alive, Orion, Atlantic, Avenue, Hemdale, Cannon, Lorimar and De Laurentiis, most of whom handled at least an occasional foreign film.

The case of Orion Pictures was particularly disappointing. Orion's art films subsidiary, Orion Classics, had been one of the more aggressive players in the market. By getting involved in pre-production deals and paying top dollar for straight acquisitions, the company secured the rights to such pictures as Pedro Almodóvar's *Women on the Verge of a Nervous Breakdown* (1988), Agnieszka Holland's *Europa, Europa* (1991), which won a Golden Globe for best foreign picture and went on to gross $5.6 million, and the top Chinese-language import, Zhang Yimou's *Raise the Red Lantern* (1992).[14]

II The survivors

Only a handful of stalwarts survived the 1980s: Miramax, Fine Line, and the Samuel Goldwyn Co. Miramax, the most successful of the three, became a 'logo that brings audiences in on its own'. Formed in 1982 by Harvey and Bob Weinstein, Miramax did not emerge from the fringes of independent film distribution until 1989, when three of the films they had acquired drew critical and commercial attention: Jim Sheridan's *My Left Foot*, which starred the still relatively unknown Daniel Day-Lewis (who went on to win the Oscar for best actor) and grossed $14.7 at the box-office; Steven Soderbergh's *sex, lies and videotape*, which garnered for writer-director Sonderbergh a Palme d'Or at Cannes and grossed $24.7 million; and Giuseppe Tornatore's *Cinema Paradiso*, which won an Oscar for best foreign film and went on to become the highest-grossing art film of 1990.[15]

Miramax adopted a straight acquisition policy from the start. By the 1990s it was releasing an eclectic slate of over a dozen pictures a year and winning more Academy Award recognition than most major film companies. Its success rested largely on its marketing skills. 'We're a publicity-driven, word-of-mouth, labor intensive distributor,' said a company executive.[16]

The ability of the Weinstein brothers to generate free publicity became legendary. Traditionally, the company acquired its pictures at film festivals. The strategy was to pick up an award-winning picture and take advantage of the ensuing press coverage to ease the picture into distribution. Take the case of Jane Campion's *The Piano*. A cultural hodge-podge financed by the French company CIBY 2000, filmed in New Zealand by a native-born writer-director with an international cast, and having Australian nationality by dint of its Sydney-based producer, Jan Chapman, *The Piano* was acquired weeks before it was shown at Cannes where it won the Palme d'Or.[17] *Newsweek* devoted a two-page article and a full-page photo to *The Piano*, describing the 'delirious standing ovation' after its screening and the 'fever pitch' of the reception a full six months before the picture was released in the US.[18]

After acquiring a picture, Miramax was not above re-editing it with a view to making it more accessible to American audiences. This controversial practice earned Harvey Weinstein the sobriquet 'Harvey Scissorhands', but the success of at least three Miramax releases – *Cinema Paradiso*, *Farewell My Concubine* and *Like Water for Chocolate* – was attributed to his snipping. Trimming fifteen minutes from the running time of *Like Water for Chocolate* helped it return its $2.5 million investment in a remarkably short time and become the highest-grossing foreign-language film in US history.[19]

To ignite interest in a new release, a favourite ploy of the company was to challenge the rating assigned to it by the Motion Picture Association of America (MPAA). Take the case of Almodóvar's 1990 *Tie Me Up! Tie Me Down!* After the film received an X rating from the MPAA, Miramax hired a prominent attorney to challenge the decision in the courts. The attorney argued that the sexual content of Almodóvar's film paled in comparison to the explicitness of certain recent Hollywood films such as David Lynch's *Blue Velvet*, and that an X rating would harm the picture financially. Deciding in favour of the MPAA, the court stated that 'the allegations of economic prejudice and discrimination are unsubstantiated and the exploitation of the X rating by the petitioners in their advertising . . . leads to the inference that this proceeding may be just publicity for the movie.' Miramax released *Tie Me Up! Tie Me Down!* without a rating and earned over $3 million as a result of this free publicity.[20] They repeated a similar ploy with *The Grifters* (1990), *A Rage in Harlem* (1991) and *Madonna: Truth or Dare* (1991), among others.

Arguably the company's most creative efforts were devoted to the marketing campaign for Neil Jordan's *The Crying Game* (1992). Miramax succeeded in making people want to see the film without knowing why. A British release with no major stars that centred on the British–IRA conflict made the picture seemingly difficult to sell to Americans. But it did have an unusual plot twist and that twist was exploited by Miramax to create a *cause célèbre* to rival the famous publicity campaign for Alfred Hitchcock's *Psycho*. Launching the picture at the New York Film Festival, Miramax handed journalists letters which read: 'The producers and the director of *The Crying Game* would like to formally request that you do not reveal all of the plot twists contained in the film.' The critics complied and so did cinemagoers. Publicised as 'America's best-kept secret', *The Crying Game* became a great crossover hit, grossing an incredible $62 million. It was also a great critical success, receiving six Academy Award nominations, including best picture, and winning writer-director Jordan the Oscar for best screenplay.[21] 'The industry', *Variety* reported, 'was staggered by the response.'[22]

Having placed a film in distribution, Miramax was quick to react to new-found opportunities. After the initial reviews of *Like Water for Chocolate* came in, Miramax opened the picture beyond the usual art house circuit to include Spanish-language theatres in Latino neighbourhoods. A total of 179 sub-titled prints were used during the run. While the run did not approach the 500-screen saturation of *The Crying Game*, it represented a remarkable market penetration for a foreign-language film.[23] To give the picture an added boost, Miramax generated an elaborate cross-promotional campaign tapping Mexicana Airlines, Mexican restaurants and radio stations, and the food, travel, book review and entertainment sections of newspapers. The novel of the same name on which the film was based was written by Laura Esquivel, Alfonso Arau's wife, who also wrote the screenplay. Published by Doubleday, the novel remained on the *New York Times* bestseller list for nineteen weeks.[24]

To protect itself from the volatility of the art film market, Miramax branched out into the genre market in 1992, and formed a new subsidiary, Dimension Pictures. *Variety* described the types of picture slated to go on the Dimension roster as 'movies that make audiences scream and buy more popcorn'.[25] Among Dimension's first ventures were a series of horror films that included such items as *Hellraiser 3: Hell on Earth* (1992) and *Children of the Corn II: The Final Sacrifice* (1992). Unlike most art films, this type of picture could be reliably and profitably sold to home video, TV and foreign markets.

Miramax's entry into the genre market mirrored the formation of Fine Line Features by New Line Cinema in 1991. Founded in 1967 by Columbia University law school graduate Robert Shaye, New Line's strategy outlined in its business plan was to 'make and distribute low-cost, low-risk films and carefully target them at specific audiences'.[26] In its early years, New Line targeted college campuses, but by the 1970s it had expanded into the theatrical market and distributed midnight movies (John Waters's *Pink Flamingos*), soft porn (*The Best of the New York Erotic Film Festival*), kung-fu pictures (Sonny Chiba's *The Streetfighter*) and art films (R.W. Fassbinder's *Despair* and Eric Rohmer's *The Marquise of O*). By keeping overhead and debt to a minimum, New Line remained solvent.

In the early 1980s, New Line expanded into film production. Searching for properties aimed at young couples on dates, New Line put up $2 million to capitalise on the renewed interest in horror and slasher films and financed the modestly priced *A Nightmare on Elm Street* (1984), a property rejected by rival studios. Featuring the creepy, razor-nailed Freddy Kreuger, *Nightmare* grossed $23 million, spawned a successful horror series, and propelled New Line to the top of the independent ranks. The Elm Street series proliferated to six films in about as many years, collectively grossing more than $500 million worldwide and fuelling New Line's subsequent growth.[27]

New Line went public with a market capitalisation of $45 million in 1986 and continued releasing ten to twelve pictures a year, consisting of both in-house productions and acquisitions. In 1990, New Line discovered a second gold mine when it distributed a film, *Teenage Mutant Ninja Turtles*, that a new regime at 20th Century-Fox had rejected. The film was acquired for $3 million and grossed more than $130 million. New Line opened the film in 2000 screens, making it the most successful independent release in US history. The sequel grossed $78 million.[28]

With profits from the Elm Street and Ninja Turtles pictures and from another gold mine, two 'House Party' films, New Line formed a home video unit and a TV production company and acquired the domestic video rights to Nelson Entertainment's 600-title film library. In addition, in 1990 Robert Shaye set up a division in New York called Fine Line Features under marketing whiz Ira Deutchman to produce and distribute sophisticated or provocative films aimed at adults. Within two years, Fine Line Features had carved a niche for itself in the art house market.

Fine Line's first major hit, Gus Van Sant's *My Own Private Idaho* (1991) starring River Phoenix and Keanu Reeves, typified the kind of picture bankrolled by the company. An American independent venture, *My Own Private Idaho* contained moonlighting Hollywood stars or recognisable supporting actors in lead roles, a proven auteur director, and an offbeat story – marketing angles that the company could parlay into a crossover success. Unlike Miramax, Fine Line did not resort to publicity stunts but relied on conventional means of promotion for its pictures. Other notable independent ventures distributed by the company included Robert Altman's *The Player* (1992) and *Short Cuts* (1993), Jim Jarmusch's *Night on Earth* (1992), and Whit Stilman's *Barcelona* (1994). These pictures were carried by the likes of Tim Robbins, Whoopi Goldberg, Winona Ryder and Andie MacDowell.

Going outside the US for product on limited occasions, Fine Line (like Miramax) searched for pictures that won awards at film festivals or were objects of critical praise. Fine Line looked to Britain for most of its imports, taking among others Derek Jarman's *Edward II* (1992), Hanif Kureishi's *London Kills Me* (1992), Charles Sturridge's *Where Angels Fear to Tread* (1992), and Mike Leigh's *Naked* (1993). Initially it steered away from the foreign-language market, but it released Maurizio Nichetti's *Volere volare* from Italy in 1992 and a Canadian–French co-production, Jean Claude Lauzon's 1992 *Leolo*, in 1994.

Following yet another tack, the Samuel Goldwyn Co., headed by the son and namesake of Samuel Goldwyn, evolved into the only vertically integrated operation in the speciality film market. Founded in 1980 as distribution arm for the Samuel Goldwyn library of film classics, the company expanded into the first-run art film market, then into film production, home video, television production and syndication, and finally into exhibition. By diversifying, the company hoped to stabilise its operations.[29]

Goldwyn typically distributed eight to ten pictures a year, a mix of English-language imports from Britain and Australia, foreign-language pictures from Europe, independent productions from the US, and an assortment of documentaries and animated features. The company's reputation rested on its British pictures, which represented the company's output and covered the gamut of production trends in Britain as film-makers there attempted to construct an alternative to commercial Hollywood product. Goldwyn's first British release was Bill Forsyth's *Gregory's Girl* (1982), a romantic youth comedy produced in Scotland and described by *Variety* as having 'enough freshness and quirky charm' to provide an antidote to the 'US public's constant exposure to vulgar comedies on the subject (from *Pom Pom Girls* to current *Porky's*)'.[30]

Other trends were represented by Richard Eyre's *The Ploughman's Lunch* (1985), a scathing satire of Margaret Thatcher's Britain at the time of the Falklands War; Alex Cox's *Sid and Nancy* (1986), based on the life of punk musician Sid Vicious; Stephen Frears's *Prick up Your Ears* (1987), from the play by Joe Orton; Gillies MacKinnon's *The Playboys* (1992), one of many recent films exploiting an Irish setting; and Kenneth Branagh's *Henry V* (1989) and *Much Ado About Nothing* (1993), popular Shakespearean adaptations in the heritage film mould.

Foreign-language pictures played a small role in Goldwyn's business, accounting for only one or two films a year. Among these were Claude Chabrol's *Madame Bovary* (1991); *The Best Intentions* (1992), written by Ingmar Bergman and directed by Bille August (whose *Pelle the Conqueror* (1987) had won the Palme d'Or at Cannes and an Oscar for best foreign-language picture); and two crossover hits, Coline Serreau's *3 hommes et un couffin* (1985) and Ang Lee's *The Wedding Banquet* (1993). (Released in the US as *Three Men and a Cradle*, Serreau's film was remade by Disney as *Three Men and a Baby*, which grossed $168 million at the box-office and spawned a cycle of American remakes of French hits.)

Although American independent productions played an even smaller role on its annual roster, Goldwyn was responsible for releasing three off-beat pictures of interest: Jim Jarmusch's *Stranger than Paradise* (1984), David Lynch's *Wild at Heart* (1990) and John Sayles's *City of Hope* (1991).

Goldwyn did not expand into other facets of the business until it was well established as a motion picture distributor and, when it did so, the company played safe. Entering the home video market in the early 1980s, the company enlarged its film catalogue by acquiring the rights to the Alexander Korda library of British films in 1984; it did not, however, launch a video distribution business of its own, relying instead on established companies in the field. Going into motion picture production, the company only backed projects that had commercial potential. Its first effort, Frank Zuniga's *The Golden Seal* (1983), was a wilderness picture designed for the family trade. And its next effort, Howard Storm's *Once Bitten* (1985), was a high-styled Dracula parody aimed at teenagers. Going into television production, the company decided to tap the syndication market rather than trying to compete with the majors for slots on network TV. Goldwyn's final expansion effort occurred in 1991 when it made a public offering of stock to acquire Landmark Theatres, a 125-screen chain of art houses in California, Washington and Minneapolis. The rationale for this acquisition was simple: if Goldwyn pictures stumbled, the company could make some money from whatever hits were playing in the art film circuit.

III Enter the Hollywood majors

The vitality of these three companies – Miramax, Fine Line and Goldwyn – convinced the majors to have another go with the art film market. Sony Pictures Entertainment, parent company of Columbia Pictures and TriStar Pictures, established a speciality film arm called Sony Pictures Classics in 1992. Apparently wanting to create a new profit source that might benefit from the occasional crossover foreign film hit, Sony simply hired the successful founding executives of the New York-based Orion Classics: Michael Barker, Tom Bernard and Marcia Bloom.

Given no production mandate (other than for the pre-purchase of projects), Sony Classics during its first month of operation acquired *Howards End*, Ismail Merchant and James Ivory's adaptation of the E.M. Forster novel. Thanks to Sony Classics' handling of the picture *Howards End* grossed more than $10 million in the first four months after release and by the end of the year had earned more than $21.3 million in over 1000 playdates. Although the picture received critical acclaim and positive word of mouth, Sony Classics distributed it slowly to create 'a slow burn rather than a flare', in the words of the company's co-president Tom Bernard. By that he meant distributing the picture on a market-by-market basis in order to keep expenses low and interest high in the run-up to the 1993 Oscars.[31] Sony Classics next acquired two films by directors whose previous films had been distributed by Orion Classics: *Olivier, Olivier* (1992) by Agnieszka Holland, and *The Story of Qui Je* (1993) by Zhang Yimou.

Following Sony's lead, Masushita-owned Universal Pictures formed Gramercy Pictures in 1992 in partnership with the Dutch company PolyGram. Unlike Sony Classics, which functioned as an acquisition-oriented distributor of foreign- and English-language independent films, Gramercy planned to produce films in-house for the speciality film market. Gramercy was not just searching for profits from crossover hits; it wanted to build relationships with new talent. As a Universal executive expressed it, 'the Gramercy start-up allows Universal the latitude to start or continue to foster relationships with quality filmmakers, ostensibly giving them the ability to promote another Spike Lee outside of the make-or-break studio atmosphere.'[32]

Despite the Sony and Universal initiatives, Hollywood did not enter the art film market in a big way until 1993, when Disney and Turner Broadcasting made their moves. In that year Disney teamed up with Merchant–Ivory and bought out Miramax Films. According to Peter Bart of *Variety*, Disney's strategy was:

> to foster an eclectic slate of projects.... While rival entertainment companies pursue the Time Warner model to become diversified, albeit debt-ridden, hardware-software conglomerates, Disney is determined to become the largest producer of intellectual property in the world. As such, the studio is committed to an astonishing 60-films-a-year release schedule starting in 1994.[33]

The producing-directing team of Ismail Merchant and James Ivory had made thirty-one films in as many years, including its breakthrough Forster adaptation *A Room with a View* (1986), which cost $3 million and grossed more than $68 million worldwide, and *Howards End* (1992), which cost $8 million and achieved a worldwide gross of more than $70 million. The Disney deal was basically a 'three-year, first-look' proposition in which Disney, among other things, guaranteed to put up half the financing for any Merchant–Ivory picture with a budget of up to $12 million in exchange for all US distribution rights. For Merchant–Ivory, the arrangement freed the team from having to raise substantial sums of money and enabled it to use the studio's highly skilled distribution arm, Buena Vista Pictures. For Disney, the deal guaranteed a flow of serious films aimed at adults without much of a downside risk.[34]

Disney's deal with Miramax was a $90 million buyout. Disney acquired Miramax's library of over 200 English-language and foreign films and agreed to finance the development, production and marketing of Miramax's movies. Although the Weinstein brothers signed five-year contracts and in effect became Disney employees, Miramax retained its New York headquarters and functioned as a fully autonomous division of Disney's Buena Vista Pictures.[35] After joining Disney, Miramax continued to dominate the independent film market by acquiring the distribution rights to Bernardo Bertolucci's $35 million epic *Little Buddha* (1994) and by financing Quentin Tarantino's *Pulp Fiction* (1994). Within a year, Miramax had broadened Disney's product and audience base and accounted for over 10 per cent of Buena Vista's total gross. Miramax's 1994 roster also led the entire industry in Oscar nominations, with a total of twenty-two; Disney, by comparison, received only nine nominations.

Turner Broadcasting entered the art market indirectly as a result of its acquisition of New Line Cinema and Castle Rock Entertainment, a Beverly Hills-based producer of top-grade films and television programmes. The founder of superstation WTBS in Atlanta and the owner of one of the largest film libraries in the business, Turner had become a principal programme supplier to cable. Adding New Line and Castle Rock to his domain at a cost of $700 million was designed to catapult Turner into Hollywood's top ranks and create a platform for global expansion on the film side. With Turner's financial backing, New Line doubled its annual movie roster to more than a dozen films and bid aggressively for big-name stars with the intent, in Robert Shaye's words, of going after 'genuine broad-based, audience-pleasing projects'.[36]

IV Conclusion

Hollywood's new-found interest in speciality films has had mixed effects. Although companies like Sony, Universal, Disney and Turner made their marketing skills readily available to smaller independent producers and foreign film-makers during the 1990s, the market became more consolidated. *Variety* reported that about one-third of 1993's 'indie' product came from just two companies: Turner's New Line–Fine Line arms, and Disney's Miramax.[37] In June 1995, the Samuel Goldwyn Co., the industry's last true independent, disclosed a $20 million loss for the previous year. Brought down by a $62 million debt load from the acquisition of the Landmark Theatres chain and a string of costly film and TV failures, the company was put up for sale.[38] In December 1995, Goldwyn was acquired by Metromedia International Group, an international telecommunications business run by billionaire John W. Kluge and the owner of the mini-major Orion Pictures. Unable to successfully meld the film libraries of Goldwyn and Orion into his business, Kluge then sold the two companies to Metro Goldwyn Mayer in April 1997 for $573 million.[39] Meanwhile, in November 1996 New Line Cinema and its art house subsidiary Fine Line announced an operating loss of $19 million and soon after were put up for sale by their new owner Time Warner, which had bought out Turner Broadcasting in September 1995 for $7.4 billion.[40] In this ruthless and competitive commercial environment, one wonders just how long the art film will remain an alternative cinema.

Notes

1 Sally Valongo, 'American Filmgoers Criticized', *The Toledo Blade*, press clipping, n.d.
2 Addison Verrill, 'Hard Going in U.S. for Foreign Films', *Variety*, 3 May 1972, p. 31.
3 During the 1980s, the art film market expanded to include certain American independent ventures produced outside mainstream Hollywood. Because the vast majority of such films were targeted at the teenage exploitation market and at pay cable and home video, this chapter will concentrate on foreign imports.
4 Jim Hillier, *The New Hollywood* (New York: Continuum, 1994), p. 163.
5 'Alien Ration', *Variety*, 21 October 1991, p. 8.
6 'Indie Boom Turns Bust', *Premiere*, May 1989, p. 31.
7 Leonard Klady, 'H'wood Foreign Rub', *Variety*, 12–18 September 1994, p. 9.
8 Deborah Young, 'Figuring Out the Arthouse Market', *Variety*, 18 May 1992, pp. 3, 85.
9 Leonard Klady, 'When Oscar Talks, the B.O. Listens', *Variety*, 4–10 April 1994, p. 7.
10 Derek Elley, 'Win Helps, but Won't Make Pic in Europe', *Variety*, 4 January 1993, p. 62.
11 William Grimes, 'Different Rules, Different Rewards for Smaller Films', *New York Times*, 31 July 1992, pp. B1, B7.
12 'Indie Boom Turns Bust'.
13 Aljean Harmetz, 'Sam Goldwyn's Little Studio that Could', *New York Times*, 18 October 1992, p. 23.

14 Lawrence Cohn, ' "Mediterraneo", 92's Most Moneyed Import', *Variety*, 11 January 1993, pp. 5, 63; Peter Bart, 'Oscar Snubs', *Variety*, 3 February 1992, p. 5.
15 John Evan Frook, 'Miramax Paradiso', *Variety*, 21 September 1992, pp. 101, 106.
16 Ibid.
17 Don Groves, ' "Piano" Wins 11 Oz Film Honors', *Variety*, 15 November 1993, p. 11.
18 David Ansen, 'Passion for Piano', *Newsweek*, 31 May 1993, pp. 52–3.
19 Betsy Sharkey, 'The Brothers Miramax', *New York Times*, 24 April 1994, sec. 2, pp. 1, 18, 19.
20 'Excerpts from the Miramax vs. MPAA Ruling', *Los Angeles Times*, 21 July 1990, p. 7.
21 Peter Stack, 'Secret of *Crying Game* Success', *San Francisco Chronicle*, 23 February 1993, p. 1+.
22 Michael Fleming and Leonard Klady, ' "Crying" All the Way to the Bank', *Variety*, 22 March 1993, pp. 1, 68, 69.
23 Lawrence Cohn, ' "Like Water" Crossover a Spanish-lingo Record', *Variety*, 21 June 1993, p. 7.
24 Susan Karlin, 'Sweet Shortcut for Hot "Chocolate" ', *Variety*, 30 August 1993, p. 1.
25 Lawrence Cohn, 'Oft Snubbed, Dubbed Euro Pix may Make a Comeback', *Variety*, 10 August 1992, p. 72.
26 'Niche was Nice: New Plan – Expand', *Variety*, 10 August 1992, pp. 35, 44.
27 Chris Mitchell, 'Shrewd Marketing Fuels Freddy', *Variety*, 10 August 1992, p. 36.
28 Bernard Weinraub, 'New Line Cinema', *New York Times*, 5 June 1994, p. F4.
29 Harmetz, 'Sam Goldwyn's Little Studio'.
30 *Variety Film Reviews*, 26 May 1982.
31 Lawrence Cohn, 'Majors are Relying on Indies in a Major Way', *Variety*, 27 April 1992, p. 3; Grimes, 'Different Rules, Different Rewards; John Evan Frook, 'Sony Unit's "Howard" Slow Rollout Pays Off', *Variety*, 11 January 1993, pp. 16, 18.
32 Richard Natale, 'Gramercy to Rescue of Smaller Pix', *Variety*, 25 May 1992, pp. 5, 7.
33 Peter Bart, 'Mouse Gears for Mass Prod'n', *Variety*, 19 July 1993, pp. 1, 5.
34 Bernard Weinraub, 'Disney Signs Up Merchant and Ivory', *New York Times*, 27 July 1992, p. B1.
35 Claudia Eller and John Evan Frook, 'Mickey Munches on Miramax', *Variety*, 3 May 1993, pp. 1, 60, 66.
36 Dan Cox, 'Turner Dough Feeds New Line's Desire', *Variety*, 25 April–9 May 1994, p. 11.
37 Leonard Klady, 'Studio Deals Spark Indie Identity Crisis', *Variety*, 13 December 1993, pp. 1, 91.
38 Martin Peers, 'Goldwyn Caught in Crunch', *Variety*, 19–25 June 1995, p. 11.
39 'Metromedia to Sell Film Units to MGM for $573 Million', *New York Times*, 29 April 1997, p. C9.
40 Dan Cox, 'New Line Sees Red', *Variety*, 11–17 November 1996, pp. 1, 73.

5
Italian genre films in the world market

Christopher Wagstaff

The important debates about the post-war development of Italian cinema have centred around two issues. The first concerns questions relating to the quality of the films that were being produced and that were attracting the greatest number of viewers. Here historians have seen the situation as one of early promise being betrayed progressively over time. The second issue concerns economic and commercial questions relating to struggles over the control of markets. Here historians have seen Italian cinema as achieving consistent success over the period 1945–70, followed by failure.[1] Discussion of these two issues has often been dominated by a preoccupation with Italy as a source of characteristically Italian 'art films' for the home market and for the art house circuit in foreign capital cities, counterposed to Hollywood as an exporter of popular genre cinema for the international mass market. This vision of Italy's place in the world cinema market needs closer examination.

Table 1   Number of tickets sold (millions)

Year	1946	1955	1960
USA	4400	2340	2129
UK	1635	1182	501
Italy	411	819	745
France	417	373	419

Immediately after the war, the international cinema market was dominated by Hollywood because of the size and monopolistic structure of its domestic market. The rapid decline in the size of that market and the effects of anti-trust actions against the monopolistic vertical integration of the American cinema industry, combined with the drop in Hollywood's largest export market (the UK, from which Hollywood was taking 25 per cent of its receipts),[2] meant that Italy (which gradually replaced the UK as the largest European market) became a progressively more important export market for the Americans. From Table 1 it can be seen that in 1946 the UK market was twice that of France and Italy put together and that by 1960 Italy, France and the UK together almost equalled the size of the US domestic market. The US administration of occupied Italy did everything it could to secure the Italian market for itself, and to prevent Italian protection of its own domestic production.

Italy's situation at the start of 1946 was one in which its export market was nil, and its domestic market was dominated by the 'dumping' policy of the Motion Picture Export Association of America (Italian films were receiving only 13 per cent of box-office receipts). What the Italian industry needed was protection for its domestic production (precisely what the Americans used their considerable influence to prevent, and precisely what would be prohibited by the GATT trade agreements), a production policy that would wrest the domestic market from American imports, and an export market of its own – all of this to enable Italian producers to gather box-office receipts large enough to cover the costs of production.

Neo-realism was a response to this situation: the production of very cheap films of high 'cultural' (as opposed to 'entertainment') quality which could be exported, which would earn respect (though not much money) for Italian films abroad, and which would carry more popular (and therefore more profitable) Italian films into foreign markets in their wake. *Sciuscià* (Vittorio De Sica, 1946) won an Oscar; *Aquila nera* (Riccardo Freda, 1946), a genre vehicle, made real money in foreign provincial cinemas. The problem with neo-realist films was that they did not have the 'entertainment' quality (known stars and conventional genre characteristics) to wrest the domestic market from American imports; they won prizes abroad, but Italians would not go to see them.

This situation gave rise to an intense debate inside the Italian cinema industry. There were those who said that it was useless to pin hopes on neo-realism, because the domestic public rejected it, with the result that the American hold on the domestic market was strengthened by the public's suspicion of Italian films; what Italy needed was a domestic production of films for 'entertainment'. On the other hand, there were those who said that without export, Italian films could never cover the costs of production; it was the 'quality' of neo-realist films that was opening the doors abroad for Italian exports, and therefore the Italian industry needed government protection and subsidy for the production of quality films for export.

Both sides had their way. Because of the damage that American film imports were doing to the Italian balance of payments, the government determined to try to replace as much as possible American films with Italian films in Italian cinemas, and it used tax rebates (a form of 'subsidy' that evaded GATT regulations), screen quotas and state support for film finance to encourage production. Because tax rebates were tied to box-office receipts, there was an incentive to make films that attracted the domestic public. These measures required defining the 'nationality' of films, in order to select films for tax rebates and for screen quotas. This nationalism had the paradoxical effect of internationalising Italian cinema. For a film to be admitted to screen quotas and to receive state credit and tax rebates, it had only to dress itself up as Italian, even if the money used to produce it came from American profits (blocked in Italy by currency exchange restrictions) earned by Hollywood films distributed in Italy. Once Italy started protecting its own films on the Italian market, foreign countries which had hitherto been hostile to Italian films while nevertheless exporting their own films to Italy (for example, the UK) saw it as in their interest to make film exchange agreements with Italy (the UK did so in 1950) which, by definition, opened up those countries' markets to Italian films. Last, but by no means least, two countries with similar interests could co-operate on a production, and give the released film 'national' privileges in both of the countries (Italo-French co-production began experimentally in 1946, and was formalised in 1949; between 1950 and 1965 Italy co-produced 764 films with France).

Notions of 'quality' gradually changed also. The 'cultural' quality characteristic of neo-realist films gave way to quality defined in terms of production values (international stars, exotic locations and spectacle), and to quality defined in terms of literary or historical value (filmed versions of nineteenth-century novels, historical films). Co-production permitted film-makers to invest in Italo-French films the sums that would confer on the films the production values associated with Hollywood imports, so as to be able to compete with American films on the combined French and Italian markets. In time this policy was modified, because the expensive co-productions did not attract large enough box-office receipts, and did not export well enough, to justify such large investments.

The Italian domestic public was wooed away from American films with a strategy of systematic exploitation of popular genres: the tear-jerkers of Raffaele Matarazzo, musicals (especially Neapolitan ones), comedies (for which a formidable corps of writers was established), vehicles for comics like Totò and Ernesto Macario, and adventures. A star system was created by recruiting young women from beauty contests. Effective dramatic Italian male leads were so scarce that post-war Italian cinema has been characterised by the use of American actors for those roles. Because of the recession in Hollywood, and its policy of runaway production in Italy, these actors were available in Rome and reasonably cheap. Their use in Italian productions increased the exportability of those films.

While the development of the domestic market is of great interest, and significantly determined the growth of exports, the reader is referred elsewhere for detailed accounts.[3] It is now necessary to turn to a brief summary of the history of Italian film exports from 1945 to 1965. From a financial point of view, the story is simple: from a time in 1945 when Italy received no significant income from exports, to the mid-1950s when 40 per cent of receipts for Italian films came from foreign earnings, and finally to the mid-1960s, where export income solidly surpassed the costs of American film imports (see Tables 2 and 3).

The Italian production sector consisted of a multitude of small companies. The one which first launched a systematic programme of export was the largest at the end of the war, Riccardo Gualino's Lux Film, which sent its films into Europe, South America, the Middle East and the United States, setting up a large number of agencies in foreign countries. But it was not the only company to export. The sale (for $20,000) of *Roma città aperta* to an American importer and the dollars it earned in the US (people have spoken of $1,500,000) started a gold rush whose disorderliness alarmed contemporary commentators.

The market that everyone wanted to break into was that of the US. Italian films had a few successes in the early years, such as *Roma città aperta*, and the odd film of Lux's like *Vivere in pace* and *Riso amaro*, but to begin with Italian films were limited to the art cinema outlets and cinemas in immigrant quarters of a few

76

Table 2 Export permits for Italian films

	1947	1948	1949	1951	1953	1955	1956	1957	1959	1960	1961	1962	1963
Argentina	51	105	31	7	27	31	96	52	40	36	45	54	50
Austria	3	2	–	32	2	24	54	42	45	21	40	12	15
Belgium	7	23	31	36	4	36	18	15	31	21	32	11	13
Brazil	11	81	69	38	3	41	32	41	52	22	77	39	21
Egypt	45	122	76	45	31	65	31	13	37	28	45	26	40
France	42	56	40	49	48	54	28	19	21	23	36	47	73
											(62)	(82)	(76)
											[29]	[32]	[21]
West Germany	–	2	23	50	47	48	36	39	68	78	65	63	79
England	9	5	8	12	18	23	35	17	20	35	15	21	52
											(34)	(43)	(68)
											[24]	[39]	[34]
Holland	13	17	29	22	32	47	55	34	32	21	37	43	48
Portugal	10	14	14	25	81	63	50	39	58	42	31	43	48
Spain	14	40	11	17	32	34	46	56	40	26	36	51	41
Switzerland	28	75	52	74	69	79	64	39	43	38	109	102	99
USA	53	42	37	69	30	57	57	42	60	82	38	43	106

Notes: The figures in round brackets for 1961–3 for France and England give, as a comparison, the number of films of Italian nationality listed as released in that year by *Annuaire du Cinéma*, *Film Français*, *Monthly Film Bulletin*. The figures in square brackets give the numbers of co-productions of Italian majority listed by the same sources. The table lists the major importers of Italian films.
Source: ANICA.

Table 3 Receipts from export of Italian films

Year	Total export permits	Receipts (billion lire) from fixed price sales	Total receipts (including percentages)
1948	827	0.3	0.6
1949	644	0.45	0.9
1950	848	0.77	1.5
1951	948	1.3	2.6
1952	1042	1.7	3.4
1953	1716	3.3	6.6
1954	2139	3.4	6.8
1955	2239	4.0	8.0
1956	2032	4.6	9.0
1957	1871	3.1	6.2
1958	2297	4.7	9.0
1959	2752	6.9	12.0
1960	3681	10.7	15.0
1961	3895	12.4	19.5
1962	3897	13.7	22.0
1963	3953	10.6	18.3
1964	3947	–	22.5
1965	2993	–	20.1

Source: ANICA.

cities, with films being sub-titled, or filmed versions of grand opera. The trade journal *Cinespettacolo* of March–April 1948 informed its reader that the US market for Italian films consisted of a minor circuit of 300 cinemas, with earning possibilities amounting to $3-5000, and a maximum of $8000 – less, that is to say, than the Brazilian market. In time it became a valuable market, with the creation of the Italian Film Export Company and the ANICA–MPEAA (Associazione Nazionale Industrie Cinematografiche e Audiovisive) Agreements,[4] and it is possible to get an idea of its proceeds for a brief period (see Table 4).[5]

It was in the year 1947 that the Italian film industry began to appreciate the true potential of the foreign market. During the previous year there had, admittedly, been much talk about export, but it was the enormous prestige that neo-realist films were gathering at festivals and in art houses, and the commercial success of *Aquila nera*, that transformed the hypothetical discussion into concrete action. The most successful neo-realist films abroad were those that contained a strong genre element: *Roma città aperta, Vivere in pace, Il bandito, Riso amaro, Domani è troppo tardi*. The artistic success of other neo-realist films which earned little either in Italy or abroad helped to boost the prestige of Italian cinema, and hence the receipts of the more commercial exports. However, many outdated or mediocre films travelled abroad on the back of the high-quality films. The list of the New York distributor Superfilm carried twenty-two Italian films for the

Table 4   Rental income by nationality in the US and Canadian markets and Italian export (in millions of dollars)

	Italy	(a)	(b)	France	Germany	UK
1956	2.3	15.0	57	2.2	0.3	1.7
1957	1.8	10.3	42	3.2	0.3	6.3
1958	1.5	15.0	59	8.3	0.5	27.1
1959	9.7	20.0	60	5.2	0.7	18.6
1960	12.3	25.0	82	5.2	0.7	23.0
1961	11.1	32.5	38	3.0	1.9	41.0
1962	8.9	36.6	43	6.4	1.0	24.0
1963	17.2	30.5	106	4.6	0.5	37.5
1964	9.4	37.5	–	3.0	1.9	49.1

Notes: (a) Total receipts from worldwide export of Italian films in millions of dollars, for the purposes of comparison (Source: ANICA).
(b) Number of Italian export permits for the USA (Source: ANICA).
The rest of the data is from Guback, *The International Film Industry*, p. 96, who took them from *Variety*; the figures are probably an underestimate (see Guback, p. 84).

1946–7 season, among which were the pre-war *I bambini ci guardano* (1943), *La corona di ferro* (1941), *La cena delle beffe* (1942) and *La donna è mobile* (1942). The following year, a list of New York distributors of Italian films showed fifty-five Italian films on offer for the 1947–8 season. In October 1947 *Un colpo di pistola* (1942) opened in Paris, and in October of the following year the Fascist propaganda film *Abuna Messias* (1939). The trade journal *Cinematografia italiana* for 11 January 1947 announced the success of Italian cinema in Argentina, Switzerland, Norway, Iraq, Spain, Egypt and the USA, calculating that the number of Italian films in circulation in foreign markets was 230, giving receipts of around one billion lire (about $1,700,000). At the same time, trade journalists expressed alarm over the tendency of Italian exporters to exploit a fashion by exporting old films capable of damaging the prestige of Italian cinema abroad.

In Stockholm the week of 8–15 November 1948 saw the opening of three Italian films: *Caccia tragica*, *Gioventù perduta* and *L'ebreo errante*. In Argentina *Vivere in pace* was earning well, together with *Il bandito*, *Un americano in vacanza*, *Aquila nera* and *O sole mio*. *Roma città aperta* was enormously successful, but was banned by the censor for being anti-Fascist, withdrawn and relaunched with the categorisation 'horror, not for the impressionable'. *L'Onorevole Angelina* triumphed in Buenos Aires. At the start of 1948 *Il bandito* opened in the two largest theatres in Istanbul, *Rigoletto*, *Carmen* and *Aquila nera* were successful in Turkey, *Fedora* and *Il mercante di schiave* did reasonably well, while the Turkish public rejected *Roma città aperta* in favour of the more entertaining genre films. *Cinematografia italiana* for 16 October 1948 listed the Italian films recently shown in two major Cairo theatres: *Chi è più felice di me?* (1938), *Oltre l'amore* (1940), *Abbandono* (1940), *La fornarina* (1942), *I due Foscari* (1942), *Tristi amori* (1943), *Resurrezione* (1943), *Campo dei fiori* (1943); and the post-war films: *Molti sogni per le strade*, *Sperduti nel buio, L'isola del sogno, Tombolo paradiso nero, Assunta Spina, La Certosa di Parma, Sotto il sole di Roma, Il corriere del re, Follie per l'opera, I fratelli Karamazov, Un uomo ritorna, Vivere in pace, L'elisir d'amore.* The trade bulletin *Unitalia Film* for December 1950 wrote:

> Egypt, as well as being the most important Muslim market, is the principal centre of distribution for the Middle-East. In 1950 alone, Egypt showed 120 Italian films, surpassing Switzerland in quantity. Italian films, however, do not get distributed as widely as their success deserves, and this could be remedied by dubbing them into Arabic and by making a sounder selection of films.

Germany opened up to Italian films after the signing of an exchange agreement in June 1950, but both this market and the Anglo-Saxon market (US, UK and dependants) – all of them markets of vast potential – had less to offer Italian cinema because of the lack of dubbing into English and German. In this period, Italian films are sub-titled. From 1951 onwards, the odd film began to be dubbed into English.

For reasons of space, it is well to proceed by taking as samples just two of the foreign markets for Italian films: France, as the most fraternal market, and the UK as one of the most impenetrable. When the British Labour government imposed the Dalton Duty on American film imports in 1947, the Hollywood majors boycotted the British market, whereupon after a few months the government capitulated, removing the duty, and replacing it with the blocking of funds. Faced with the absence of US films for a while, UK distributors were totally indifferent to the possibilities offered by the importing of high quality European films, even though the latter were generating for themselves a critical esteem and a success with audiences that was rapidly increasing worldwide. The fact that the Dalton Duty hit all imports, not just American ones, made the British position even more vulnerable to pressure from the Americans. The journal *Documentary News Letter* of the time commented:

> It must be remembered that one of the main reasons why European films are not shown more widely here is the determination of the US-influenced section of the Trade that they shall not be shown. Had it been possible to encourage the entry of European films while taxing the entry of US films the general audience in this country – after a period of resistance no doubt – would have benefited a great deal.[6]

When, in January 1950, Italy communicated to the British Board of Trade, through the British Embassy in Rome, a proposal for a joint commission to examine the question of film exports, the Board of Trade replied saying that since the British public were 'not interested in dubbed films', they could offer nothing in return.[7] The Board of Trade was accepting the theories of British distributors as true, and no one considered putting dubbed films to the test.[8] Nevertheless, that same year the British Film Producers' Association signed an exchange agreement with ANICA.

In 1946 no Italian films were imported into the UK, and in France just *Roma città aperta*, in November. In 1947 *Il barbiere di Siviglia, Roma città aperta, Sciuscià* and *Vivere in pace* were released in the UK, while in the following year just *Enrico IV, Quattro passi tra le nuvole, Rigoletto* and *Paisà*. In 1949 of the five Italian films released four were Lux Film productions: *Don Bosco* with an English spoken commentary, *Un americano in vacanza*, *L'Onorevole Angelina*, *Caccia tragica*, while the fifth was *Ladri di biciclette*. Apart from the pious *Don Bosco*, and the operas, the films were definitely considered 'art' films, and were shown only in specialist theatres in London. When we see this situation change, we know that we are dealing with a wider distribution of dubbed Italian films for a mass audience.

Things were very different in France. In 1947 the Italian imports were more numerous and consisted of neo-realist films together with comedies and adventure films like *Il cavaliere senza nome* (1941) and other pre-war genre vehicles. In 1948 the imports numbered thirty-eight, many of them either dubbed or distributed in two versions: one dubbed, the other sub-titled. Films imported only in sub-titled versions can easily be identified as art films, whereas films for mass audiences were frequently dubbed. Around this time French exhibition started to split between Paris and the art house audience on the one hand, and the provinces and a mass audience on the other, with the French market absorbing different types of Italian film for the different markets. In the mid-1950s the *salles de quartier* and rural cinemas were generating more that 50 per cent of national box-office receipts.

Table 5 is an attempt to illustrate statistically the process of change, in which Italy developed from being an exporter of 'art' films to one of popular genre films, using the designation of 'peplum' for a whole series of minor adventure formulae going from mythological epics (they were not often very 'epic') to sword-and-sandal formulae (one film, for example, contaminates the corsair formula with Robin Hood – *Robin Hood e i pirati* (Giorgio Simonelli, 1960) – and was shot on the bare coastline of Puglia). It will be seen that France was at first, understandably, a far better market for popular Italian films than the UK, but that in the 1960s the UK became a significant importer of popular adventure formula films for a mass market (partly with a B-movie function).

In the 1970s, television viewers did not identify the individual films of the 'Kojak' series by their titles; they knew them as a weekly appointment with Kojak. This serialisation of film narratives was used by Italian exporters, notably in the era of the spaghetti Western.[9] The German titles of Italian Westerns illustrate this:

Italian title	German title
Django	Django
Non aspettare, Django, spara	Django – dein Henker wartet
Chiedi perdono a Dio, non a me	Django – den Colt an der Kehle
Per 100.000 dollari ti ammazzo	Django – der Bastard
Texas, addio	Django – der Rächer
Execution	Django – Die Bibel ist kein Kartenspiel
7 dollari sul rosso	Django – dei Geier stehen Schlange
Ciakmull, l'uomo della vendetta	Django – Die Nacht der langen Messer
Quella sporca storia nel West	Django – die Totengräber warten schon
Momento di uccidere	Django – Ein Sarg voll Blut
Dio perdoni la mia pistola	Django – Gott vergrib seinem Colt
Lo voglio morto	Django – ich will ihn tot
Cjamango	Django – Kreuze im blutigen Sand

Italian title	German title
Uno di più all'inferno	Django – Melodie in Blei
Django spara per primo	Django – Nur der Colt war sein Freund
Starblack	Django – schwarzer Gott des Todes
Le Colt cantarono la morte e fu ...	
tempo di massacro	Django – sein Gesangbuch war der Colt
La vendetta è il mio perdono	Django – sein letzter Gruss
Il suo nome gridava vendetta	Django spricht das Nachtgebet
Quel caldo maledetto giorno di fuoco	Django spricht kein Vaterunser
Bill il taciturno	Django tötet leise
Sentenza di morte	Django – umbarmherzig wie die Sonne
Django il bastardo	Django und die Bande der Bluthunds
Preparati la bara!	Django und die Bande der Gehenkten
C'è Sartana ... vendi la pistola e	
comprati la bara!	Django und Sabata – wie blutige Geier
Una lunga fila di croci	Django und Sartana, die tödlichen Zwei
T'ammazzo! ... Raccomandati a Dio	Django, wo steht Dein Sarg?

In the UK, films imported from Italy underwent a similar process, and further-more were cut to serve as the B-movie in double bills. *Daniele Cortis* (Mario Soldati, 1946) arrived in the UK in 1957 with its title changed to *Elena* (because Sarah Churchill played the female lead) cut from 109 minutes to sixty-one, and in the same year *Legione straniera* (Basilio Franchina, 1952) was cut from eighty-five minutes to fifty-eight. The year 1963 saw the release of the following Italian productions (or Italian majority co-productions) for the 'art circuit': *8½* (Fellini), *RO.GO.PA.G.* (Rossellini, Godard, Pasolini, Gregoretti), *I Basilischi* (Wertmüller), *I compagni* (Monicelli), *Il gattopardo* (Visconti), *La rabbia* (Pasolini and Guareschi), and the following French majority co-productions with Italy: *Les Carabiniers* (Godard), *Le Feu follet* (Malle), *L'Immortelle* (Robbe-Grillet), *Le Jour et l'heure* (Clément), *Judex* (Franju), *Landru* (Chabrol), *Muriel* (Resnais), *Le Mépris* (Godard). It was also the year that saw the release of a very different kind of Italian film. Fortunato Misiano owned the production company Romana Film which targeted its films in the early years at a southern audience, particularly around Naples, with revealing titles (often those of famous Neapolitan songs of the period) like *Dove sta Zazà?*, *Monaca Santa*, *Marechiaro*, *Santo disonore*, *Gli innocenti pagano*, *Verginità*, *Ergastolo*, *Processo contro ignoti*, *Rimorso*, *In amore si pecca in due*, *Desiderio 'e sole*, *Lacrime d'amore*, *Lettera napoletana*, *Pescatore 'e Pusilleco*, *Scappricciatiello*, *Suonno d'ammore*, *Maruzella*, *Tormento d'amore*, *Serenata di Maria*, *Carosello di canzoni*, *Ricordati di Napoli*. People who worked for Misiano have recounted to me how they expected to get paid less working for him than for other producers, and how the films were made one 'inside' the other (so that a scriptwriter would be asked to develop a script to use existing sets from another film). These were cheap, popular films for a very circumscribed domestic market. In 1963 the titles were *Golia e il cav-aliere mascherato*, *L'invincibile cavaliere mascherato*, *Sansone contro il Corsaro Nero*, *Sansone contro i pirati*, *Zorro contro Maciste*. When one realises that Zorro and the *cavaliere mascherato* (masked rider) can be as interchangeable as Samson, Goliath, Maciste and Hercules, the new operation becomes clear. Some

	FRANCE						UK					
	(a) Film	(b) Art %(a)	(c) Gen %(a)	(d) Cop maj Ital	(e) Cop min Ital	(f) Tot part Ital	(a) Film	(b) Art	(c) Gen	(d) Cop maj Ital	(e) Cop min Ital	(f) Tot part Ital
1947	17(42)	35	29	–	–	–	4(9)	75	25	–	–	–
1949	21(40)	38	38	–	–	–	5(8)	60	0	–	–	–
1951	27(49)	33	48	–	–	–	13(12)	54	23	–	–	–
1953	48(48)	9	–	–	–	–	21(18)	19	–	–	–	–
1955	52(54)	15	–	–	–	–	28(23)	11	–	–	–	–
1957	35(19)	9	–	–	–	–	21(17)	10	–	–	–	–
1959	38(21)	9	–	–	–	–	12(20)	25	–	–	–	–
1961	62(36)	15	P40	29	37	99	58(15)	24	P26	24	26	84
1963	76(73)	7	P37	21	47	123	63(52)	13	P46	30	17	80
1965	77	7	P33	23	71	148	47	8	P47	24	26	73

Notes: The figures in this table give only an imprecise indication of the situation. The nationality or majority participation indicated are those assigned (not always accurately) to the films by the journals consulted.

(a) *Number* of Italian and Italian majority co-productions; in round brackets, the number of export permits (*source: ANICA*) for Italian films to be exported to that particular country in that year.

(b) *Percentage* of (a) that can be called 'art films' – a purely personal indication.

(c) *Percentage* in (a) that in the period 1947–51 consists of 'genre' films. for the 1960s the figures preceded by the letter P are the percentage of 'peplum'-type films. This column presents as statistics what are in fact the author's own rather problematic judgments, and the distinction between genre and art films becomes decidedly hazardous for the 1950s – hence the blanks.

(d) For the 1960s, the number of films in (a) which are majority Italian co-productions.

(e) For the 1960s, the number of films (not included in (a)) which are minority or tripartite Italian co-productions.

(f) Total number of films benefiting from some Italian participation (i.e. (a) + (e)).

Sources: Annuaire du Cinéma Français, Le Film Français, Monthly Film Bulletin.

of these films were destined for export, while others made 'inside' them were destined for the customary local market.

Golia e il cavaliere mascherato (directed by Piero Pierotti) was exported to France in 1964 as *Goliath et le chevalier masqué* (minus five minutes), and to the UK in 1965 as *Hercules and the Masked Rider* (full length). *L'invincibile cavaliere mascherato* (an Italo-French co-production directed by Umberto Lenzi) went to Germany in 1963 as *Robin Hood in der Stadt des Todes*, and to France and the UK with straight translations of the Italian title, barely cut. *Zorro contro Maciste* (again directed by Lenzi) went to the US in 1963 and to the UK in 1965 as *Samson and the Slave Queen* uncut, to France in 1964 as *Maciste contre Zorro* three minutes longer, and to Germany in 1964 as *Kampf der Unbesiegbaren*. All of this means that Romana Film's notion of production (cheap for a local market) and the notion of co-production (costly for an international market) had come to a remarkable convergence.

Remaining with the year 1963, but returning to the question of tailoring Italian formula films for the B-movie UK (and French) market, it is worth seeing what happened to some other small Italian productions. Leone Film's *Maciste, l'eroe più grande del mondo* (Michele Lupo, 1963) was cut from ninety-two minutes to eighty and retitled *Goliath and the Sins of Babylon* for the US in 1964 and the UK in 1965, and with a running time of ninety-five minutes was released in France in 1964 as *Le Retour des Titans*. *Sandokan, la tigre di Mompracem* (yet another film directed by the busy Umberto Lenzi in 1963) lost twenty-seven minutes in its release the following year in the UK as *Sandokan the Great*.

Perhaps just one example from 1963 will suffice to give an idea of the minority co-production activities of Italian producers in the field of popular genre cinema. In the year before the release of *Per un pugno di dollari* (*A Fistful of Dollars*, Sergio Leone, 1964), Carlo Scala's company, Atlantis Film-Società per il commercio e le industrie cinematografiche nazionali ed estere, which specialised in co-productions with Germany and other countries, was a minority partner (together with a French company, and with an associated Yugoslav company) in the Rialto Film Preben Philipsen (Berlin) production of the film *Winnetou I* (its German title; in Italy it was called *La valle dei lunghi coltelli*, in France *Révolte des indiens apaches*; directed by Harald Reinl, and based on Karl May's well-known novels). This Western was exported to the US in the summer of 1965 as *Apache Gold*, that is to say following on the success of Leone's first Western, released in the US in 1964. In France and the UK, the bubble of the peplum had yet to burst, and so the vogue for Italian Westerns had to wait until Leone's film's release in 1966 in France, and 1967 in the UK (although it was a Spanish minority co-production, it was not released in Spain until August 1973).

It has not been possible to give a complete picture of Italian cinema's place in foreign markets, and instead the choice has been made to proceed by means of sampling, and by looking in more detail at the beginning (1946–7) of the development of export and the end (1960s), to illustrate the transformation of Italy from a producer of essentially 'Italian' films for an art house public to a major exporter of popular genre films for a mass audience.

Notes

1 For an examination of that failure, see Christopher Wagstaff, 'Italy in the Post-War International Cinema Market', in Christopher Duggan and Christopher Wagstaff (eds), *Italy in the Cold War: Politics, Culture and Society 1945–1958* (Oxford and Washington: Berg, 1995).

2 PEP (Political and Economic Planning), *The British Film Industry* (London: PEP, 1952), pp. 98–102.

3 See Wagstaff, 'Italy in the Post-War International Cinema Market', and Christopher Wagstaff, 'A Forkful of Westerns: Industry, Audiences and the Italian Western', in Richard Dyer and Ginette Vincendeau (eds), *Popular European Cinema* (London: Routledge, 1992).

4 See Lorenzo Quaglietti, *Storia economico-politica del cinema italiano 1945–1980* (Rome: Editori Riuniti, 1980), the chapter 'La complicata storia dell'Ife'.

5 Thomas Guback, in *The International Film Industry: Western Europe and America Since 1945* (Bloomington: Indiana University Press, 1969), p. 86, notes that around $4,000,000 of the receipts for 1960 came from four peplum films starring Steve Reeves, and that 75 per cent of the receipts for 1963 were from spectaculars like *Barabbas* and *Sodom and Gomorrah* which had been made with American money. Nevertheless, the period covered by *Variety*'s collection of this data coincides with the period of issue of the largest number of Italian export permits for films to the US.

6 *Documentary News Letter* vol. 6 no. 59, October 1947, p. 110, cited in Margaret Dickinson and Sarah Street, *Cinema and State: The Film Industry and the British Government 1927–84* (London: BFI, 1985), p. 182.

7 Dickinson and Street, *Cinema and State*, pp. 182–3.

8 *Unitalia Film*, December 1950, p. 13.

9 For further discussion of this and similar questions, see Wagstaff, 'A Forkful of Westerns', p. 255.

6
Émigrés or exiles? The French directors' return from Hollywood

Janet Bergstrom

> My friend, I think the good film about France
> will be made by one of us in France itself.
> > Jean Renoir to Jean Benoît-Lévy, 1944

> It was not necessary in 1941 to make a film in the United States
> about the Resistance. Even today one feels that it is too soon.
> > Jean Fayard reviewing Renoir's *Vivre libre* (*This Land Is Mine*), 1946

> The word 'lynching' isn't French.
> > Georges Sadoul reviewing Duvivier's *Panique*, 1947

In early February 1944 Jean Renoir received a letter from screenwriter Philip Dunne, then chief of production for the Overseas Branch of the Bureau of Motion Pictures, Office of War Information, requesting his services as a film-maker.[1] Dunne underlined the urgency of the situation: the Allied invasion of northern France was imminent and the film in question was meant to play a role in it. He specified the staff and facilities Renoir would have at his disposal and included a rough outline which he had received from Captain Burgess Meredith, the actor, then in England, who would soon join Renoir and Dunne in New York to work on the film. Their project, Dunne explained, had a 'dual purpose: first, to tell our troops about the land which they will enter when the invasion begins; second (and more subtly), to show the French the kind of indoctrination we are giving to American troops. The theme of the picture is that America admires and respects France and that our troops enter French territory as friends and liberators not as conquerors or imperialists.' Dunne added, 'Meredith wants to be sure that you understand that the treatment has received the approval of French authorities in England, including leaders of the underground.' Who were those French authorities and leaders of the underground, one wonders? At the time, apparently no further information on this point was deemed necessary.

In May, back in Hollywood after *A Salute to France* had been shot, Renoir wrote to his friend Jean Benoît-Lévy, the French producer and former director then living in New York, about his disappointment at the way the film had been handled, and in particular how his attempts to represent a realistic portrait of France in the

US had been frustrated. This letter gives us some insight into Renoir's perception of the cultural gap between himself and the well-intentioned Americans who worked with him on the project, and it foreshadows, as well, a more serious problem he will encounter after the war with the French reception of *This Land Is Mine*:

> I did everything I could do for this film. I am fairly sure I succeeded in only two things: one was to get rid of all the excuses in the script that Captain Meredith wanted me to shoot. I stand behind the conviction that we don't need to make excuses to anyone and that under the same circumstances any other nation would have given up ground as we had to. Second, I was able to have Bernard Lamotte, who is French, design the sets. With his help, I was able to eliminate a lot of grotesque characterizations that this country stubbornly insists on giving our countrymen – what they look like, how they dress, the way they act, where they live and work, what they eat and drink.
>
> It is unfortunate that a film about France had been conceived so thoughtlessly by our American friends. I don't want to accuse anyone. Phil Dunne is a man full of good will, probably gifted with real talent. But he has too many things on his mind. France, the problem that is primary for us, is only one of twenty problems rushing through his mind every day. Meredith is a brilliant guy. ... What is bizarre is that our friends thought of him to produce a film about a country he doesn't know.
>
> Everyone has been very nice to me, but I have done all this in an atmosphere of disrespect and superficial discussion about problems that, as a French person, fill me with trepidation. ... My friend, I think the good film about France will be made by one of us in France itself.[2]

On the eve of the Allied offensive to liberate his country, Renoir could invoke the image of 'the good film about France' that he imagined would be made after the war by a French director in his native environment. But when the French émigré directors returned to France after the war was over, they discovered that in many important respects their country was no longer the same. Indeed, how could one characterise France after it had been liberated, or, according to de Gaulle's version of history, after it had liberated itself?[3]

In *The Vichy Syndrome*, Henry Rousso argues that the internal divisions that split the country as a result of the Vichy regime constituted nothing less than civil war.[4] De Gaulle's myth of national unity – the idea that France had collectively resisted the Occupation, thereby equating the entire country with an abstracted idea of the Resistance that took the place of the resistants themselves – was, aside from his personal political objectives, meant to stabilise French society in the face of the desire to avenge the victims of the German Occupation and its Vichy supporters. The Vichy regime and collaborationists were directly responsible for imprisoning 135,000 people, interning 70,000 suspects and firing 35,000 civil servants. Sixty thousand freemasons were investigated, 6000 harassed and 549 (of 989) died in the camps. The Vichy government, with German-paid assistance, deported 76,000 French and foreign Jews, less than 3 per cent of whom survived, and sent 650,000 workers to Germany as conscript labourers. As well, Vichy 'waged unremitting battle against the Resistance and all other opponents of the regime. Today ... there can be no doubt that many victims of the era were claimed not by the foreign occupation or military conflict but by internal struggles in which Vichy figured as the initial issue.'

On the other side, the Free French and the Resistance also spilled French blood, both literally and figuratively:

> Roughly 10,000 people were killed without trial or other legal authorization by the Provisional Government; a good half of these summary executions were carried out prior to 6 June 1944 (D-Day), thus *en pleine Occupation*. Of 160,287 cases examined by military and civilian courts, 45 percent ended in dismissal or acquittal, 25 percent in *dégradation nationale* (national dishonor) and loss of civil rights, and 24 percent in prison terms, a third of these being terms at hard labor for a limited period or for life. Finally, 7037 people were sentenced to death, and perhaps 1500 were actually executed.

Moreover, Rousso reminds us that thousands of deaths resulted from battles in which Vichy soldiers opposed the Free French in West Africa and Syria. 'Civil wars', Rousso points out, 'have always been the hardest to deal with afterward, for in a foreign war the enemy goes home when hostilities end – in a civil war the "enemy" remains.' Rousso's thesis is that

> the civil war, and particularly the inception, influence, and acts of the Vichy regime, played an essential if not primary role in the difficulties that the people of France have faced in reconciling themselves to their history – a greater role than the foreign occu- pation, the war, and the defeat, all things that, though they have not vanished from people's minds, are generally perceived through the prism of Vichy.

This succinct account can serve as an index of the deep-seated difficulties in renegotiating cinematic representations of French national and individual ident- ity following the war. In retrospect, the assertion of French identity seems effortless in the films of the 1930s: even the bleakest depictions at the end of the decade – *Pépé le Moko*, *La Bête humaine*, *Quai des brumes* and *Le Jour se lève*, to take the most commonly mentioned examples – featured popular anti-heros, often personified by Jean Gabin, who were tragic figures caught up in circum- stances that might have turned out differently and whose inherent French identity (and cultural superiority) is taken for granted, often in contrast to foreigners. Film-makers in the post-war period, on the other hand, had a hard time depict- ing French national and individual identity, particularly when dealing with contemporary subjects. What it meant to be French could easily become a source of controversy. The easiest way to avoid a no-win representation of Vichy and its aftermath was to situate films in an earlier time, especially the turn of the century, or to make films based on established literary works – two strategies that had also characterised much of Vichy cinema – or, a more restricted option, to make films that glorified the Resistance. Apart from the Resistance films, a new mood of cyn- icism often took the place of the tragic or resigned pessimism of the late 1930s in films set in the contemporary post-war period.

This chapter is about the disphasure between the desire the French émigré directors – René Clair, Julien Duvivier and Jean Renoir – had while still in the United States to make that good film about France when they returned to their native country and the first films they eventually did make there after the war. That disphasure, for Renoir and Duvivier, passed first through fiction films they made to help the French cause from Hollywood – *This Land Is Mine* (1943) and *The Imposter* (1944), respectively – and the reaction to these films several years later, when they were released in France after the war. Part of the anxiety and turmoil of national identity during the war years and the post-war period for these directors came from an estrangement born of the realisation that they had become, in some sense, members of two national cultures, but that in so doing, Duvivier and Renoir (if not Clair) had lost as much as they had gained. The war had put them out of synch with France in a way that could not have been imagined in advance and that was experienced with great difficulty.

Most of the writing on émigrés in Hollywood during the Second World War has been devoted to exiles from the German film industry. It has been well documented how Germany lost almost all of its cinematic talent in the exodus of 1933. By 1940, many of those people had relocated to the US to try to find work, sometimes after having established a strong second career in France (such as Siodmak and Ophuls).[5] After the war, the German film industry was no more than a shadow of what it had been at the end of the Weimar Republic. Few of these expatriates chose to return except for temporary projects, and most didn't even do that. The situation with French émigrés in Hollywood was different. Relatively few French film personnel left their country after the Armistice with Germany in 1940, and only three of them were established directors: Clair, Duvivier and Renoir. Although adjustments were made, the French film industry remained largely intact throughout the Occupation. The return of the French émigrés after the war was not only viable, it was expected. As John Russell Taylor pointed out, emphasising an important difference between the German and French émigrés, 'It is much easier somehow to be exiled by your own choice, rather than out of desperate necessity, from a defeated country than to be exiled from a country that is at war with the country in which you have settled and which has deprived you of citizenship and made you in a very real sense a stateless person.'[6]

Clair, Duvivier and Renoir had much in common. They were in their forties when they arrived in Hollywood, they had begun making films in the silent period, and they had all achieved international eminence. In 1940 they were the most important directors in France, along with Feyder, who spent the war years in Switzerland, and Carné, who remained in France. Clair, Duvivier and Renoir all returned to their native country after the war, although not at the same time. Just as their reasons for leaving France differed – none of the three was Jewish – so too did their attitudes to leaving their American homes and careers for an uncertain future in France; in fact, each of them was considering future projects in or with American studios even as he returned to his native country. Although the duration of their exile could be measured in years – Clair and Duvivier were in Hollywood for about five years before seeing France again in 1945, while Renoir stayed away for six more years – it marked them irrevocably. The social and cultural dissonance these directors experienced on returning to film-making in France is an important factor to take into account when trying to understand the complexities of post-war French cinema, especially considering the key role they had played in creating a distinctive national cinema there during the 1930s.

In America, these directors were always referred to, and referred to themselves, as French. We can see this in press coverage of their activities, interviews, studio publicity releases, personal and professional correspondence, and so forth. Professionally, they had matured as film-makers within an industry that was very different from the American system. They were respected as authors, they could enter into every phase of production they wanted to, and they had been able to develop their own working methods and styles. Style and cinematic objectives differed greatly from Clair to Duvivier to Renoir, but in Hollywood they all struggled with a decision-making hierarchy, a unionised division of labour and a timetable that was much different than it had been in France.

We can see Renoir's situation in unusual detail because of the voluminous correspondence he bequeathed us which is especially rich during the war and post-war years. When the Vichy government broke diplomatic relations with the United States following the Allied invasion of French North Africa in early November 1942, mail services were cut off between France and the US until the autumn of 1944 and were not normalised again until the spring of 1945.[7] Renoir, who had corresponded regularly with family and close friends, wrote many letters as soon as the mail began to circulate again to try to find out what had happened to his loved ones and closest colleagues during this long, anxious time. In turn, he created vivid descriptions for them of his work, his aspirations and disappointments, and his everyday life in Los Angeles. Again and again Renoir explained that none of his American films had achieved real success considering what he had hoped to accomplish, yet he still believed he had a better chance to make good films there than in France. In May 1946, Renoir wrote with poignant simplicity to his old friend, the screenwriter of *La Grande Illusion*, Charles Spaak, that he felt suspended between two worlds: 'Unfortunately, nothing I have done since *The Southerner* is worth very much. It isn't that one cannot make good films here; it is as easy and even easier than in France. It is simply that ideas don't come to me. All my imagination is used up trying to represent to myself, during all of the war, what could be happening on the other side, that other side where you, most of your friends and mine had to stay.'[8] To his nephew, Claude, who had worked as his cinematographer on *La Bête humaine*, Renoir described his estrangement in more practical terms: 'Since the war ended, my ideas have been very confused. They are barely beginning to become clear and I don't think that if I went to Paris now, I would have anything worthwhile to offer a producer. I probably have more ideas which would apply to America, and that is why I want to try and make a good film here, taken from a personal story.'[9] And in a letter to his lifelong friend Pierre Lestringuez, Renoir expressed his growing realisation that he felt profoundly at odds with the new France as well as the US:

> I believe that the post-war period is going to bring us bigger changes than the last one, of 1918; changes in life and manners, and therefore changes in taste. I don't want to lose contact, but from time to time, I feel that I've lost it. I feel out of step with the immense childishness of the new generations, whether French or American. I am indifferent to the preoccupations of most of my comrades, and it is possible that certain problems that seem fundamental to me seem futile to them.[10]

This disphasure was much different from the internationalism all three directors had known earlier in their careers. René Clair was the first of the three to become an international success. We tend to forget how far Clair's appeal had reached by the early 1930s, when he was frequently compared with Chaplin. *Sous les toits de Paris* (1930), a French-German co-production, and *A nous la liberté* (1931) were enormous successes worldwide. Entire issues of the German illustrated revue *Film Kurier* were devoted to each of them. That Chaplin borrowed from *A nous la liberté* for *Modern Times* pleased Clair enormously: it is well known that he refused to sue his idol for copyright infringement. After such heady acclaim, Clair was not prepared for failure, and when *Le Dernier Milliardaire* (1934) opened to negative reviews and a poor box-office, Clair left France to pursue opportunities in England. There, he released *The Ghost Goes West* in 1935 and *Break the News* in 1937. Between these films, he visited the US for two weeks, at which time he told the press he was considering going to Hollywood after fulfilling his obligations in England.[11] Instead, Clair returned to France in the autumn of 1938 with the intention of remaining, as he later remembered, although 'the prospects of returning home weren't at all pleasant because the industry was in its usual financial crisis and my brief experience as a producer gave me the horrors.'[12] He was in the middle of shooting *Air pur* when the production was halted by the impending German invasion. (The film was never completed.) Clair left for Hollywood with his wife and son where, between 1940 and 1945, he directed and co-wrote four films: *The Flame of New Orleans*; *I Married a Witch*; *It Happened Tomorrow*; *And Then There were None*, which he also produced.

By 1940, Duvivier had accumulated an impressive amount of experience shooting films outside of France. He was the first French director to make a film in Germany after the First World War: *L'Ouragan dans la montagne* (1922), a Franco-German co-production,[13] and he made a second, *Le Logis de l'horreur*, the same year. In 1931, he shot *Les Cinq Gentlemen maudits* in Morocco, and in 1932 he made an imaginative French/German dual-language film in France, *Allo Berlin/Ici Paris*. In the 1920s he made two films in Belgium, *Maria Chapdelaine* was shot on location in Quebec in 1934, *La Bandera* in Morocco and *Golgotha* in Algeria in 1935, and *The Golem* in Prague in 1936. In 1938 he was invited to Hollywood following the huge success of *Pépé le Moko* and *Un Carnet de bal* (1937), where he directed *The Great Waltz*. Although he had options to continue in Hollywood, Duvivier returned to France and completed three more films (the last of them, *Untel père et fils*, rescued from the lab even as the Germans advanced) before setting out for Hollywood again in 1940 at the age of forty-four. During his second American stay, he directed four films: *Lydia*; *Tales of Manhattan*; *Flesh and Fantasy*, produced by Duvivier and Charles Boyer; *The Imposter*, produced by Duvivier from his original script.

In 1940, Renoir's international profile was quite different from the universal populism of René Clair or the resourceful professionalism that characterised Duvivier and perhaps the later Clair, their differences notwithstanding. Because of the immense international cultural stature of his father, Renoir was able to develop a cosmopolitan and rather bohemian taste in art, especially the popular arts, and friendships with artists. He could travel in different circles and had a broader frame of reference. For his first major film, *Nana*, Renoir chose the German actors Werner Krauss, world-famous as Dr Caligari, and Valeska Gert, and ended up shooting half of the film in a Berlin studio in the winter of 1925–6. In Germany again in 1929, Renoir had a walk-on part in G.W. Pabst's *Diary of a Lost Girl* and a role in *Die Jagd nach dem Glück*, directed by Rochus Gliese, which starred his wife Catherine Hessling. And in 1932 he went to Berlin with his producer Pierre Braunberger, who was looking for financial partners, where he met Paul Klee and the art dealer Alfred Flechtheim, and investigated cabarets. Throughout the 1930s, Renoir worked closely in France with a number of German collaborators such as Karl Koch, who was his co-writer off and on from 1933 to 1940, renowned silhouette animator Lotte Reiniger, who was Koch's wife, writer Carl Einstein, cinematographer Theodor Sparkuhl, and composers Hanns Eisler and Kurt Weill.[14] Through Koch, Renoir came to know Brecht and Lotte Lenya at the time the *Threepenny Opera* was a hit on the Berlin stage, and they visited him at his home in Meudon, near Paris, with Eisler and Weill. Renoir recounted in his autobiography how Brecht's secretary came with a concertina, and that the old French songs Brecht encouraged him to sing reappeared in new German versions.[15] In 1940, after the disastrous French reaction to *La Règle du jeu*, Renoir left France for Italy, where he began a film version of *La Tosca*, but he was able to film only the first shots when the war made it necessary for him to return to France, after turning over the film to his co-writer Karl Koch, where he remained briefly before leaving for America. Unlike Clair and Duvivier, Renoir had no previous experience making films in the Anglophone world. In fact, when he arrived in Hollywood at the age of forty-seven, he did not speak English. Nonetheless, he made five films in the US between 1941 and 1946: *Swamp Water, This Land is Mine, The Southerner, Diary of a Chambermaid, Woman on the Beach*, and he participated in making *A Salute to France* for the Office of War Information. Unlike Clair and Duvivier, however, and for rather complex reasons, Renoir did not return to France when the war was over; rather, he shot an independent production in India (*The River*) followed by a French–Italian co-production in Italy (*The Golden Coach*) before he finally made another film in France in 1954 at the age of sixty, *French Cancan*.[16]

While in Hollywood building their new careers, these émigrés were involved in various activities in support of France. René Clair was not interested in making films related to the war, but after his brother, Henri Chomette, died from polio while serving in the French Army in Morocco, Clair volunteered his services as a translator for the French and Allied troops in North Africa. His letter was passed to the head of the French Mission in Washington, General Béthouard, who met with Clair and asked him to leave immediately for a more important mission in Algiers, namely to organise the Cinema Division of the Army. When Clair learned that no resources had yet been allocated for this mission, he wrote a report detailing the material his unit would need. After many delays, he was ready to leave for North Africa in January 1944 when he discovered that the equipment which had been authorised had still not been purchased. Many months of Clair's activity ended in a trip not taken and a report in which he explained why the French cinema had not recorded the historic Allied invasions of North Africa or of northern France.[17]

Renoir and Duvivier each made a feature film to counter anti-French sentiment in the US: *This Land Is Mine* (1942) and *The Imposter* (1944), respectively. *This Land Is Mine* is the story of collaboration and resistance, secret denunciations to the foreign occupiers, sabotage against them and the emergence of an unlikely hero, an apparent coward (Charles Laughton), who ends up mobilising the community against the foreign occupiers as well as the local businessman who works with them. The location of the film was France in Renoir's original treatment, but it was deliberately left unspecified in the film. One explanation for this was given in the preface to the published screenplay, namely, to convey the idea that this story could happen anywhere: 'The locale is symbolic of all occupied countries and hence resembles no one precisely. Neither sets nor manners should be too foreign. We make a complete translation of an alien people. They speak plain English and we avoid any accents except in the Germans. They speak as you do, they have about the same habits as you have, they could be yourselves.'[18] Moreover, RKO was worried about negative box-office fallout if the film was too explicitly sympathetic to France, since there was a widespread belief in America that France's quick capitulation meant that the populace was collaborating will- ingly with the German occupiers. Nonetheless, many details remained that tied it to France. At the end, for instance, the schoolteacher (Laughton) reads the 'Declaration of the Rights of Man' when he takes the stand at his trial to protest against those who take away freedom of speech, thought and action. He is con- demned to death, yet this public act of resistance, which is, exactly as Renoir wanted it to be, the opposite of the usual heroic image of the underground fighter, strengthens the resolve of his community against the occupying forces.

Although he tried hard to do so, Renoir was not able to maintain the realist style in this film that he had developed during the 1930s in France.[19] Financial constraints forced him to cut corners and to work in a way that he was not used to, which had many negative effects, including having to use sets left over from *The Hunchback of Notre Dame*. To cut costs, Renoir's friend and co-producer, Dudley Nichols, prevented Renoir from opening the film with a complicated tracking shot using a crane. His reaction to this interference was so strong that he cut every single tracking shot from the film, which changed the visual style he had planned completely, as Alexander Sesonske has documented.[20] In the end, *This Land Is Mine* did not evoke an authentic milieu of any kind and its one- dimensional characters were sometimes strident. Early in the production, Renoir wrote to his son, Alain, who was serving in the US Army in the Pacific:

> I have finished writing the scenario I have done with Dudley Nichols for Laughton. We are delighted. It is very violent and shows, I hope clearly, that certain European leaders have preferred to see the Nazis penetrate their own country rather than grant some advantages to the workers. It is the story of collaboration, conscious or not, honest or dishonest, that we are trying to explain.[21]

By the time the film had been completed, however, the life had been drained from the screen representation of these deeply felt convictions.[22] None the less, the film seems to have been effective in helping American audiences become more sym- pathetic to the cause of the occupied French people and more willing to help them in the great European military offensive soon to come, rather than to see them as Hitler's allies.

In 1944, nearly two years after Renoir's film, when the Americans were engaged in heavy fighting in Europe, Duvivier produced and directed *The Imposter*, with Jean Gabin in the title role. Here too, the objective was to win American support for the French cause. While the film is reminiscent of Duvivier's earlier success in France with Gabin in *La Bandera* (1935), *The Imposter* was tightly anchored to events in France immediately following the capitulation to Germany. Where French accents are deliberately avoided in *This Land Is Mine,* nearly all the actors have or adopt French accents in *The Imposter.* Where *This Land Is Mine* is deliberately abstract in order to universalise the theme of ordinary citizens reacting to occupation by a foreign military power, *The Imposter* begins with a map of France, then focuses on Paris and slowly moves south-west across the map along the Paris–Bordeaux road, stopping at Tours. A fateful date is superimposed on the screen: 14 June 1940, the day the Germans marched down the Champs Elysées. The film is full of specific information, and gives a rather concrete sense of the confusion and disorientation following the French capitulation. Soldiers and civilians alike are heading south as best they can. Soldiers who survived the brief conflict with the Germans cannot understand what happened and feel betrayed:

> 1ST SOLDIER: I lost my company – or they lost me.
> 4TH SOLDIER (bitterly): With me it started at Sedan. They sent three of us to clean out a pillbox. When we came back – no regiment.
> 5TH SOLDIER: My outfit was in Belgium.
> 1ST SOLDIER: Then orders: fall back, fall back. [. . .]
> 2ND SOLDIER: What a beating!
> 4TH SOLDIER: Up in Champagne – not one plane. They were all in Belgium.
> 5TH SOLDIER: In Belgium they told us they were all in France.
> 2ND SOLDIER: No planes, no tanks. (Looking down) Not much feet left, either.[23]

At the Atlantic port of St Jean de Luz, just south of Biarritz near the Spanish border, Pétain's infamous speech is heard on the radio announcing his acceptance of the Armistice. The crowd becomes more bitter and confused, since they expected Pétain to announce the relocation of the government outside occupied Paris. Rumours spread that the French government will fall back to its military forces in the colonies, spurring soldiers to board a ship for Dakar. En route, they hear de Gaulle's famous radio speech of 18 June: 'Soldiers of France, arise, wherever you may be.' When they learn that Dakar has been declared loyal to Vichy, they head further south, finally landing in Pointe Noire. Most of the film takes place in French Equatorial Africa. Superimposed maps appear again, detailing the soldiers' journey to Brazzaville, where they enlist in the Free French Army, and their ascent of the Congo River to the place they have been ordered to establish a communications site, which they name DeGaulleville.

The film begins before this, with Clement's (Gabin's) miraculous (or ironic) escape from Tours when a German bomb blows up his prison at the very moment he is to be guillotined. (He was a scapegoat, convicted of killing a policeman in an open fight between striking factory workers and the police.) To avoid being arrested again, he takes a uniform and papers from a dead soldier, and joins the throngs of people trying to escape from the city as the roads are strafed from German aircraft. The cynical attitude that characterises him at the outset is gradually transformed by his experiences with other men in battle, men who have volunteered to fight for the Free French in Africa. Under his assumed name, Lafargue, he gains a sense of belonging and moral values he had never known before. But his false identity is discovered, and he is court-martialled and stripped of all honours, including those he earned for himself in battle at Koufra. His demotion results in his transfer to the most dangerous theatre of action, but four of his comrades volunteer to go with him: they have wanted to be at the front all along. Another date appears on the screen: March 1942. At the Libyan oasis of Fezzan, Clement/Lafargue takes on a suicide mission and dies a hero's death as he blows up a machine gun site, saving his friends and winning territory from the enemy. After the battle, we see an endless field of unmarked wooden crosses through the eyes of Gabin's closest friend, paying his respects. The ending written in the script is even stronger: Lafargue's ghost is seen marching triumphantly with his comrades after their victory. The producers ran into trouble with the Production Code Administration because the film seemed to be glorifying suicide, and perhaps that was why the original ending was dropped.[24]

Both *This Land Is Mine* and *The Imposter* were made for specific strategic purposes in America in 1943 and 1944. They were intended to make the French capitulation to the Germans understandable to an American audience, to make French people more sympathetic so that American public opinion would see France as an ally in need of and deserving liberation despite the high cost that would be paid by American soldiers. Neither film was intended to be shown in France. After the war, however, the flood of American films coming into French theatres carried both films along with it. In fact, they were released in Paris on the same day, 10 July 1946. While *The Imposter* did not receive much praise, *This Land Is Mine* was a disaster.

An excerpt from one of the reviews conveys a sense of how strongly people reacted against the portrayal of their activities during the Occupation from the other side of the Atlantic:

> One can imagine that Jean Renoir, the author of *Grand Illusion*, has some excuses for having made a stupid and offensive film in America. He arrived as an émigré in a country that he barely knew and he had to submit to some of the exigencies of Hollywood. But I think that a real artist never has to make excuses. The sculptor breaks the statue that hasn't met his standards; the painter burns the canvas that isn't successful. The man who presents the public with a work signed with his name carries all the responsibility for it.
>
> In this case, Renoir's responsibility is very serious. After all, he had Charles Laughton, which proves that he was held in some esteem. In a film about France, he didn't even insist on the reproduction of French costumes and French customs. ... It was not necessary in 1941 to make a film in the United States about the Resistance. Even today one feels that it is too soon. So how, at that time and from over there, could one know the moral climate of our country, the exact nuances of the occupation, the indispensable details of our daily life? Jean Renoir passed over all of it in a cavalier manner. He made everything too simple, a horrible melodrama stuffed with inaccuracies, with academicism, empty phrases, mindless patriotism of the worst kind.[25]

When one takes into account how Renoir was thwarted in his attempts to create a realistic French ambience, in spite of his lack of first-hand knowledge of the country under the Occupation, it must have been difficult to hear deliberately offensive criticism that did not (and could not) take into account the production problems or the situation in the US that he was addressing.

Indeed, that was the crux of the issue: French critics could not know Renoir's situation or the American attitude toward the French in 1942 because of the same distance that divided Renoir from France. Word of negative reviews in French papers came back to Renoir, who reacted strongly and emotionally, as we can see from this letter to his brother Claude:

> I read in a Hollywood newspaper that *This Land Is Mine* was very badly received in Paris because the subject of the Resistance was treated in an unorthodox way in the film. I won't hide from you that this news has hurt me badly. It wasn't easy to insist on a subject of this kind at a time when everything French was considered in America to be in the service of the enemy. It seemed to me that my first duty was to explain to Americans, through film, which is 'my medium,' that anti-Nazi feelings were there in occupied Europe, despite everything. I think I succeeded in doing that, and the proof is the many letters I received from soldiers that I can sum up in these few words: 'Until now, I thought that the French were all bastards; your film made me think about it, and now I think that I was probably too harsh.'
>
> Besides, Resistance fighters from different countries, among them a delegation of Russian cameramen sent on leave to the US for their heroic acts during the war, saw the film and told me that it represented the state of mind of an occupied city and the insinuating manner in which the Germans had acted very well.
>
> On the other hand, I think that RKO was wrong to release a work [in 1946] that was contemporary in 1942. But that doesn't mean that, if what I read is true, I am prepared to forget the deep pain that this lack of understanding on the part of my countrymen has caused me. I told you at the beginning of this letter that I felt a strong desire to remain here. This incident only reinforces my feeling that I don't want to return to find people whose heroism during the war forces my admiration but whose susceptibility seems regrettable to me.[26]

The Imposter was preceded by an explanatory title which shielded the film from much of the disdain heaped on *This Land Is Mine* and lowered the artistic stakes:

> *The Imposter* is not a comedy or a drama or a documentary: it is a message. A message sent by the French in America to friends who must be reassured and to enemies who had to be silenced. This film was begun at the end of 1942, when the world suspected France and many persisted in believing that she had accepted defeat willingly. It was out of the desire to certify that our country had never stopped fighting that a French director solicited an American company for the means to make known to everyone the reality of the Free French Forces.[27]

The French version of *A Salute to France* was prefaced by a similar introduction, in which the actor, Claude Dauphin, in military uniform, explained the film's purpose. But *This Land Is Mine* had no introductory explanation and was further handicapped by being shown dubbed in French – a practice Renoir detested but apparently was helpless to prevent.

The same reviewer who castigated Renoir's film devoted a smaller column on the same page of his paper to *The Imposter* saying, among other things:

> It's a bad film, full of heavy, false moments, not to mention the execrable melodrama that serves as its plot. Nonetheless, it is a lot less bad than Renoir's film because the action takes place almost entirely outside of France and so one is less shocked at every moment by the lack of correspondence to reality. It is also less slow and boring. . . . Let's be fair. The story is worthless. The false heroism, the false sentiments, the false situations are smothered in syrup. It is too bad that the epic of French West Africa and Leclerc didn't find a serious historiographer in the cinema.[28]

Another reviewer, who refers to Gabin's role as 'Pépé le Moko de la défaite' ('Pépé le Moko of the defeat'), underlined the distance between the French directors in America and the people who had lived through the defeat and the Occupation:

> We are at once thankful, moved and outraged. Duvivier proved his indisputable good will with his *Imposter*. Nonetheless he offends our sense of logic and decorum at every moment. *The Imposter...* is history seen by a Frenchman who was not there during our exodus and our defeat and by Americans who didn't experience them. We cannot help being annoyed to see our army in disarray, represented by little men who, naturally, have mustaches and exchange pessimistic remarks in 'American.' ... Duvivier probably succeeded in creating excellent propaganda for us in America. But for us French, with six years distance, it is not possible to swallow this exodus, this defeat without revolting against it.[29]

When Clair and Duvivier returned to France in 1945, they were not welcomed by everyone. To some, they were opportunists who had escaped the deprivations of the war years to advance their careers in the lucrative American studio environment. Duvivier left Paris for London, intending to work on a film with Alexander Korda. There he met screenwriter Charles Spaak and, together, they planned *Panique* (1947), based on Simenon's 1933 novel, *Les Fiançailles de M. Hire*, which they re-cast as a dark post-war morality tale. Not surprisingly, the critics recoiled from this film, shocked by its portrayal of mob violence that, they claimed, was unrealistic and absolutely unFrench. One wonders if the profound cynicism of Duvivier's first post-war French film was partly a response to the negative reaction to the idealised and heroic resistants he had portrayed in *The Imposter*. In *Panique* not one single member of the community represents positive moral values. Moreover there is nothing by which one could even measure moral value. Even Clouzot's *Le Corbeau* had portrayed French society less cynically. Michel Simon, who played M. Hire, described his role as follows:

> In *Panique*, I made no concession to anecdote. I wanted to create a character free from every social convention. The individual who never smiles, who does not say hello. He falls from the sixth floor of a building, pursued by the hatred of his entire neighborhood. The people disperse, ashamed of what they have done. Why was he killed? Because he didn't shake their hand. Because he didn't say, 'Thanks, I'm fine, how are you?' In the period of the worst demagoguery, the critics sabotaged this film.[30]

In October 1946 Duvivier left no doubt about the seriousness with which he intended his portrayal of post-war France to be taken:

> Why *Panique*? Because it was an inevitable reaction for me. I arrived in Hollywood where I saw optimistic films with traditional happy endings for five years. So I wanted to treat a subject more in tune with the present situation. Of course I know that it is much easier to make sweet, charming poetic films with beautiful photography, but my nature pushed me toward themes that are bleak, dark, bitter.
> What does *Panique* say? It says that people are not nice, that the crowd is stupid, that independent people are always wrong ... and that they inevitably end up falling into line with the rest. Obviously, we are far from people who love each other, who are the rage on the screens of Hollywood, but I have the strong impression that we are passing through a period where people do not love each other. For me – the public will tell me later what they think – *Panique* is the most significant film of my career because in it I wanted to say something.[31]

Claude Beylie commented on Duvivier's reference to the 'present situation' as a 'possible allusion to the atmosphere of collective psychosis and informing on people which reigned in France under the Occupation and did not let up – quite the contrary – during the period of the purges (*l'épuration*). The fact that Hire (Hirovitch) was Jewish takes its meaning from this situation.'[32] This character is never explicitly identified as Jewish, but many critics have assumed that he was, which adds, of course, to the seriousness of the representation of the cruelties perpetrated against him by so many individuals in his community, culminating in the mob shouting for his blood until, isolated, terrified and innocent, he does indeed fall to his death before everyone's eyes.

French critics reacted strongly. Georges Charensol wrote that *Panique*'s script, written by Charles Spaak, was 'unrealistic and without humanity'.[33] In July 1947 Georges Sadoul wrote in *Les Lettres Françaises*:

> The word 'lynching' is not French. If gossip would be enough to have an unfortunate man killed who was only guilty of looking unpleasant, how many collective murders would have been committed during these past years! In 1944 part of France found itself without police and without a governing body, even without contact with the central government, and you only needed to hold out your hand to have a gun. Even so, were there many lynchings – I'm not talking about innocent people, but of known and recognized criminals?
>
> If the scenes where we see the crowd mobilize and assemble against the unfortunate Monsieur Hire are so unconvincing, it is because these collective murders do not exist in French customs or psychology, and that this exceptional case is represented as a normal and natural event. The lack of a minimum of believability meant that the *social atmosphere* dreamed of by Charles Spaak was not realized if the author wanted to prove that the *crowd* is necessarily stupid and evil. ...
>
> *La Belle Équipe* [was] one of the rare works, along with those of Renoir and René Clair, that showed real Parisian people; ... the perfect success of *Pépé le Moko* [was] a masterpiece of the *underworld* (le milieu). ... Despite the perfect craft that he demonstrates in all [the films he made in America], Duvivier proved in each case that his loss of the French environment prevented him from doing his best.[34]

Duvivier left France again for England where he made *Anna Karenina*, and then persevered in a long career of international productions, making films in Britain, Italy, Spain and West Germany as well as many in France.

Renoir had made it clear to his family as early as 1941 that he intended to become an American citizen. His ambivalence toward the French film industry and the postwar French climate is explicit throughout his correspondence. He delayed a long time returning to his native country. Even after the bigamy lawsuit brought by his first wife, Catherine Hessling, had been settled in June 1949, Renoir waited six months to see France again, and then he spent only thirty-six hours there.[35] The following year, Renoir passed through France briefly, and in 1951 it seems that he was in France only three times, for periods of two to three weeks. Although according to his biographer Renoir moved back to France in May 1951 to resume his film career, in fact he had made arrangements before leaving the US to go to Italy almost immediately to prepare *The Golden Coach* and he never moved back to France to live.[36] Renoir did not make a film in France again until 1954, *French Cancan*. By then, he was sixty years old, he had not lived in his native country for fifteen years and he was an American citizen whose residence would remain Los Angeles until he died.

His duty as a French artist, Renoir stated over and over, was to make good films in the French manner, in Hollywood or elsewhere. As he wrote at the end of a long letter in 1944 against dubbing to the actor Pierre Blanchar, president of the Comité de libération du cinéma, 'France has just suffered terrible losses. We have fewer men, fewer factories, less gasoline, and fewer airplanes than our powerful friends. Let's show them that at least there is one treasure which our enemies have not been able to take from us, our artistic integrity.'[37] Renoir never stated that the duty of the French artist was to live in France, but French critics obviously believed this to be necessary.

The first post-war French films of both Renoir and René Clair are set in the past, long before the émigré/deserter or collaborationist conflicts resulting from Vichy. For Renoir, it was *French Cancan*, a huge success which was widely reviewed as an ode to life, colour and the *belle époque* as seen in his father's paintings. Although this story of the birth of the Moulin Rouge through its founder, Charles Zidler, played by Jean Gabin, has a darker side with regard to Renoir's sexual politics as I have tried to show elsewhere,[38] its vibrant surface captivated the French public. Many reviewers – not just one – stated that Renoir needed only to set foot on French soil again for him to be able to make a truly French film.

René Clair's first post-war film, *Le Silence est d'or* (1947), was a French–American co-production situated in 1906 and the early days of silent films. It was seen as a typical Clair fantasy in keeping with his earlier career, but perhaps Clair's portrait of an ageing film director (Maurice Chevalier), in love with a young woman who falls in love, in turn, with his own assistant, is more tender and heartfelt. Clair told interviewers after the war that he was eager to return to France to see his parents:

France had just been liberated, and more than anything I wanted to see my parents, who were quite old by then. While I was at home, I received offers to make a film there. The most interesting came from a consortium composed of RKO and Pathé, who had just signed a co-production agreement with each other. I wasn't at all sure of what to do. My son was in the American army stationed on the West Coast, and I wasn't too eager to put all that distance between us, for one thing. I returned to Hollywood in October, and then the film [*Ten Little Indians*] came out at the end of the month in New York. It did quite well commercially, so RKO offered me an irresistible deal: I would write, produce and direct two films for them, one in France with Pathé, and then one back in Hollywood with RKO. They signed me without even asking me what sort of pictures I would be making. [...] Bronia and I returned to France in July [1946], I finished the script, and that fall we began shooting *Le Silence est d'or*.

After all those years in England and America, I wanted to return to my old vision of Paris – singers, little people in the streets, neighbourliness, familiarity. But all that had been changed by the war. Paris had become a different place; it had a different atmosphere. I wanted to recapture that old spirit. [...] So I decided that I would have to make a period picture in order to get back to the pre-war atmosphere. I was feeling nostalgic about my art and the early days of my career as well as about Paris, so I decided to set the picture in the heroic days of the birth of motion pictures. My principal character would be someone on the order of Feuillade, with whom I had worked as an actor. I originally wrote the part for Raimu, in his style, which was rather lower-class, solid and emotional, instead of the middle-class charming and witting character the film ended up with. That change occurred because Raimu was at first under contract for another film, then fell ill and died.

When he died, I wondered how I could make the film I had written for him and I soon realized I couldn't. It occurred to me that my old friend Maurice Chevalier might be able to do the part if I rewrote it. I was reluctant to suggest it to him, since he had never played anything but juvenile leads. When I finally did ask him, we both knew perfectly well that accepting a role like this would spell the end of that type of part for him for the rest of his career. I was very touched by his acceptance of the role: I took it as a profound gesture of confidence and friendship on his part.[39]

The sense of genuine love and loss in Clair's tribute to early French cinema was also influenced by the fact that his mother died just after he began shooting and his father followed her only five weeks later.

The first film Renoir made in France after the war was quite different in tone from Clair's, and it was also made much later, in terms of this volatile period, in 1954. His first European film following the war, *The Golden Coach*, was a Franco–Italian co-production made in Italy. Like so many of Renoir's ambitious films, it had been dismissed critically and was unsuccessful in France, and had added to Renoir's reputation as a film-maker who had lost his way. *French Cancan*, with much more distance than Clair's film (one need only compare the roles and comportment of Maurice Chevalier and Jean Gabin), was, I believe, a calculated bet on nostalgia on Renoir's part to try to win back a French audience for his films in the aftershock of, most importantly, the negative reaction to *La Règle du jeu* (which Renoir never got over), then to the reaction against his American films when they were released in France after the war, and most recently to *The Golden Coach*.

The entire first issue of *Ciné-Club*, published in 1947 as the 'organ of the French federations of ciné-clubs' (president Jean Painlevé; Secretary General, Georges Sadoul) was devoted to René Clair, calling him the most French of French directors and welcoming him back so that he could nourish his native film industry in its time of need. In the same issue, the director of the Centre National de la Cinématographie, Michel Fourré-Cormeray, wrote a column in which he explained that the French film industry would not be able to compete with others (meaning, the Americans) in terms of the numbers of films it produced, but it could compete successfully when it came to quality. The mission of the ciné-clubs, therefore, should be to educate the public to understand what quality meant in the cinema. It is in this context that the journal presented Clair, with a profile that showed how his roots in the Dada and Surrealist avant-garde artistic movements of the 1920s (he had made *Entr'acte* in 1924) could still be felt in his new film. Further, *Le Silence est d'or* was described as a loving tribute not only to silent cinema, which Clair had been one of the first to revive as a film critic in his youth, but more specifically to his mentor from the silent days, Louis Feuillade, who was by then recognised as one of the great inventors of a uniquely French tradition in cinema.

In this time of heavy contestation about the past and the future in French cultural life, Clair made a statement that signalled his withdrawal from contemporary portrayals of his day:

When people say that the cinema should 'serve' this or that, I can't help thinking that, in the dictionary, serve is dangerously close to servitude. If Shakespeare lived today, censors would disapprove of the uselessness of *A Midsummer Night's Dream*. Questions about the real and the contemporary also come up about the novel. A literary journal asked recently: 'Should a novelist bear witness to his time?' I would have preferred a more modest question. For instance: 'Can a novelist bear witness to his time?' That is by no means certain. Often the most important works have been inspired by the time of their authors' youth or an earlier period. The Abbé Prévost of *Manon Lescaut*, the Stendhal of *La Chartreuse de Parme*, the Tolstoy of *War and Peace*, or, closer to us, the Proust of *Swann*, were they, in these novels, witnesses to the time in which they wrote them?

One isn't a witness to one's time because one has decided to become one. Sometimes one becomes a witness by accident, when posterity judges us worthy of it. The one who wants to be a witness at any cost risks producing false testimony.[40]

Jean-Pierre Jeancolas observed in *15 ans d'années trente*: 'France in the 1930s was convinced that it was a great power. Hadn't France won the First World War? Occupied France perceived itself as a great power that had been humiliated. It was between 1944 and 1946 that the French became conscious of the fact that their country was only a secondary power. Between 1940 and 1945, the health of French cinema wasn't bad. At least, it could pretend. It was in 1946 that it nearly died.'[41]

If we return to Renoir's hope in 1944, in the face of his disappointment over *A Salute to France*, that it would be a French director in France who would make that good film about his country, one wonders what, in fact, could count as a good film about France in the context of the Franco-French conflicts resulting from Vichy? While Clair and Renoir, many years after him, chose to return with nostalgic, bitter-sweet portraits of love adventures amidst the newly emerging entertainment milieux (the movies; the Moulin Rouge and Montmartre as tourist attractions) of France's *belle époque* before the trauma of the Great War, films which were met with relieved enthusiasm, this was certainly not what Renoir had in mind in 1944.

One of the Paris reviews of Duvivier's *The Imposter* ends with this lament, as if in reply: 'Ah! Where is *Pépé le Moko*?'[42] This sigh of regret, which was echoed by critics reviewing many dark post-war films, such as those of Yves Allégret, did not simply mean that Duvivier's very French pre-war gangster film was better than *The Imposter*. Rather it signalled the widespread feeling that those memorable films that were decried as defeatist and pessimistic in the late 1930s were preferable to the cynical tone adopted by so many directors after the war. In fact, it was not just *Pépé le Moko* or *Quai des brumes* or those other darkly unforgettable films of the late 1930s that were regretted: what was really wanted was a return to the past and an image of France untarnished by all that Vichy stood for. Paradoxically, the decade that was so heavily criticised during its shaky existence had become, in retrospect, one version of the good old days.

Notes

I would like to thank Emmanuelle Toulet, Bibliothèque de l'Arsenal, Paris, for her generous assistance. Translations are my own unless otherwise noted.

1 Letter from Philip Dunne to Jean Renoir, 4 February 1944. Jean Renoir Collection, UCLA.
2 Letter from Jean Renoir to Jean Benoît-Lévy, 26 May 1944 in *Lettres d'Amérique*, presented by Dido Renoir and Alexander Sesonske (Paris: Presses de la Renaissance, 1984), pp. 150–1. Part of the history of this project is recounted in Alexander Sesonske's

unpublished ms. '1944: *A Salute to France*' (n.d.), pp. 107–25. A summary of his account may be found in Renoir, *Lettres d'Amérique*, pp. 149–51. A great deal is still unknown about the history of this project. Christopher Faulkner provides a description of the English-language version of the film in *Jean Renoir: A Guide to References and Resources* (Boston: G.K. Hall, 1979), pp. 134–5. The official OWI summary, reel by reel, including the names of historical figures and places as well as extensive cross-referencing by subject, is available through the National Archives in Washington at the following Web address: http://www.nara.gov:80/cgi-bin/starfinder/26172. Apparently it has not previously been known that all but the last reel of the French version of the final film (four of five reels) are held in the Film Archive at the Academy of Motion Picture Arts and Sciences, which was the West Coast repository for the OWI during the war. I would like to thank Michael Friend for providing access to the film, and Alexander Sesonske, who made available to me his unpublished manuscript on *A Salute to France*.

3 'Paris! Paris outragé! Paris brisé! Paris martyrisé! Mais Paris libéré! Libéré par lui-même, libéré par son peuple avec le concours des armées de la France, avec l'appui et le concours de la France tout entière, de la France qui se bat, de la seule France, de la vraie France, de la France éternelle.' From de Gaulle's speech at the Hôtel de Ville in Paris on the evening of 25 August 1944. The speech is reproduced in its entirety in connection with the exhibition 'Paris Libéré' (Paris, 1994) at http://www.paris. org/Expos/Liberation/Speech/speech.html (copyright 1994–6 Norman Barth: nbarth @paris. org).

4 Henry Rousso, *The Vichy Syndrome: History and Memory in France since 1944*, trans. Arthur Goldhammer (Cambridge, Mass: Harvard University Press, [1987] 1991), pp. 7–10; sources for figures cited pp. 336–7.

5 Although Ophuls had taken out French citizenship papers in the late 1930s, he was never considered a French director by the press until the New Wave critic-film-makers canonised him in the 1950s.

6 John Russell Taylor, *Strangers in Paradise: The Hollywood Émigrés 1933–1950* (London: Faber and Faber, 1983), pp. 218–19.

7 Jean-Pierre Azéma, *De Munich à la Libération, 1938–1944* (Paris: Seuil, 1979), pp. 277–81; Renoir, *Lettres d'Amérique*, pp. 131–3.

8 Renoir, *Lettres d'Amérique*, pp. 223–4, 10 May 1946.

9 Jean Renoir, *Jean Renoir: Letters*, edited by David Thompson and Lorraine LoBianco (London: Faber and Faber, 1994), p. 177, 13 May 1946; Renoir, *Lettres d'Amérique*, p. 229.

10 Renoir, *Letters*, p. 176, 11 May 1946; Renoir, *Lettres d'Amérique*, p. 227.

11 From an interview with the author, in Celia McGerr, *René Clair* (Boston: G.K. Hall, 1980), pp. 130–1.

12 From an interview with the author, in R.C. Dale, *The Films of René Clair* I (Metuchen, NJ: Scarecrow, 1986), p. 273.

13 Pierre Leprohon, *Anthologie du Cinéma* IV (Paris: L'Avant-Scène, 1968) pp. 203–14, 250–5. Leprohon's study seemed to be the most reliable to date for the information in this paragraph.

14 Célia Bertin, *Jean Renoir: A Life in Pictures*, trans. Mireille Muellner and Leonard Muellner (Baltimore: Johns Hopkins University Press, [1986] 1991). See pp. 62–175 passim and the filmography, pp. 351–75.

15 Jean Renoir, *My Life and My Films* (London: Collins, 1974), pp. 163–4.

16 On this subject, see my essay 'Jean Renoir's Return to France', *Poetics Today* vol. 17 no, 3, Fall 1996.

17 Georges Charensol and Roger Régent, *50 ans de cinéma avec René Clair* (Paris: La Table Ronde, 1979), pp. 141–8; see also Clair's later, less detailed interviews with Dale in *The Films of René Clair* I, pp. 341–2.

18 Dudley Nichols, *This Land is Mine* in John Gossner and Dudley Nichols (eds), *Twenty Best Film Plays* (New York: Crown, 1943), p. 834. Although Nichols wrote the script with Renoir, Nichols received sole credit.

19 Alexander Sesonske, 'Jean Renoir in America: 1942, *This Land is Mine*', *Persistance of Vision* nos 12–13, 1996, pp. 103–35.

20 Eugene Lourié, *My Work in Films* (New York: Harcourt Brace Jovanovich, 1985), pp. 76–7. Sesonske documents this with amazing figures comparing the number of shots, their duration and whether they are moving or static with *La Règle du jeu*, '*This Land Is Mine*', pp. 129–30.

21 Cited in Sesonske, '*This Land is Mine*', p. 77; Renoir, *Letters*, p. 138.

22 Sesonske gives many examples of things omitted in shooting or during editing. His analysis of the film's formal structures shows that Renoir's message survived subtly in symmetrical structural patterns despite the drastic changes.

23 *The Imposter*, script. Dimitri Tiomkin Collection, Doheny Library, University of Southern California.

24 See the PCA file on *The Imposter*, Margaret Herrick Library, Academy of Motion Picture Arts and Sciences.

25 Jean Fayard, review of *Vivre Libre* (*This Land is Mine*), *Opéra*, 24 July 1946.

26 Renoir, *Letters*, p. 183; the final paragraph was omitted from the English translation (translation modified slightly); Renoir, *Lettres d'Amérique*, p. 238, 26 July 1946.

27 Reproduced at the beginning of Jean Arlan's review in *Cité-Soir*, 14 July 1946.

28 Fayard, review of *Vivre Libre*.

29 Monique Berger, *Le Populaire*, 30 July 1946.

30 Paul Guth, *Michel Simon* (Paris: Calmann-Lévy, 1951), pp. 123–4; cited in François Guérif, *Le Cinéma policier français* (Paris: Henri Veyrier, 1981), p. 93.

31 Julien Duvivier, *Cinémonde*, 29 October 1946. The first part of this citation is included Claude Beylie's 'Les Trois Visages de Monsieur Hire', *L'Avant-Scène* nos 390–1, p. 4, n. 2.

32 Ibid.

33 Georges Charensol, *Les Nouvelles Littéraires*, 16 July 1947.

34 Georges Sadoul, *Les Lettres Françaises*, 24 July 1947 (emphasis in the original).

35 Sesonske's and Bertin's accounts differ slightly; Renoir's voluminous correspondence adds more precise details about his movements. See Jean Renoir Collection, UCLA, in addition to the two published books of correspondence: *Letters* and *Lettres d'Amérique*.

36 Bertin, *A Life in Pictures*, pp. 258, 260; Renoir, *Letters*, pp. 263, 269.

37 Renoir, *Letters*, p. 162, 31 December 1944 (translation modified slightly); Renoir, *Lettres d'Amérique*, p. 165.

38 See Bergstrom, 'Jean Renoir's Return to France'.

39 Dale, *The Films of René Clair*, pp. 361–2: interview with the author.

40 René Clair, *Comédies et commentaires* (Paris: NRF, 1959), pp. 339–40; cited in Marc Edelmann and Noëlle Giret (eds), *René Clair* (Paris: Cinémathèque française, 1983), p. 67.

41 Jean-Pierre Jeancolas, *15 ans d'années trente: le cinéma des français 1929–1944* (Paris: Stock, 1983), p. 8.

42 Fayard, review of *Vivre Libre*.

7

'D' for disgusting: American culture and English criticism

Richard Maltby

In matters of taste, more than anywhere else, all determination is negation, and tastes are perhaps first and foremost distastes, disgust provoked by horror or visceral intolerance ('sick-making') of the tastes of others.... The most intolerable thing for those who regard themselves as the possessors of legitimate culture is the sacrilegious reuniting of tastes which taste dictates shall be separate.

Pierre Bourdieu[1]

The generation of the 50s grew up on American movies, comics, and music: American mass culture was not an imported entity but part of our own daily experience, of the rebuilding of our postwar, post-Fascist, neo-capitalist identity. ... America was to us both the disease and the antidote. ... There was no need to go on beyond America to find alternatives to America.

Alessandro Portelli[2]

In a 1989 article about the effect of new communications technologies on cultural identity, David Morley and Kevin Robins proposed that 'American culture' has come to possess the capacity to reposition social, cultural and geographical frontiers. America, they argued, 'is now part of a European cultural repertoire, part of European identity'.[3] But how far the post-modern geographies of satellite broadcasting and the Internet have redefined concepts of cultural nationality remains open to question. America – or rather, what we might now call a Virtual America constructed from the exports of its culture industries – has been 'within' European identities, challenging and contesting definitions of the 'national' since at least the 1920s, when a State Department official described the way in which access to American popular culture combined with immigration restriction to convert 'the longing to emigrate ... into a desire to imitate'.[4] In 1937, for instance, an editorial in the *Daily Express* complained that British cinemagoers 'talk America, think America, and dream America. We have several million people, mostly women, who, to all intent and purpose, are temporary American citizens.'[5] The familiar foreign territory of Hollywood populated by this fantasised citizenry was not to be found on the other side of the Atlantic; rather, it would be more accurate to argue that American popular culture has always inhabited a virtual geography, one in which the location of 'America' has been no more exactly defined on the map than the borders of Ruritania, Freedonia, or any of Hollywood's other mythical European kingdoms.[6]

Recent debates over GATT have revived European rhetorics of cultural nationalism and, along with them, academic interest in the problematic definitions of the 'national' in ideas of 'national cinema' and 'national culture'. But American popular culture has long been so much a part of everyday life in other countries as to question the sense in which it can be considered to possess a specifically American national identity. The 'Americanisation of the world' has actually involved the circulation across national boundaries of a multinational popular culture which recognises no frontiers but acknowledges a principle of production and marketing inelegantly termed the 'glocal': 'a standard overall design with the flexibility to build in local variations to meet individual markets'.[7] What Dick Hebdidge has called 'the ubiquitous spectre of Americanisation', has functioned as a trope of displacement, from economic base into the virtual geography of cultural nationalisms imbued with fears of homogenisation and anxieties over the desire to imitate.[8]

In this chapter I am more concerned with examining the diverse forms of resistance to American culture than with the marginal economic effectiveness of any 'European challenge' to Hollywood's hegemony. Relatively stable national production industries have existed in Europe, making product for predominantly domestic consumption. But, however popular their product, these European popular cinemas have remained subaltern industries, subordinated by the competing hegemonic powers of Hollywood's commercial imperium on one side and cultural nationalism on the other. On the one hand, the stability and material prosperity of any particular domestic industry has been principally governed by the role played by American investment and distribution; withdrawal of American investment – for instance in Italy in the early 1970s – has brought about the collapse of the national production industry.[9] On the other hand, these popular cinemas have also consistently failed to meet the 'cultural' qualification required to achieve the status of 'national culture', according to the definitions proposed by the cultural apparatuses of the European nation-states. The ideal of a national cinema that meets both commercial and cultural criteria is by definition not far short of an oxymoron, at best occurring only in the isolated instances of individual films, and certainly not with sufficient frequency to sustain the notion of a national cultural industry.[10]

By contrast, Hollywood has remained substantially free from comparable cultural criteria, and therefore significantly less constrained by an obligation to behave as if it were a national cinema. Europeans have frequently failed to perceive the ways in which American purveyors of American culture do not recognise their product as part of a national culture. This mutual misperception may account for the striking rhetorical gap between European denunciations of cultural imperialism poisoning 'the souls of our children ... who are to be turned into the docile slaves of the American multi-millionaires',[11] and the cultural imperialists' insistence that 'US culture is not pernicious,' because 'we're only talking leisure, entertainment, here.'[12] The rhetorical gap points to a divergence of understanding larger than one measured simply by economic self-interest. It can be argued that the 'American culture' resisted by nationalists has been a national culture only outside the geographic boundaries of the United States, where it has been represented as the cultural Other of a defensively defined and often equally invented 'traditional' national culture.

Since the 1920s, concerns about Americanisation have provided European cultural elites with the material with which to debate issues of modernity, national identity and the constitution of 'culture'. As cultural Other, American culture has appeared dangerous to elites because it is radically democratic; at a variety of levels, it challenges hierarchies of discrimination, taste and class. To a significant extent, this danger is contained by its being classified as 'entertainment', and the interchangeability of the terms 'entertainment', 'popular culture' and 'American culture' indicates the ways in which ideas of aesthetic distinction have been intertwined with elite definitions of nationalism in the perception that 'Americanisation' involved a process of 'levelling down' moral and aesthetic standards. From this perspective, the 'American culture' for which Hollywood was a metonym was not 'culture' at all. In the two sets of terms 'American culture' and 'national culture', the word 'culture' does not, clearly, mean the same thing: it is inclusive and anthropological in 'American culture', and exclusive and discriminating in 'national culture'.

Part of the process of resistance to 'Americanisation' involved the identification of alternative criteria by which its commercial hegemony might be not so much countered as discounted through distinction: most commonly, through the distinction between art and popular culture or entertainment. This distinction is typically constructed as a binary opposition. While 'art and literature are rooted in a fundamental dissonance between appearance and reality', popular culture 'deals in certainties': offering assurance that things are under control, that ambiguity will be resolved, that violence is assimilable, that disorder will resolve into order, that sexuality is not anarchic, that death is not real, that injustice is a temporary state, that rebellion is a predictable phase which will be subsumed eventually in a necessary corporate stability.[13]

In liberal democracies, the distinction between art and entertainment has for most of this century been legally enforceable, in that the protection from legal restrictions offered to art under rights of free speech and free expression has been denied to entertainment. The definition I have just quoted makes the rationale for this distinction relatively clear: unlike art, entertainment is not supposed to be socially disruptive. Thus the boundaries of national culture are reinforced by criteria of taste and quality, and cultural frontiers are policed by the institutions of censorship and criticism. Regimes of censorship ensure that entertainment conforms adequately to its socially prescribed role; regimes of criticism define entertainment as trivial, and maintain the distinction.

More recent approaches to cultural nationalism offer an alternative recognition of what 'American culture' is and how it may be understood. In Richard Kuisel's phrase, American culture is 'everyone's second culture',[14] an idea elaborated by Tom O'Regan's suggestion that Hollywood's dominance is 'a function of it being better placed to handle the *diminishing value attached to programming when it circulates outside its home market*'. O'Regan invokes the concept of ' "*Americanicité*" [or Americanness]: the construction of an imaginary "America" by different social formations. "*Americanicité*" is a cultural matter (the French version of America is not the Australian), it links "local audiences" to "global media product" and so facilitates Hollywood's circulation.' American culture – Hollywood – is locally appropriated, and put to specific, situated cultural uses. But its 'American' identity makes it multinational: 'a global resource which simultaneously transmits transnational aesthetic values and encourages local audiences to customise for appropriate local resonances.' At some level, purveyors of American culture who claim it is not pernicious recognise this: Hollywood is, as O'Regan observes, 'not in the business of erasing the difference between it and its foreign markets, but turning it to its own advantage'.[15]

But for other cultural elites, reluctant to abandon their own culture's claim to universal significance, being reduced to the role of supplying exotic local colour to add gloss to the universal truths of American culture is an unedifying position. Paradoxically, the defenders of 'traditional' national cultures have been forced to exaggerate the influence and transformative power of 'American culture' in order to demonstrate how threatening it is, in a mirror image of its producers' denial. Defenders of 'traditional' European identities have used the explicitly political mechanisms of trade barriers and censorship to counter the hegemonic influence of Hollywood. Quotas and subsidy legislation quantify the 'national' as a percentage of exhibition or employment. Censorship, on the other hand, seeks to establish the national as a quality by asserting cultural difference as a form of national moral superiority. In the remainder of this chapter I want to look at two instances of the transgression of cultural boundaries, when the forms or concerns of American culture located themselves in Britain and provoked a defensive reaction from the institutions of censorship and criticism that challenged the legitimacy of the particular trans-Atlantic cultural practices involved.

The virtual 'American culture' resisted by Europeans is in part their own creation. That 'indigenous American form' film noir, 'the unique example of a wholly American film style', bears a French name, commonly assumed to derive from Marcel Duhamel's *Série noire* imprint of crime novels.[16] In his autobiography, Duhamel explains that his decision to create the *Série noire* resulted from his translating three novels, *This Man is Dangerous* and *Poison Ivy* by Peter Cheyney, and *No Orchids for Miss Blandish* by James Hadley Chase.[17] In pursuit of the relativities of Americanness, it is an irony worth noting that both Cheyney and Chase were British. But it is perhaps more than just an irony: the publisher of a German imitation of Cheyney explained that the appeal of the American setting lay in its otherness:

> Detective novels set in Germany are mostly boring – and if not boring, then incredible. The neighbouring countries around us have been shown to be commonplace by streams of tourists. . . . Only America is left to us. It is the only place where the reality of things cannot be checked personally by most European readers. American crime is still credible.[18]

This perception of American culture as fantastic and therefore credible deserves more exploration than it can receive here. In Britain, however, the trans-Atlantic cultural operation involved in this imagining of America was seen as particularly transgressive. *No Orchids for Miss Blandish* was the subject of an essay written in 1944 by George Orwell, in which he contrasted the 'moral atmosphere' of Chase's novel with that of E.W. Hornung's *Raffles, the Amateur Cracksman*, written in 1900. Orwell lamented 'the change in popular attitude' he identified, and related it specifically to a process of Americanisation. Chase was the target of his criticism precisely because he was 'an Englishman who seems ... to have made a complete mental transference to the American underworld', and his offence was compounded by the fact that he had achieved this transference without having visited the United States.[19] Instead he had imitated the American culture of what Orwell called 'Yank Mags', imported into Britain literally as ballast in the holds of ships.[20] The book was, he believed, 'a new departure for English sensational fiction, in which till recently there has always been a sharp distinction between right and wrong and a general agreement that virtue must triumph in the last chapter'. In the America of Orwell's imagination, 'both in life and fiction, the tendency to tolerate crime, even to admire the criminal so long as he is successful, is very much more marked.'[21]

The threat that this 'half-understood import from America' posed to English cultural values was articulated in an essay Orwell wrote two years later, on the 'Decline of the English Murder'. Life, it appeared, was imitating 'lowbrow fiction'. The perfect English murder, a domestic poisoning committed by a dentist whose guilty passion for his secretary made murder seem 'less disgraceful, and less damaging to his career, than being detected in adultery', was being replaced in the popular imagination by a well-publicised case known as the Cleft Chin Murder, committed by two characters who might have emerged from the pages of Chase's novel. Karl Hulten was an American army deserter who described himself, untruthfully, as a 'big-time Chicago gangster'. Elizabeth Jones was an eighteen-year-old ex-waitress who described herself, equally untruthfully, as a striptease artist 'and declared that she wanted to do something dangerous, "like being a gun moll"'. Together, they committed several petty but violent robberies, and a random killing. What offended Orwell's aesthetic sensibility was that 'there was no depth of feeling to ... the whole meaningless story.' Instead of the aura of domestic repression that made the English murder memorably tragic, the Cleft Chin Murder's background was that of 'the anonymous life of the dance-halls and the false values of the American film'.[22] Its cultural significance lay in its importation of inadequately motivated crime.[23]

Orwell's critique of 'American culture' – what he described as his 'header into the cesspool' – partook of the common currency of bourgeois English cultural criticism. For the anxious critics of Americanisation, the 'shiny barbarism' of Americanness represented a pseudo-culture of unconvincing imitation.[24] It was inorganic, unnatural and therefore particularly disgusting. The English rhetoric of Americanisation is a discourse of the *abîme*, filled with references to contamination and pollution as much as invasion, and expressions of anger and disgust at the unnatural abominations produced by the encounter. British cultural criticism also seldom describes the products of its own culture as either meaningless or violent, whereas violence, particularly sets of violent gestures centred on the use of guns, is a part of the fantastically credible representations of *Americanicité*.[25]

The Motion Picture Production Code's restrictions on classical Hollywood's explicit representation of sexual behaviour, and its insistence on 'compensating moral values' ensured that European censors found themselves more exercised over American violence than American sex. The danger of social disruption caused by imitation formed the most common basis for European censorship of the violence in American films.[26] The concern was, as always, over a deviant

response to 'realism' on the part of inadequately socialised viewers who were, par-
adigmatically, delinquent adolescents: the readers of Orwell's 'Yank Mags', partly
Americanised, like Elizabeth Jones, in their language and their moral outlook.[27]
For the British critics of Americanisation, imitation existed at two levels: what
Trevelyan called 'the danger of stimulation and imitation' on the part, for
example, of Teddy Boys watching *The Wild One*; and the formal imitation of
American content, which was a form of the same thing, but which, apparently,
carried much greater dangers of cultural contagion, since it confused the cat-
egories of the fantastic and the real.

When the British company, Renown, filmed *No Orchids for Miss Blandish* in
1948, it was treated as a cultural abomination by British newspaper critics in one
of their occasional bouts of collective moral outrage. C.A. Lejeune in the *Observer*
declared herself 'ashamed to have to report' that 'this repellent piece of work ...
was made in England', and devoutly hoped that it would 'never be considered for
export; let our shame be confined, at least, to our own country'.[28] Lejeune's com-
ments were echoed in all the press reviews: several critics called it a 'disgrace' to
the British film industry.[29] Even the *Monthly Film Bulletin* described it as 'the most
sickening exhibition of brutality, perversion, sex and sadism ever to be shown on
a cinema screen,' and condemned the British Board of Film Censors (BBFC) for
their 'extraordinary oversight' in passing 'this monstrosity ... for public showing'.
In the *Sunday Times*, Dilys Powell wrote her review as 'A Letter to the Censor', in
which she contrasted a number of recent deletions by the BBFC with their
decision to pass *No Orchids*. Ironically suggesting that the Board's duties 'consist
in saving me and other members of the public from contamination by the cinema',
she argued that 'if you must refuse us the serious, the educated inquiry into
human character and the nature of the living world, defend us also from the dully
nauseating.' Alternatively, she suggested, the Board 'should add to the number of
your certificates: "U" or universal, "A" for adult, "H" for horrific, one more category, "D" for disgusting'.[30] However ironically, Powell's proposal to expand the
system of classification indicates the policing function that criticism possessed in
relation to censorship. Although the Board initially reacted to the public outcry by
protesting that 'We don't know what the excitement is about ... as far as we are
concerned it is a normal gangster film, no more brutal than many made in
Hollywood,' the BBFC president, Sir Sidney Harris, subsequently publicly apolo-
gised to the Home Office for having 'failed to protect the public' adequately. As the
critics' rhetoric indicated, the 'excitement' was about the transgression of cultural
boundaries involved in the imitation of 'American culture'. Tom Dewe Matthews
claims that *No Orchids for Miss Blandish* turned 'the clock back on British film
censorship by ten years'.[31]

It has become something approaching a critical orthodoxy to argue, against
Orwell and Hoggart, that the impact of American popular culture on its European
consumers has been 'positive', to the extent that it provided them with 'a repertoire
of cultural styles and resources' which have been used to undercut the cultural
hegemony of traditional elites.[32] Leaving aside the ways in which this argument
works as a convenient tactic in politically defending the study of American culture, it also supplies the mirror image to the arguments of those elites who sought
to resist the incursions of American culture, and confirms that their anxieties were

not misplaced. The post-war 'levelling down' – that is, democratisation – of cultural value occasioned by 'Americanisation' destabilised the presumptions of moral and aesthetic distinction that had been supported by the regimes of censorship and criticism that had exercised responsibility over popular taste. But if cultural difference was rendered uncertain, it was not eradicated.

In 1964, the secretary of the BBFC, John Trevelyan, declared that it could no longer 'assume responsibility for the guardianship of morality' or prohibit the exhibition of films showing 'behaviour which contravenes the accepted moral code'.[33] This permissiveness was, however, also a matter of distinction, and the licence afforded to films 'of real artistic quality' was much greater than that extended to movies 'made solely for commercial profit'. The value judgments embodied in this distinction were crucial to the increasing liberalisation of British censorship during the second half of the 1960s. These changes paralleled, but did not run exactly in synchronisation with, the decomposition of the Production Code and the introduction of a ratings system by the Motion Picture Association of America (MPAA) in 1968. Precisely when a greater degree of international standardisation in the classification of movie content might have been imposed, a distance between the two systems was reasserted. Far from welcoming Hollywood's introduction of a rating system comparable to Britain's, Trevelyan expressed himself 'gravely concerned' about it.[34] In keeping with its task of asserting cultural difference as a form of moral superiority, the BBFC applied a different set of restrictions to the same material, particularly over the representation of violence. What had been hailed in 1967 as the 'New American Cinema' came to be characterised by British critics as 'the New Violence of Hollywood', frequently interpreted as symptomatic of Vietnam, the assassinations and 'the gruesome public interest' aroused by the Manson killings – the panoply of fantastic American violence.[35]

The abandonment of the Production Code had permitted, in principle, the reclassification of some Hollywood movies as art, allowing them to escape from the restrictive thematic confines of 'American culture'. That reclassification was, however, resisted by several defensive strategies of censorship and criticism that attributed a preoccupation with violence to 'American culture', and in doing so asserted a moral superiority over it. Because this preoccupation was seen as not only dubious but also contagious, the critical policing of this boundary was seen to be a matter of cultural difference as well as of artistic acceptability, and the two arguments were combined into an instrument used to distinguish 'Hollywood' from its alternatives.

Where the MPAA was criticised for an essentially quantitative approach – its 'habit of counting nipples and four-letter words to help them decide on a rating'[36] – the BBFC's response relied on subjective judgments of 'quality'. Art was distinguished from commerce on the basis of an undefined notion of 'integrity' that might apply to the aesthetic organisation of the film or the personality of the filmmaker, but which manifested itself most frequently in an assessment of the moral seriousness of the work in question. What might constitute moral seriousness was the topic of a dialogue between censorship and criticism in 1971, a dialogue conducted quite explicitly within the specifically British framework established by the tradition of cultural criticism represented by Hoggart and Orwell, and focused most clearly around the release of Straw Dogs.

As in the case of *No Orchids*, the controversy that surrounded *Straw Dogs* was initiated and to an extent sustained not by a pro-censorship lobby group but by the critical reception of the film, and the context of censorship concealed, to a significant extent, the anti-American cultural concerns of their position. What stirred the controversy around *Straw Dogs*, as it had around the British version of *No Orchids* in 1948, was the presence within the work itself of a transgression of national cultural boundaries: the work both contained and was itself evidence of the contamination of American influence. The plot of *Straw Dogs* itself represented an American invasion of sorts, in David Sumner's provocative incursion into the Cornish landscape, resulting in the deployment of an American sensibility about violence in this English context. In a common interpretation, 'The American, considering himself a man of peace and disgusted by the violent society he lives in, comes to England partly to escape and partly to dissociate himself from the violence only to discover that the violence lies within himself.'[37]

Although the BBFC had declared the movie to be 'tremendously enjoyable for the most part, and compulsive viewing', the press reception was vitriolic in its denunciation of the movie as an abomination: 'brutal, vicious, sadistic, repulsive'; 'unnecessary and obscene'; 'ridiculous, pretentious and very nasty indeed, both artistically and morally'.[38] And as with *No Orchids*, critics turned their disgust on the censor's standards: 'To have made such a vicious and degrading film appears an aberration of judgment on someone's part. To pass it for public exhibition in its present form is tantamount to a dereliction of duty.'[39] The attack on censorial standards was carried further in December by a letter in *The Times*, signed by thirteen film critics writing for the national press, declaring that the movie was 'dubious in its intention, excessive in its effect', and likely to contribute to public concern over the effects of cinematic violence.[40]

At one level, the discussion concerned where the quasi-legal boundary between art and entertainment lay: where an art of excess was a form of social criticism, an entertainment of excess was a form of cultural debasement. The majority of critics found *Straw Dogs* so offensive and its violence so gratuitous because it lacked the moral certainty they required of popular culture: Orwell's preference in 'lowbrow fiction' for 'a sharp distinction between right and wrong'.[41] David Robinson argued that extreme violence could be justified when it was employed 'as a means to induce revulsion against violence'.[42] But the ambiguity of *Straw Dogs*, the complexities of its excess, rendered it problematic, and the absence of an allegorical setting refused to distance that ambiguity. As an 'American director ... who is esteemed for his Westerns', Peckinpah could be credited with technical virtuosity but not thematic complexity by British critics as yet unpersuaded by auteurism.[43] Derek Malcolm concluded that: 'this is simply a brilliantly made, thoroughly bad film,' and even the most sympathetic of its reviewers declared that 'one emerges superficially harrowed, but no more enlightened than one is by reading newspaper accounts of horrors such as the Moors murders.'[44]

The critical rhetoric of verisimilitude and contagion indicated that the movie's transgression was in part generic: Malcolm saw it as an inadequate horror movie, 'out-Hammering Hammer' only in the *grand guignol* of its conclusion. More frequently reviewers asserted that *Straw Dogs* would have been much more acceptable had it been a Western, so that its excessive representation of violence could have been more evidently allegorical. As it was, the movie's alleged generic vulgarity in failing to distinguish 'between a West Country pub and a Western saloon', was offered as evidence that the director did not know where he was.[45] *Straw Dogs* compounded this confusion of categories by failing to fulfil a necessary obligation to 'realism' that apparently came literally with the territory, as though reviewers were 'looking for documentary truth about a particular part of England'.[46] This was, obviously, an argument that would work only in Britain. Criticism of *Straw Dogs* elsewhere – and most obviously in the US – was noticeably free from a concern with the accuracy of the accents, remarking instead, for instance, on Peckinpah's use of 'the brooding monochromes of the Cornish countryside to construct a self-contained universe of indifferent terrors'.[47] But British reviews of *The Wild Bunch*, for instance, had equally dwelt very little on the historical and ethnographic accuracy of this representation of Mexico, since the Mexico in question was not Mexico but an allegorical landscape.

A Clockwork Orange, produced in Britain by Stanley Kubrick, was released in London a month after *Straw Dogs*. The two movies were almost invariably linked in editorials on censorship, and contrasted by critics, for whom Kubrick and Peckinpah offered almost perfect points of comparison. In the judgment of the BBFC, Kubrick's 'use of music, stylisation and other skills ... succeeded in distancing audiences from the violence ... and keeping the effect within tolerable limits'.[48] This point was reiterated by many critics, who found its violence neither contaminating nor disgusting, but admirably alienating, a proper way to handle the subject. Moreover, Kubrick's movie had a clearly articulated thesis about the dehumanising effects of violence, where Peckinpah's did not.[49] More importantly for a discussion of critical anti-Americanism, *Straw Dogs* was set in an impossible version of Britain which was being used as the site for the expression of a universal American mythology. The recognisably British environment that *A Clockwork Orange* projected was taken, by English critics at least, to be a successful, exportable, allegorical landscape of universal relevance. Critics made categorical distinctions between the two movies, and blamed *Straw Dogs* for the abuse heaped on *A Clockwork Orange*. However, the aesthetic distinction they made failed to persuade others with a more straightforward anxiety about the desire for imitation. Despite its aesthetic distance, *A Clockwork Orange* was accused of creating copycat crimes; its English violence was, apparently, only too recognisable in the behaviour of young men brought before the courts.[50] Although *Straw Dogs* seemed to encapsulate with particular clarity an English disgust at the contagion brought by American culture to the English pastoral landscape, its fantastical version of Cornwall at least ensured that its lack of 'realism' would not stir anxieties about imitation.

Notes

1 Pierre Bourdieu, *Distinction: A Social Critique of the Judgement of Taste*, trans. Richard Nice (Cambridge, MA.: Harvard University Press, 1984), p. 56.
2 Alessandro Portelli, 'The Transatlantic Jeremiad: American Mass Culture and Counterculture and Opposition Culture in Italy', in Rob Kroes, Robert W. Rydell and Doeko F.J. Bosscher (eds), *Cultural Transmissions and Receptions: American Mass*

Culture in Europe, European Contributions to American Studies vol. XXV (Amsterdam: VU Press, 1993), pp. 130–1.

3 David Morley and Kevin Robins, 'Spaces of Identity: Communications Technologies and the Reconfiguration of Europe', Screen vol. 30 no. 4, Autumn 1989, p. 21.

4 James True, Printer's Ink (4 February 1926), quoted in Charles Eckert, 'The Carole Lombard in Macy's Window', Quarterly Review of Film Studies vol. 3, Winter 1978, pp. 4–5.

5 Quoted in Jeffrey Richards, The Age of the Dream Palace: Cinema and Society in Britain 1930–1939 (London: Routledge and Kegan Paul, 1984), p. 63.

6 Ruth Vasey, The World According to Hollywood, 1918–1939 (Madison: University of Wisconsin Press; Exeter: Exeter University Press, 1997).

7 Phil Dourado, 'Little Glocal Difficulties', Independent on Sunday: The Sunday Review, 5 September 1993, p. 63.

8 Dick Hebdidge, 'Towards a Cartography of Taste 1935–1962', in Hiding in the Light (London: Routledge, 1988), p. 52.

9 See Christopher Wagstaff's chapter in this volume.

10 'A genuinely popular European cinema seems to be an impossibility.' Ien Ang, 'Hegemony in Trouble: Nostalgia and the Ideology of the Impossible in European Cinema', in Duncan Petrie (ed.), Screening Europe: Image and Identity in Contemporary European Cinema (London: BFI, 1992), p. 28.

11 Maurice Thorez, General Secretary of the French Communist Party, 1948, quoted in Jean-Pierre Jeancolas's chapter in this book.

12 Peter Hoffman, President of Cinemavision, when he announced plans to distribute Hollywood movies in India and eastern Europe in 1992. Quoted in Joanna Coles, 'Eastern Promise for Recession-Hit Movies', Guardian, 17 May 1992.

13 C.W.E. Bigsby, 'Europe, America and the Cultural Debate', in C.W.E. Bigsby (ed.), Superculture: American Popular Culture and Europe (London: Paul Elek, 1975), p. 15.

14 Richard Kuisel, Seducing the French: The Dilemma of Americanization (Berkeley: University of California Press, 1993), p. 237.

15 Tom O'Regan, 'Too Popular by Far: On Hollywood's International Reputation', CONTINUUM vol. 5 no. 2, 1992, pp. 311, 318, 332, 343.

16 Alain Silver and Elizabeth Ward (eds), Film Noir: An Encyclopedic Reference to the American Style (Woodstock, NY: Overlook, 1979), p. 1.

17 Marcel Duhamel, Raconte pas ta vie (Paris: Mercure de France, 1972), p. 491.

18 Quoted in Klaus Kunkel, 'Ein artiger James Bond: Jerry Cotton und der Bastei-Verlag', in Jochen Vogt (ed.), Der Kriminalroman; zur Theorie und Geschichte einer Gattung (Munich: W. Fink, 1971), p. 564.

19 George Orwell, 'Raffles and Miss Blandish', in Decline of the English Murder and Other Essays (Harmondsworth: Penguin, 1965), pp. 63, 69.

20 According to Orwell, this mode of transport 'accounted for their low price and crumpled appearance'. Since the war, he added, 'the ships have been ballasted with something more useful, probably gravel' (ibid., p. 72).

21 Ibid., pp. 73–4.

22 Ibid., pp. 12–13.

23 Contrary to Orwell's hope that the case would not be long remembered, it was twice filmed, in 1948 as Good Time Girl, and in 1990 as Chicago Joe and the Showgirl. Both the story and the scandal are, of course, also echoed in both the story and the scandal surrounding Natural Born Killers (1994). Part of its resonance lies in its exaggerated fulfilment of official fears of the 'sexual delinquency' that would result from Britons' first direct experience of American popular culture. A 1943 emergency Home Office study observed that: 'To girls brought up on the cinema, who copied the dress, hairstyles, and manners of Hollywood stars, the sudden influx of Americans, speaking like the films, who actually lived in the magic country and had plenty of money, at once went to the girls' heads. The American attitude to women, their proneness to spoil a girl, to build up, exaggerate, talk big, and to act with generosity and flamboyance, helped to make them the most attractive boyfriends. In addition, they "picked-up" girls

easily, and even a comparatively plain and unattractive girl stood a chance.' Quoted in John Costello, *Love, Sex and War: Changing Values 1939–1945* (London: Collins, 1985), p. 281.

24 Richard Hoggart, *The Uses of Literacy* (Harmondsworth: Penguin, 1958), p. 213. For Hoggart, as for Orwell, the principal victim of this 'shiny barbarism' was the culture of British working-class youth, the 'juke-box boys' who spend their evenings in 'harshly lighted milk bars', affecting 'drape suits, picture ties, and an American slouch', 'living to a large extent in a myth-world compounded of a few simple elements which they take to be those of American life'(ibid., p. 203).

25 British cultural criticism has seldom acknowledged a concern with a native poetics of violence. British violence seems, rather, to be understood as a form of psychopathology, most frequently identified as falling within the horror genre – in fictional forms (Hammer) and in revisiting particular crimes of sexual violence (Jack the Ripper or the Moors murders, for instance). By contrast, American cultural critics such as Robert Warshow have at least tentatively explored the poetics of violence. Robert Warshow, *The Immediate Experience* (New York: Doubleday, 1962).

26 In the early 1950s, for instance, a spate of reports from European censor boards expressed concern with the depiction of violence and organised crime in American movies. In 1954, the American Embassy in Oslo was 'thankful' that the Norwegian film censor had banned *The Wild One* because 'it presented practically all the standard misconceptions about America that our enemies stress, such as claims that we are uncultured, rude, bombastic, impatient, lawless and addicted to mob violence.' Quoted in Paul Swann, 'The Little State Department: Washington and Hollywood's Rhetoric of the Postwar Audience', in David W. Ellwood and Rob Kroes (eds), *Hollywood in Europe* (Amsterdam: VU University Press, 1994), p. 190.

27 This 'Other viewer', the figure of misinterpretation, has remained an archetype of the censorship argument, and is as frequently present in contemporary debates over the regulation of television and pornography as in the early years of cinema. It has also been an important figure in high cultural critiques of popular culture. It is often identified as a child, the figure towards whom the idea of moral guardianship can most unproblematically be extended. Its essential perceptual feature is its inability to discriminate fiction.

28 C.A. Lejeune, *Observer*, 18 April 1948.

29 Milton Shulman in the London *Evening Standard* called it 'a disgrace to British films'; Leonard Mosley in the *Daily Express* (16 April 1948), 'a nasty and wicked disgrace to the British film industry'.

30 Dilys Powell, 'A Letter to the Censor', *Sunday Times*, 18 April 1948.

31 James C. Robertson, *The Hidden Cinema: British Film Censorship in Action, 1913–1975* (London: Routledge, 1989), pp. 96, 92; James C. Robertson, *The British Board of Film Censors: Film Censorship in Britain, 1896–1950* (London: Croom Helm, 1985), p. 174; Tom Dewe Matthews, *Censored* (London: Chatto & Windus, 1994), p. 122.

32 Tony Bennett, 'Popular Culture and Hegemony in Post-War Britain', in *Politics, Ideology and Popular Culture* (1) (Milton Keynes: Open University Press, 1982), p. 2.

33 Quoted in Matthews, *Censored*, p. 174.

34 Quoted in Guy Phelps, *Film Censorship* (London: Victor Gollancz, 1973), p. 55.

35 Alexander Walker, *National Heroes* (London: Harrap), p. 24.

36 Stephen Farber, *The Movie Rating Game* (Washington, DC: Public Affairs Press, 1972), p. 89.

37 Tom Milne, *The Times*, 26 November 1971.

38 BBFC quoted in Matthews, *Censored*, p. 200; Arthur Thirkell, *Daily Mirror*, 26 November 1971; Margaret Hinxman, *Sunday Telegraph*, 27 November 1971; Patrick Gibbs, *Daily Telegraph*, 26 November 1971.

39 Alexander Walker, *Evening Standard*, 25 November 1971.

40 *The Times*, 17 December 1971.

41 Orwell, *Decline of the English Murder*, p. 76.

42 David Robinson, *Financial Times*, 26 November 1971.

43 Gibbs, *Daily Telegraph.*
44 Derek Malcolm, *Guardian*, 25 November 1971; Milne, *The Times.*
45 Walker, *Evening Standard.*
46 Charles Barr, 'Straw Dogs, *A Clockwork Orange* and the Critics', *Screen* vol. 13 no. 2, Summer 1972, p. 21.
47 Jay Cocks, *Time*, 20 December 1971.
48 *Evening Standard* report, quoted in Barr, *Straw Dogs*, p. 27.
49 Barr, however, pointed out the irony that *Straw Dogs* enacted the thesis about violence that *A Clockwork Orange* articulated. Barr, *Straw Dogs*, p. 20.
50 In sentencing an offender in a *Clockwork Orange* case in 1973, a judge in Manchester Crown Court expressed the hope that 'those salacious creatures who appear to dominate what is called show business today are compelled to earn a more respectable and honourable livelihood instead of inciting young persons to violence at the expense of their victims ... cases like yours present, in my view, an unassailable argument in favour of the return as quickly as possible of some form of censorship.' Quoted in Phelps, *Film Censorship*, p. 281.

Part III

8
New Wave interchanges: *Céline and Julie* and *Desperately Seeking Susan*

Laura Mulvey

In his 'Letter on Rossellini' published in *Cahiers du cinéma* in April 1955, Jacques Rivette remarks:

> There are films which begin and end, which have a beginning and an ending, which conduct a story through from its initial premiss until everything has been restored to peace and order, and there have been deaths, a marriage or a revelation; there is Hawks, Hitchcock, Murnau, Ray, Griffith. And there are films quite unlike this, which recede into time like rivers to the sea; which offer us only the most banal of closing images: rivers flowing, crowds, armies, shadows passing, curtains falling in perpetuity, a girl dancing till the end of time; there is Renoir and Rossellini.[1]

Rivette was writing at a time when a major, qualitative shift was transforming cultural and critical perception of cinema. This shift first emerged in Paris, articulated in the first instance by the critics of *Positif* and the *Cahiers du cinéma*, with which Rivette and others who were to become directors of the French New Wave were closely associated. It called into question the critical and popular perception of an opposition between European cinema as art (and therefore to be valued) and Hollywood cinema as commerce (and therefore valueless). For Rivette the only difference that mattered between movies made on one side of the Atlantic or the other was that of two approaches to cinema as such. Rivette celebrates any cinema which advances awareness of the cinematic, wherever it might be found, and irrespective of given political or aesthetic preconceptions. This celebration, or self-consciousness, which Rivette calls modernist in Rossellini and Bernard Eisenschitz sees as Brechtian in Tashlin, leads on to a different sense of cinematic awareness in the New Wave directors.

There is a difference between the self-awareness of the New Wave directors as the 'first generation to make films with an awareness of past cinema' and the movie 'quotes' and allusions that characterise the later self-conscious Hollywood trend which culminates, I suppose, in Quentin Tarantino. The aesthetics of self-referentiality are not uniform. Nevertheless, an 'exchange of movie fantasy' can be mapped across the exchange of movie culture that crisscrossed the Atlantic from the days of New Wave *Cahiers* onwards. And although the terms 'Europe' and 'Hollywood' would continue to perform a negotiating function between two film cultures, both for critics and for directors, the aspiration to understand cinema across its divisions would produce new approaches to cinema aesthetics and thus, necessarily, new kinds of cinemas.

To elaborate these points, I shall focus on a curious trans-Atlantic journey of cinematic influence, tracing the influence of Hollywood on Jacques Rivette's *Céline and Julie Go Boating* (*Céline et Julie vont en bateau*, Films du Losange, 1974) and on the influence that Rivette's film then had on Susan Seidelman's *Desperately Seeking Susan* (Orion Films, 1985). Hidden beneath the traces of the exchanges that appear on the surface lies a cat's cradle of other trans-Atlantic crossings, and I want to unravel some of the strands here.

The late 1950s were a pivotal period for the relationship between Hollywood and Europe and between 'old' and 'new' cinemas. It was during the late 1950s that a number of the *Cahiers du cinéma* writers made the transition from criticism to direction, first of all with shorts such as Godard's *Charlotte et son Jules* (1958), Truffaut's *Les Mistons* (1958) or Rivette's *Le Coup du berger* (1956), and then with features – Chabrol with *Le Beau Serge* (1958), Truffaut with *Les Quatre cent coups* (1959), Godard with *À bout de souffle* (1959), Jacques Doniol Valcroze with *L'Eau à la bouche* (1959), Eric Rohmer with *Le Signe du lion* (1959), Rivette with *Paris nous appartient* (1960). This was also a moment of transition for Hollywood. As the traditional studio system of production went into crisis, the number of independent production companies mushroomed, allowing certain Hollywood directors greater freedom just as the French critics highlighted the neglected place of the director in Hollywood cinema. Although the French critics are best known for their polemical re-evaluation of Hollywood, they were interested first and foremost in *cinema*, regardless of whether a picture was the product of a Hollywood genre or of Italian neo-realism.

Then, in the early 1960s, a few indigenous American voices began to speak up for their own popular cinema. The most famous of these was Andrew Sarris, whose special issue of *Film Culture* in 1963 was devoted to a reappraisal of Hollywood which reformulated and articulated important aspects of the *Cahiers* position.[2] But it took some years before the majority of critics and intellectuals in the United States got round to taking their own system of production – the studio system – and its products seriously. The French delirium over Frank Tashlin and the British admiration for Douglas Sirk seemed only to confirm the suspicion that love for Hollywood was a strange and unaccountable European aberration. By the time American opinion came round, the studio system was in crisis. Television had made huge inroads into the audience and, by a strange paradox, was to prove the vehicle that introduced a new generation to the kind of Hollywood cinema the French critics loved. So while Godard, Rivette, Chabrol and their friends had discovered Sam Fuller at the Cinémathèque in Paris, Martin Scorsese discovered him, and so many others, on American television. Hollywood films of the studio period were to provide a source of cinematic passion and resource for cinematic reference of a kind that led directly to the Tarantino style of the 1990s.

Céline and Julie was Rivette's tenth film and commercially his most successful. (Most of his other films, before and after, are uncompromisingly austere, often very long, and only ever to be seen in specialised venues.) Although still challenging at a rambling 142 minutes, *Céline and Julie* was well received and, revolving as it does around the friendship between the two young women (played by Juliette Berto and Dominique Labourier), came across as more accessible than his other movies. But it still bears witness to the director's ongoing reflections on the aesthetics of cinema as such.

The film was shot on 16mm, and later blown up to 35mm. The combination of the 16mm Éclair camera and Nagra tape recorder, first introduced around 1960, contributes significantly to the film's style. The cheap location filming permitted by this technology rapidly acquired its own stylistic resonances and associations, generating a specific kind of cinematic space. *Céline and Julie* is very much a Paris film. The fictional world in which the two women meet, make friends and embark on their adventures is above all the world of the Paris streets in which the film is shot and set. Often hand-held, and including a slight shakiness, the camera follows and frames the protagonists. Figure and frame relate in such a way that on- and off-screen space merge and flow into each other imperceptibly. Sometimes shots are elongated far beyond the limit of narrative content, so that a casual rhythm of movement builds up, overwhelming narrativity and paying attention to the details of the everyday that a tightly organised *mise en scène* is forced to exclude. Although the protagonists remain central to the action and lead the camera's movement, they are often framed in such a way as to integrate large elements of cityscape and to incorporate casual, marginal and fortuitous moments of the everyday into the scenario. This bringing together of dramatic action with chance incursions on to the screen is a particular pleasure of 16mm fictional location shooting. In *Céline and Julie* the camera, often watching the action from a distance, picks up the movement of passers-by, children playing, cats pausing for a moment on their way, cars cutting off the corner of the frame, wind moving the leaves on the trees. All these elements are integral to the space and mobility of the film and are all also outside the exact control of director or cinematographer.

For its part, *Desperately Seeking Susan* was Susan Seidelman's second film. The director describes herself as having been formed by studying film at university. Her film studies course at New York University offered an intensive exposure to European cinema that could not be matched by ordinary distribution circuits or television. 'I rarely went to the movies as a kid,' Seidelman has said, 'unless they had Natalie Wood. But here [at NYU] I saw *Wild Strawberries*, *The Four Hundred Blows*, *Breathless* – the typical text-book art movies.' And, speaking of *Desperately Seeking Susan*:

> My film took Jacques Rivette's as a point of departure but I also drew on aspects of Hollywood studio comedy while *Céline and Julie* is more typical of the European avant-garde. Both films are about a puzzle, which is sophisticated enough almost to be like an intellectual game in which one gets lost.[3]

Desperately Seeking Susan is a Hollywood movie, but it belongs on the margins of Hollywood. The script, written by Leora Barish (also highly film-literate), went the rounds of the studios until it was picked up by Barbara Boyle, then senior vice-president at Orion Pictures and in charge of their low-budget productions. She promoted the film's 'distinctly female point of view' and brought in Susan Seidelman, who had previously made the very low-budget, punkish *Smithereens*

(1982), to direct. Compared to *Céline and Julie*, its style is, in Rivette's terms, more 'Hitchcock' than 'Rossellini'. But from a Hollywood perspective it is typical of the kind of film made by the 'mini-minor' studios that flourished in the 1980s. Working through independent producers and making (by Hollywood standards) very low-budget movies, these studios picked up the new generation of film graduates. Jim Jarmusch, Gus Van Sant, Spike Lee and others were able and prepared to take risks for these minor studios that the majors could not afford. While the majors still had to maximise their audience and their profits, small low-budget productions could target specific and differentiated audiences. As Timothy Corrigan puts it: 'If the conglomerate blockbuster admitted an audience too large to be defined and actually addressed, these smaller production companies redefined that audience as a plurality of special interests and a plurality of positions.'[4]

Just as *Céline and Julie* is a Paris film, *Desperately Seeking Susan* is a New York film, and likewise dependent on technological advance (and the circumstances of independent production) to facilitate its location work. Faster film stocks, sharper lenses and more portable equipment (especially lights) transformed 35mm location work in the 1980s, opening up narrative itself. Charles Eidsvik has drawn attention to the way new tools and stocks made location work cheaper and easier, especially facilitating the shooting of night-time exteriors as exemplified in *Desperately Seeking Susan*.

> The additional location flexibility made possible by the new visual tools made location work cheaper and easier. More low light locations could be used, and they could be used in new ways. The city night locations of a *Desperately Seeking Susan* or [Scorsese's] *After Hours* were predicated on new tools and stocks. Certainly night exteriors are not new; the ease with which they can be put into films is.

Both *Céline and Julie* and *Desperately Seeking Susan* are women's films. In both of them women hold centre stage. Although directed by Rivette, *Céline and Julie* was largely scripted (or improvised) by its actresses: Juliette Berto and Dominique Labourier for the main story, and Marie-France Pisier and Bulle Ogier for the film-within-a-film, 'Phantom Ladies over Paris'.

I   Same-sex friendship

Céline and Julie's crazy, zany relationship is based on the Jerry Lewis/Dean Martin partnership of the early 1950s, which was, of course, in turn based on existing stage and screen comic double-acts. Tashlin's *Artists and Models* of 1955 was, according to Rivette, a particular influence. In that film, the Lewis character exists in a world of comic-book fantasy within the already cartoon-like world created by Tashlin's style. These 'two worlds' clearly prefigure the construction of other world inhabited by the Phantom Ladies in *Céline and Julie*. More immediately important, however, is the way the theme of same-sex friendship, which is the emotional centre of the film, is played out through an evocation of the traditional comic double-act inherited by the cinema from music hall and vaudeville. Juliette Berto and Dominique Labourier both 'perform'. Their performances are non-naturalistic in a way that sometimes seems at odds with the naturalism of the location settings. They exaggerate their actions, drawing attention to the physicality of gestures, movements or looks. This is particularly so for Berto, who plays, as it were, the Jerry Lewis side of the friendship. She has described her performance as based on 'cartoon-like movements . . . everything Céline does is very visual, her movements are staccato'.

This combination of same-sex friendship between women and highly accentuated performance also evokes another Hollywood movie of the 1950s, Howard Hawks's *Gentlemen Prefer Blondes* (1953). Here Jane Russell as Dorothy plays the straight-guy (Dean Martin, as it were) while Marilyn Monroe as Lorelei plays the comic fall-guy (as it were, Jerry Lewis). Both Monroe and Lewis create a comedy of bodily excess, an overwhelming physicality that goes beyond conscious control and creates havoc in its wake. The fact that one involves an overstatement and the other an understatement of sexuality only confirms that it is the combination of sexual innocence and excess that creates the comedy in the first place. In *Céline and Julie*, Céline is a cabaret magician whose performance is also overtly sexual, but in a way that is more stylised, almost a citation of erotic spectacle, than erotic in itself. And in both films the other partner in the relationship, Dorothy or Julie, takes the place of her friend in a grotesque impersonation of their erotic performances.

Lorelei is supremely acquisitive. Her attitude to diamonds is magpie-like. A trace of this motif can be found in Rivette's story of 1970s Paris in the form of Céline's relationship to the 'things' she carries with her in a capacious bag (which apparently holds her whole life) and the wild stories she tells of exotic conquests around the world. More obviously, these traits of Céline's return in Susan. She too carries a bag (in this case, a large, fifties-style hat-box) which contains everything she owns, mostly the strange assortment of objects she has accumulated in thieving-magpie fashion: cutlery and ashtrays mix with Egyptian ear-rings, her collection of clothes, and so on. She too is nomadic, inhabiting a fantastic world of romance and adventure. While Madonna's stylised sexuality consciously recycles the erotic spectacle epitomised by Marilyn Monroe, her mannered, almost awkward performance is much closer to the gestural acting of Céline and Julie than is Rosanna Arquette's conventionally played Roberta.

Leora Barish, who wrote *Desperately Seeking Susan*, has also readily acknowledged that her script pays homage to *Céline and Julie*. The influence was, indeed, noted at the time of release, with the critic Dan Yakir saying that it was 'as if a couple of Jacques Rivette femmes had met for breakfast at Tiffany's. Unlike *Céline and Julie*, however, *Desperately Seeking Susan* does not have the double-act motif and the film is more about one woman's fascination with another woman – her wild life-style and her glamorous image – but at a distance. Roberta and Susan do not actually meet until the final moments of the film, while the two women's friendship is central throughout *Céline and Julie*. *Desperately Seeking Susan* ends up like the movies in Rivette's first category: 'There are movies that begin and end . . . there is Hawks, Hitchcock . . .', movies that have a proper resolution, 'a marriage or a revelation'. Céline and Julie, on the other hand, actively disrupt each other's lives and relationships – anything that might take them away from each other and their fantastic enterprise. And they end up, perhaps, in Rivette's second group, 'receding into time like rivers to the sea', as they go boating with little Madeleine.

II   Cinema, day-dreaming and other worlds

Céline and Julie Go Boating is a film about crossing the frontier between the every-day and the day-dream. The 'other world' within the fictional world of the story is explicitly a metaphor for the cinema itself. As we, the spectators, watch Céline and Julie on the screen, they in turn become spectators of the melodrama 'Phantom Ladies over Paris'. But whereas we can only watch the screen world, they find magical ways of gaining an entry into it and participating in its events. In *Desperately Seeking Susan*, the metaphor is considerably naturalised, but the resid-ual traces of *Céline and Julie* bring it into relief.

In the first instance, both films characterise one woman as 'dreamer' and the other as 'dreamed'. But while the relationship between Céline and Julie quickly closes into equality and solidarity, Roberta's fascination with Susan is closer to that of the Lacanian mirror-phase. In order to be more perfect, the image of bod-ily mastery and glamour must stay out of reach, on the other side of the looking glass. But both films explore the relationship between looking and curiosity, between one woman's secret observation and pursuit of another.

While the 'source' scene in *Céline and Julie* can illuminate and inform an under-standing of *Desperately Seeking Susan*, it also draws attention to the important divergences between the two films' sense of storytelling. Both start by suggesting that one protagonist 'conjures up' the other, who brings the story and its adven-tures in her wake. Julie, who works in a library, is studying magic and the film opens with her experimenting with certain signs that seem to engineer Céline's appearance – rather as Alice's dream conjures up the White Rabbit who then leads her into Wonderland. As Rivette puts it: 'We decided that Dominique [Labourier – i.e. Julie] would set off in pursuit of Juliette [Berto – i.e. Céline] and they would both fall, not into the rabbit hole but into fiction.' Céline is a magician too, it turns out some time later, performing, in net tights and a top hat, traditional cabaret magic acts in the same genre as those in *Desperately Seeking Susan*.

Céline drops a scarf. Julie picks it up and runs after her. The scarf creates a con-duit into another diegetic world, just as Susan's jacket carries Roberta across one world into another. Julie's polite attempt to restore the discarded object mutates into a long sequence in which she semi-secretly follows and observes Céline as she moves through the streets and staircases of Paris, as she stops to put on lipstick, steals from a stall in a street market. Julie follows more in the manner of a mutu-ally acknowledged chase than a voyeuristic surveillance. In the equivalent scene in *Desperately Seeking Susan*, Roberta's surveillance of Susan is surreptitious and unacknowledged. Gradually, Céline and Julie come to occupy the same screen space, framed together within the same shot, closing the gap between the voyeur and the exhibitionist, the day-dreamer and the object of fantasy. Thus Céline appears in the first instance as a figment of Julie's desire for 'something' and 'for something to happen' and the topographical relation between them is initially that of subject of desire and its object, the space separating the day-dreamer and the world conjured up in the day-dream. But the spatial distance between them narrows and is finally closed. They become co-conspirator day-dreamers, together embarking on an adventure in another fantasy world.

The two women meet, become friends, and then comrades and co-conspirators in pursuit of the mysterious scenario unfolding in 7bis rue du Nadir des Pommes. This is the space of the 'second diegetic world' of *Céline and Julie Go Boating*, which is given the 'sub-title' [*sic* – in English] 'Phantom Ladies over Paris'. The house emerges out of a conflation of Céline's fantasy and Julie's memory, probably both equally unreliable but combining into a collective mechanism for the construction of a metaphor for the space and drama of the cinema itself.

The 'second diegetic world' – that is, the world of the Phantom Ladies – is contained in a *grand bourgeois* house. Although both Céline and Julie play the role of Miss Angèle, the nurse/nursemaid, they can only *see* the scenario unfold through magical means. (You cannot, after all, see what's happening on the screen when you're acting in a movie.) By means of magic sweets they become spectators of the drama, sitting together, as it were, in front of a screen.

Both diegetically (in terms of the story) and stylistically (in terms of cinema), the space of their spectatorship and the space of their screen are separated. The *mise en scène* of the 'second diegetic world' is essentially that of a melodrama. Its construction of space and time is diametrically opposed to the 16mm-type construction of space and time characterising Céline and Julie's 'everyday'. Each shot is framed and focused, tableau fashion, around a highly artificial gesture, action or event. The colours are pastels with a diffuse white dominating, sometimes contrasted with a soft black or saturated red. Each shot is perfectly constructed, with the frame literally framing the contained space, which is then exquisitely organised along planes of action in perspective and proportion. Bulle Ogier, Marie-France Pisier and Barbet Schroeder act out a drama of desire, paranoia and repression, around and about Madeleine, the little girl. The two spectators soon understand that the drama is endlessly repeated in its melodramatic fragments in the course of one 'eternal day'. Over and over again, Camille cuts her hand; over and over again, Sophie faints on the floor.

As Céline and Julie become more and more fascinated by the spectacle, their desire to know 'what's going to happen next', 'which one is the murderer', 'who is seducing whom', etc., overcomes their initial contempt for the 'grand tragedy in mothballs'. As they piece together the fragments of scenes into some kind of order, it becomes clear that the story has to lead to Madeleine's death. They enter into the screen story and manage to divert its narrative out of its predestined groove.

In *Desperately Seeking Susan* the fictional topographies and the New York city geography are marked out in a way that relates to *Céline and Julie* but with a quite altered significance. Leora Barish says, 'Susan, on a certain level, is the product of Roberta's imagination.' Roberta also 'conjures up' Susan. First of all, the audience is introduced to them in their different worlds, as the story cross-cuts between Roberta's world of boredom and longing and Susan's world of excitement and self-sufficiency. In this sense the film 'fills in' Susan's image for the audience's parallel desire, in anticipation of her arrival for Roberta. In this pre-credit sequence Susan represents *image as such*; in characteristic Hollywood style, she condenses femininity, sexuality and spectacle. Susan belongs to the world of adventure, everything that is not 'everyday'. She stands for cinema itself, conflating erotic fascination and dramatic action. *Desperately Seeking Susan* maintains the topography of distance between Roberta's fascinated curiosity and Susan's image and it is in the space between the two that Roberta's adventures occur. *Céline and Julie* starts with one woman trying to control the look and the film's way of looking, and then brings the two women together, finally aligning their looks into mutual fascinated curiosity as they watch the screen. This in turn affects the spectator's relation to the screen and the nature of the spectacle it displays. The film audience recognises the metaphor for cinema as it materialises, and wonders about it and its complexities with detachment. In *Desperately Seeking Susan*, the film spectator is inexorably involved, even though confronted with scenarios which tell of cinematic desire, voyeurism and identification.

Roberta's 'conjuring up' uses space to emphasise the distance between the two women, not only in terms of the topography of the desire but also in terms of the geographical and social space. As Roberta looks out from the everyday banality, as she feels it, of Fort Lee, New Jersey, her desire is spoken, as in a fairy tale, by Gary's voice-off intoning 'all your fantasies can come true.' Although the voice stands for commodification and suburbia, it acts as a vehicle for Roberta's longing to take off. Roberta moves towards the window and looks out, across her own reflection, into the darkness. The next shot materialises her longing in the form of the bridge between New Jersey and Manhattan. Topographically, the image marks the site of separation and boundary, the river, and at the same time the bridge represents the desire to cross into the space of day-dream, the 'other' world. The river separates two contrasted social spaces, highly connotative for American audiences, playing on the fantasy resonance of Manhattan as a site for escape, day-dream, adventure, from the everyday banality of the suburbs. The next shot shows a long-distance bus crossing the bridge, with its destination New York City there to emphasise the point. The image is flattened on to the screen surface by a long lens, and accompanied by evocative extra-diegetic music. As Susan gets off the bus the camera follows her closely with a crane shot and holds her tightly in frame as she moves. In the Atlantic City scene she had snapped herself with a Polaroid camera; in the Port Authority washroom scene her image is highlighted, redoubled as it were, by her reflection as she chooses a new flamboyant get-up in front of the mirror.

Although Céline and Julie are differentiated in terms of image, and certainly colour-coded differently in clothes and in interior *mise en scènes*, they are not socially and psychologically separated. Julie may have initially played Alice to Céline's White Rabbit, but the story of their friendship is one of shared and exchanged fantasies, finally realised in their mutual 'conjuring up' of the Phantom Ladies' screen world. Roberta's place as dreamer and spectator is reinforced by a short scene, early in the film, which shows her as the classic reader of romance. In tears, she watches *Rebecca*, as Laurence Olivier says to Joan Fontaine: 'It's gone ... gone for ever ... that funny young lost look I loved. I killed it. I killed it when I told you about Rebecca.' This short extract is a reminder to the audience of Rebecca's presence as pure imago, fantasised by the second Mrs de Winter as essentially glamorous, eternally desirable and inevitably superior to her own sense of self, mundane, physically clumsy and lacking mastery over her own presence in the world. Rebecca – although, of course, we never see her – obviously has the glamour and mystery of movie stars. This parallel establishes and contextualises Roberta's fantasy of Susan.

When Roberta crosses the bridge and sees Susan for the first time, she watches

Susan, and then Susan and Jim's embrace, through a telescope that flattens the image and gives it a hazy, diffused look. It is at this point that Susan is most precisely identified with the screen, as framed space, and the site of glamour and identification processes. This sight sets up visually the space between Roberta's world and the world of excitement, danger, fascination and romance that she wants to gain access to. The next sequence replays the sequence from *Céline and Julie* in which one woman follows the other, but whereas there a complicity exists between the two, here Susan and Roberta occupy different, contrasting conceptual spaces. After the first two shots they are not included in the same frame or the same shot, and the sequence is organised around Roberta's point of view.

When Susan disappears, she bequeaths, as it were, a magical object to Roberta, the jacket which fills the gap left by her absence. The jacket will provide the means of transporting Roberta into the other world where she in turn will get caught up in danger and romance by temporarily 'becoming' Susan. From this point on, the two women's paths diverge into different, though complementary, narrative strands. Roberta's amnesia precipitates her into a melodrama, acting (as indeed it often does in melodrama) as a magical means of transport out of the everyday. Suddenly the film is taken over by genre, complete with McGuffin (the ear-rings), misrecognitions, gangster plot, a love affair, a villain. The contrast between Roberta and Susan shifts again. It is up to the audience to recognise that Roberta has crossed over into a world organised around the narrative codes of the genre movie. Roberta is now the main vector of the narrative; Susan is partially edged out (even, at one point, as far as Fort Lee itself). Roberta gets a job at the Magic Club – another point of contact with Rivette's film.

Although Roberta has effected her transition into the 'second diegetic world', the film still differentiates between the two protagonists cinematically in such a way as to maintain Susan's privileged image as glamour. The cinematographer, Ed Lachman, has described his lighting and camera strategy for the film – how for example Rosanna Arquette is shot in soft colours, using a pastel range, while Madonna has more saturated colours and chiaroscuro. The framing is perhaps even more significant. In Lachman's words: 'In Rosanna's world the camera is more or less static and the action happened within the frame, whereas in Madonna's world we wanted the camera to be more prophetic and move with the characters through her world.'[5] Indeed, looking closely at the film it is remarkable that Madonna is not only shot almost always on the move, but tightly framed. It is Rosanna Arquette who carries the film's dialogue sequences, with lines delivered in comparatively deep space. Madonna's dialogue is sparse and her lines are often delivered either off screen or away from the camera (even, perhaps, post-synchronised). This stylistic contrast may have to do with Madonna's lack of experience as an actress. *Desperately Seeking Susan* was her first film and she hit major stardom when the film was in production. But whatever the reason, the shooting strategy intensifies Madonna's construction as image – in close-up and to a certain extent removed from the normal rules of continuity shooting. At times she appears almost like a silent star, with the full force of cinematic glamour invested in her image, in tension with the naturalistic codes of the rest of the film.

Susan's image and its cinematic construction place her in the position of 'metaphor for cinema', comparable, therefore, to the Phantom Ladies in *Céline and Julie.* By the time Susan and Roberta finally meet it is clear that *Desperately Seeking Susan* is a hip, 1980s version of the rite-of-passage story so dear to the American cinema. The narrative has taken Roberta through a process of personal transformation, from the immaturity of the day-dreaming reader of romance to finding a real-life 'prince', from *petit-bourgeois* marriage and consumer philistinism in New Jersey to the bohemian libertarianism of the East Village, from an insecurity about how she appears to the ability to construct her own image. In this respect the story deviates from the old melodramas which would have returned the heroine home. *Desperately Seeking Susan* liberates Roberta into a Manhattan lifestyle and a more satisfactory sex life, and Susan may well have detached herself from living in a genre movie and be prepared to settle down. At the end, she and Jim are in the cinema audience when Dez and Roberta's kiss burns the celluloid on screen, Susan's exhibitionism has, perhaps, relaxed to the point where she can be audience rather than image. The movie and the movie metaphor have come to an end.

In contrast, the *Céline and Julie* story shows little interest in transforming the heroines. Although each one, at a certain point, impersonates the other and manages to sabotage her residual links with the demands of real life, their social status is not at issue. Perhaps, at the end, when they go boating with Madeleine, they have moved on to a different fictional plane and invented a new cinematic existence, liberated from the rigidity and repression of the melodrama, beyond Hawks and Hitchcock, beyond Rossellini and Renoir. It is hard to tell. As you go back and watch *Céline and Julie Go Boating* all over again, and then again, trying to figure out if it has a message, the images on the screen tend to shed their content and dream themselves into the pure arabesque which Rivette associated with pure cinema.

Notes

1 Jim Hillier (ed.), *Cahiers du Cinéma*, Vol. 1 (London: Routledge and Kegan Paul/BFI, 1985).
2 In the book which grew out of the *Film Culture* issue, *The American Cinema* (New York: E.P. Dutton, 1968) Sarris acknowledges his debt to an American predecessor in the field, Eugene Archer, whose knowledge about and passion for Hollywood were an inspiration to all who knew him. Patrick Bauchau, also credited by Sarris as an influence, brought cinephilia to London from Paris during the early 60s.
3 *Film Comment*, May/June 1985. See also *The American Cinematographer*, Vol. 66 no. 7, July.
4 Timothy Corrigan, *A Cinema without Walls* (New Brunswick, NJ: Rutgers University Press, 1991).
5 *Film Comment*, May/June 1985.

9
Tinsel and realism

Peter Wollen

It is often argued that the dominance of American films in a foreign country – Britain, for example – threatens to prevent the emergence of a distinctively national cinema which would express (in this case) authentic British values and a genuinely British outlook and self-image. Plainly there is a dimension of truth in this – the overriding hegemony of one culture must necessarily reduce that of all others to subaltern status – but I want to raise some specific issues which, in my view, complicate the question. I shall begin by looking briefly at the history of Hollywood's own representations of Britain and then move on to some issues which I believe have important cultural implications and, in the last analysis, political implications too.

In the 1930s, Hollywood began to make a substantial number of films which were set in Britain, or in the British Empire, or were based on British stories, plays or novels. These were, of course, studio rather than location pictures, made in Hollywood itself. Most historians suggest that, at least in part, this was because of the American success of Alexander Korda's British-made *The Private Life of Henry VIII*, released in 1934, which suggested that British subjects could be commercially viable. If so, this was a paradoxical outcome. Korda himself – and many other British commentators – saw the success of *Henry VIII* as evidence that British films, rather than British subjects, could succeed in penetrating the American market. Yet in reality, despite all his efforts to reduplicate the commercial success of *Henry VIII*, this never happened. Instead, Hollywood itself began to exploit the potential of films which fell into what we might now label the 'British costume heritage' sub-genre, films which were largely based on classics of English literature or on adventure stories drawn from Britain's imperial past and present.

From 1935 to 1940 alone, the heyday of the sub-genre, Hollywood made two Shakespeare films (the Reinhard–Dieterle *Midsummer Night's Dream* and the Cukor *Romeo and Juliet*), as well as two major Dickens films (*A Tale of Two Cities* and *David Copperfield* – Cukor again) far pre-dating the British Shakespeare and Dickens cycles made by Olivier and Lean. Hollywood also made film versions of *Wuthering Heights*, *Vanity Fair* (i.e. Mamoulian's *Becky Sharp*, the show-piece Technicolor film), *Jane Eyre* (in 1944), *Treasure Island*, *The Barretts of Wimpole Street*, *The Adventures of Sherlock Holmes*, *Tom Brown's Schooldays* and *Peter Ibbetson*, and many others by lesser-known writers. Hollywood followed up Korda's *The Private Life of Henry VIII* with Ford's *Mary of Scotland* and Curtiz's

The Private Lives of Elizabeth and Essex, based on Lytton Strachey's biography. Between 1935 and 1940, they made no fewer than four Kipling pictures – Ford's *Wee Willie Winkie*, Fleming's *Captains Courageous*, Stevens's *Gunga Din* and Wellman's *The Light that Failed*, in comparison with Korda's solitary *Elephant Boy*.

The successful English novelist Hugh Walpole worked in Hollywood on *David Copperfield* and *Little Lord Fauntleroy* but fled home when he was assigned *Kim*. And Hollywood also left Korda far behind with a tidal wave of Empire films – *Charge of the Light Brigade*, *Clive of India*, *Lives of a Bengal Lancer*, *Stanley and Livingstone* – along with a succession of swashbucklers, notably the Curtiz–Flynn films such as *Captain Blood*, *Robin Hood*, etc., as well as quasi-swashbucklers like *Mutiny on the Bounty*. The fact is that the British were quite unable to compete in commercialising their own flag-waving heritage, based on recycling their own self-image, although a number of actors did very well out of it in Hollywood, certainly sustaining the Hollywood Cricket Club.

The lesson to be learned, it seems, is that if a subaltern cinema comes up with a successful formula – albeit one which, like *Henry VIII*, was considered quintessentially English – the dominant (American) cinema is quite capable of assimilating it and reflecting it back to its country of origin. Indeed, in 1938, only five years after his own *Henry VIII*, Korda himself noted: 'No film made during the past year by a major British company comes to my mind as imitative of America. Indeed, if we went by choice of subject alone we might easily reverse the criticism. *Mutiny on the Bounty*, *David Copperfield*, *Mary of Scotland*, *Little Lord Fauntleroy* and a dozen others might more than prove a case against America.'

Korda went on to note that American films succeeded not only in assimilating subjects from other countries but reducing them to what he called a 'lowest common multiple'. In the same vein, Hitchcock famously pointed out that Switzerland is a country best known for its chocolate and its cuckoo clocks and so it should always be shown as encumbered with these stereotypical attributes, according to the same rule of what he called the 'lowest common denominator'. Similarly Holland is full of windmills and England is full of foggy Limehouse streets, impeccable butlers, Cotswold villages, medieval castles, country-houses with giant fireplaces and mullioned windows, chirpy Cockneys, Victorian aunts and stiff-lipped army officers mantled with imperial glory. This all adds up to what is now called 'heritage' – Britain even has a Ministry of Heritage, which also embraces the arts – and national heritage is indeed made up of 'l.c.d.' myths and stereotypes, which are just as available to outsiders as to insiders. In fact, as they are now perpetuated principally for consumption by tourists, they may well be more available to outsiders. Domestic fantasies of history and identity are subtly re-edited to accommodate the projection back on to the home country of foreign fantasies.

So far, so good. I was surprised, however, when I turned my attention away from what we might consider 'tinsel' – the obviously fantastic – to what we might consider 'realism'. In 1943 the great British producer Michael Balcon, best known for his early work with Hitchcock and for the films he made after the Second World War at Ealing Studios, went down to Brighton from London – first class on the Brighton Belle, I presume – to address a gathering of the Film Workers' Association and to publicly confess to them his 180 degree change of heart. In the past, he now considered, he had paid no heed whatever to realism:

What I am telling you, in fact, is a frank admission that I was not at all concerned with the sociological aspect of films [i.e. what today we would call the cultural aspect]. If I realised their potential importance it was not from the same point of view in which today I regard them as important. I visualised merely a prosperous industry giving employment to many thousands of people, providing a profitable investment, and so on.

It was the Second World War which had changed Balcon's mind and led him to abandon 'tinsel' and embrace 'realism', the authentic representation of Britain on the screen, rather than theatrical flim-flam and the primacy of entertainment values. 'Entertainment' now fell to third place on Balcon's list of desirable qualities in films, after 'the projection of our own ideas' and even after 'instruction'. Balcon's choice of nationalist 'realism' before cosmopolitan 'tinsel' became a kind of article of faith for critics, film-makers and public figures who wanted to foster a national cinema in Britain. Heritage and identity must be realism, they all agreed, not tinsel.

This view, that national cinema should, almost by definition, be a realist cinema, is very limited, to say the least. During the second half of the 1940s, when British film-makers still believed that they might be able to compete against Hollywood, before the crushing defeat of Harold Wilson's ambitious plans to challenge the Americans, the most successful films exported were films like *The Seventh Veil* and *The Red Shoes*: flamboyantly romantic melodramas – everything Balcon meant by tinsel. These films were not particularly welcomed by the British critics, who found them visually and emotionally excessive. In fact, in Julian Petley's words, they were 'desperately disliked' by the English critics. Yet, in many ways, they tell us more about England and Englishness than any films made in the realist tradition, precisely because they expose wild fantasies, however delirious, which realism seeks to suppress. Strange films, like films by strangers, are often the most revealing. Nonetheless, the realist imperative, enunciated by Balcon and by the critics, led to a long-lasting critical emphasis on realism as the destiny and duty of a truly British cinema, in contra-distinction to Hollywood tinsel.

This led, among other things, to a series of films being made which showed the seamy underside of British life and introduced the working class into the equation for the first time. Prominent in the new genres which grew out of the turn towards realism was the 'spiv' film, which had its heyday between 1945 and 1950, the years of the first post-war Labour government, the reforming Attlee government, which brought the working class – or its representatives – to real power for the first time in British history, nationalising key industries, instituting the Welfare State, with the National Health Service (known in America as 'Socialised Medicine') as its centrepiece, reforming trade union law, starting the process of decolonisation and dismantling the Empire, and so on. The 'spiv' film was the first British genre, albeit a crime genre, to be based in a working-class milieu. 'Spivs' were racketeers, who wore wide-lapelled suits and flash neckties, a type originating from the black-market economy which grew up during wartime and post-war scarcity and rationing. The 'spiv' film has some (misleading) similarities to American film noir.

It was for this reason that when I started to look at the history of the 'spiv' film, in such sharp contrast to the traditional upper-class film image of Britain, I was surprised to find that it had actually been anticipated in Hollywood, by none other than Clifford Odets, in his 1944 film, made for RKO, *None But the Lonely Hearts*, starring Cary Grant and Ethel Barrymore, which portrayed the petty criminal underworld in contemporary London. Robert Murphy, Britain's expert on the 'spiv' film, notes the first British stirrings of the new genre in 1945, one year after Odets's film. The genre as a whole did not really take off until mid-1947, after which there were no fewer than nine spiv movies released in fourteen months.

After 1948, the genre began what turned out to be a rapid decline. The last of the batch was Edmond T. Gréville's *Noose*, a film with two American stars – Joseph Calleia as the gangster and Carole Landis as a fashion reporter obsessed with Christian Dior's New Look, which signalled an end to wartime austerity – and with Nigel Patrick as the charismatic spiv. *Noose* was based on a stage play by Richard Llewellyn, who is best known in film circles as the author of *How Green Was My Valley*, a story of working-class life set in a Welsh mining village, which was made into a Hollywood film by John Ford in 1941. What is significant here, however, is that Llewellyn also wrote the book on which Odets based his *None But the Lonely Heart*. In fact, low-life or riff-raff realism, to use Murphy's term, as exemplified in the spiv genre, seems to have appeared in Hollywood before it did in England itself.

Indeed, the spiv genre returned to Hollywood again at its close. The two final films of the genre, as Murphy notes, both released in 1950, were Jules Dassin's *Night and the City*, in which Richard Widmark plays the spiv Harry Fabian, a club tout who has a tragic fantasy of controlling London's wrestling arenas, and Carol Reed's *The Third Man*, with Orson Welles as the classic black-market spiv-racketeer, Harry Lime – which was, of course, a David Selznick production. I think it is true to say that four of the five great spiv films had foreign directors – Gréville (who was French) for *Noose*, Odets for *None But the Lonely Heart*, Dassin for *Night and the City* and Cavalcanti (the great Brazilian director) for his wonderful *They Made Me a Fugitive*. The fifth was Robert Hamer's marvellously dreary *It Always Rains on Sunday*. In fact, I would argue that the best films about any country are frequently made by foreigners, who tend to have an unusual perspective.

Odets's film, for example, is at first sight a strange concoction, with its weird gallimaufry of accents, ranging from pure Hollywood through Barry Fitzgerald's heritage brogue and Cary Grant's half-remembered Bristolian twang, through to some fairly passable South London bit players. But the core of the film comes from Llewellyn's novel, which is a model of popular street-smart vernacular writing. Odets, of course, adapts it to suit his own preoccupations, but the under-lying theme of his script remains characteristically British: crime as a way out of a working-class lifestyle felt as a kind of imprisonment by the sensitive and ideal-istic central character. The same theme can be found in Carol Reed's pioneering *The Stars Look Down*, in which three classic avenues of escape from the working class are posited: crime, football and education.

In *None But the Lonely Heart*, Ernie Mott, the central character, begins as a drifter with fantasies of becoming an artist, but ends up involved with a small-time racketeer, a 'wide boy' in Llewellyn's phrase, who is based in a South London garage and, having acquired a nightclub and a slot-machine arcade, is branching out into shaking down pawnbrokers ('had to wallop the old bloke') and doing smash-and-grab raids on Brompton Road furriers. Odets gives the film a topical anti-Fascist inflection by linking the violence-and-racketeering theme implicitly to Nazism, a Brechtian tactic (as in *Arturo Ui*) supported by his use of Mordechai Gorelik as set-designer and Hanns Eisler as composer, both of whom worked with Brecht and were probably his closest associates in America. Odets, for example, highlights the significance of the fact that the pawnbroker beaten up by the spiv's two enforcers is Jewish, and thus makes Ernie Mott's change of heart about the value of the criminal road into a kind of moral decision against Fascism, linked to the war by a single shot in which the shadows of planes passing overhead move across his face.

None But the Lonely Heart could almost have served as a model for Cavalcanti's *They Made Me a Fugitive*, with its expressionist design style and its strange and eerie details of the London criminal-cum-proletarian milieu – the meal of sheep's heart, the budgerigar brought in to be pawned, the awe at the first refrigerator in the street, the arcade with its Test Your Strength machines and peep-shows, the startling appearance of Dan Duryea in the fish-and-chip shop (Special Today – Fresh Hake) and Ernie Mott's perfect pitch, which leads him to comment 'E-flat!' when the getaway car he is in crashes into a lorry. The driver is dead and the horn is jammed, droning away on the same note.

The fascination I feel for *None But the Lonely Heart* springs primarily, I think, from the strange confrontation of Odets's very American protelatarian-cos-mopolitan aesthetic with its very English source-material and subject-matter. Odets draws both on the 'new masses' vision of the vernacular representation of proletarian life, as well as on the much more intellectualised aesthetic and alle-gorical style which he takes from Brecht. This vision, when turned on to 1940s South London, somewhere round the Walworth Road or maybe Coldharbour Lane – it is slightly vague – gives a new kind of surreal gloss to standard British realism which differentiates the film from Carol Reed or Pen Tennyson films, which the English critics loved. But, this surreal gloss proved very congenial for the riff-raff spiv film, which the critics hated.

If we look at the 1960s, we find the same phenomenon – the most extraordi-nary films about England were made by Kubrick, Lester, Losey, Polanski and Antonioni. More recently Terry Gilliam's *Brazil* gave us an unforgettable vision of the Thatcher years. And if we look the other way round at cinematic representa-tions of Los Angeles, rather than London, we might remember films by Polanski and Antonioni (again) as well as by Agnès Varda, Jacques Demy, Wim Wenders, Ridley Scott, and so on. Outsiders – and I might include 'internal outsiders' in this category – often see things about a country which insiders miss or discount or repress. They 'make strange', as the Russian writer Victor Shklovsky would have put it (and he wrote one of the best books about Berlin). Insiders are not necess-arily the best judges of their own society or the best able to portray it.

National culture and national self-expression, as we all know, tend to be self-serving and mythologising (all the more acutely so, perhaps, if, as we have seen, foreigners prove even better at mythologising than the locals and drive the locals on to ever-greater feats of self-deception). In fact, I would like to go still further: – national culture, by definition, is mythologising, self-serving and, at the same time, self-mutilating, designed as it is to focus a group identity by creating shib-boleths and stereotypes. This is very well demonstrated in books like Benedict

Anderson's classic study of the idea of the nation as an 'imagined community', by Eric Hobsbawm's work on 'the invention of tradition', by Robert Hewison's study of 'the heritage industry', and Asip Nandy's dissection of the destructive effects of the Indian Empire on domestic British culture.

This is not to say that countries do not need a national cinema – whether Britain, France, Germany, Greece, the United States, Brazil or Burkina. On the contrary, the conclusion I would draw is that we need as many national cinemas as possible – not in order to multiply national mythologies, under the guise of safeguarding national culture, but to allow as many diverse, critical and estranging views as are possible. In this sense, the French view that domestic culture needs to be defended gets everything the wrong way round. On the contrary, it is American cinema that needs to be challenged. Just as Hollywood appropriated British culture, so Europe should appropriate American culture. The success of British 1960s music – the Beatles, the Rolling Stones – shows the way forward. In addition, Europe should press for the American film market to be opened up. A market share of 5 per cent or less is unacceptable. Americans always argue for market share when they negotiate with Japan and they clearly understand how internal markets can be culturally distorted.

The problem with the American dominance of global cinema, from an American point of view, is not that it prevents Britain (and other countries) from developing cultural identities for themselves, but – and this is not so often realised – it also threatens to deprive America itself of views of America from outside. American dominance simply reinforces America's own powerful, yet provincial cinematic myths about itself, locking itself into a national culture entirely of its own making, structured around terrifying misrecognitions and appallingly narcissistic fantasies. World cinema, I hope, will one day be truly cosmopolitan and, to be cosmopolitan, it requires a diversity of cinemas around the world, not simply so that each one can speak with its own voice, but so that an array of different voices will intrude on every kind of national self-obsession and self-congratulation. Domination by just one voice, by just one complacent national industry, is harmful not simply to everyone else in the global market but also, above all, to America itself, the land of Forrest Gump.

10
The beautiful and the bad: notes on some actorial stereotypes

Geoffrey Nowell-Smith

Hollywood has a hegemonic project, the spokesman for which for many years has been Jack Valenti, president of the Motion Picture Association of America (MPAA). In Mr Valenti's engagingly blunt opinion, the only films that audiences need to see are the ones they want to see, and these are Hollywood films. I shall leave on one side the economic and economic-ideological implications of this attitude – its free market assumptions and the question of whether in fact the domination of Hollywood is solely the expression of the free market rather than the operation of a barely legal monopoly. Instead I want to look at what has to be the case about the product – movies – if it is to be successful in all corners of the world and not just in the place where it is produced.

As is well known, the American automobile industry has great difficulty in persuading the rest of the world to buy American cars. Ford and General Motors are worldwide corporations, but they build different cars in Germany and Britain for sale in European markets than they do in the United States. Meanwhile the American public itself increasingly buys Japanese cars in preference to American. In the case of movies, however, the American product, barely modified except in dubbing and censorship, is a worldwide currency, apparently overriding the cultural specificity of each market in which it is sold.

Much of the success of American films is straightforwardly industrial. Films cost different amounts to make, but they cost the same amount to show. It follows therefore that an industry that can afford to make a product high in perceived production values is at an advantage compared to industries which can only afford to produce cheap-looking films but have to sell them at the same price. This advantage, once gained, is self-reinforcing. It's also the case that Hollywood films are carried to the rest of the world on a rising tide of American-led consumerism. They represent an image of what the world wants, and would appeal even if they were junk.

But American movies are not just carried along with the tide. To a great extent they created it. They are not like American cars, which have symbolic value but nobody buys, or baseball caps, which everybody buys in spite of not having a clue about baseball. They are what created the romance around cars and baseball and the sundry Americana of modern consumerism.

How do we account for this? In particular, how do we account for the fact that a product, initially designed for home-market consumption, is so successful in export markets that it has acquired between 50 per cent and 80 per cent of the market in almost all countries in which it is freely – if monopolistically – traded?

What I want to examine are some of the ways in which Hollywood in the studio period adjusted – both consciously and unconsciously – to a situation in which export sales already accounted for up to 40 per cent of its revenue and in which therefore the product had to be acceptable and indeed positively attractive in foreign markets. If the hegemonic project was to be achieved, and the Hollywood movie was to become worldwide currency, it had to produce, within its general worldview, adequate representations of persons, groups and nations at which it was targeted.

In the 1920s, the target audience for Hollywood movies was the white American middle class – the one that went to the downtown and suburban theatres where seat prices were high and most revenue was generated. The films also went to country districts and poor neighbourhoods and abroad and earned additional money, but this was secondary. The industry could therefore afford to neglect the susceptibilities of audiences outside the target area – blacks, for example, marginal groups or foreigners. Increasingly, however, these formerly secondary markets became part of the equation, domestically and internationally. In the 1930s for example, the Motion Picture Producers and Distributors Association of America (MPPDA), as it then was, became very concerned about the effects that casual negative stereotyping of foreigners in a particular movie might have on the industry's position in the market in question. Since dictatorships were particularly prone to take offence, and also possessed the means to retaliate, appeasement became industry practice – quite in line with foreign policy in general.

Far more interesting than these crude manoeuvrings to appease dictators, or than the cynical multi-culturalism (i.e. multi-marketism) of today which accommodates to the pink dollar by purifying its stereotyping of gay people, are the subtler mechanisms by which Hollywood in the studio period negotiated its representations of various forms of otherness, not so much to make them acceptable and inoffensive – which after all is easy – as to make them more adequate to its hegemonic project.

Hollywood's treatments of race and ethnicity, gender and sexual difference are now well-worn themes, and rightly so. Less attention has been paid to other aspects of cultural difference such as nationality which are nevertheless very important for an industry striving for worldwide dominance.

The discourse of the Hollywood movie has two important attributes which have really not changed very much over the years. It is normalising, and it is imperial. By normalising I mean that there is always a norm and whatever threatens it has either got to be defeated or brought within it. The films which are regarded as progressive or liberal are those which broaden the area of presumed normality; reactionary films narrow it. Progressive films domesticate the other; reactionary films zap it. A landmark liberal film like *Guess Who's Coming to Dinner* takes the norm of the white family and demonstrates that the intrusion of Sidney Poitier is not ultimately a threat, and the family norm can be extended to include blacks. Ditto films about homosexuals. What is difficult to accommodate within the Hollywood film is difference which persists and cannot be normalised.

European films are often, but by no means always, a bit more open towards what is outside the norm. (Think, for example, of Lindsay Anderson's *If...*, where the love relationship between the two boys is neither normal nor perverse, it just is.)

Connectedly, the Hollywood film is strongly imperial. This is part of its European heritage and an attribute that it shares with much of European cinema and literature. The Hollywood cinema normalises the American view of Europe and the Euro-American (white, western) view of the rest of the world. Foreign parts are a sort of playground in which the American or European characters disport themselves, on which they impose their values and from which they, occasionally, learn. But on the rare occasions on which they do learn, it is their learning process, rather than the culture from which they do the learning, that is the focus of interest. The physical representation of foreign places is often done in the studio, and the embodiment of foreigners and other races is often done through American and other white-western actors.

This being the case – and in broad terms it is the case – what is it that masochistically draws foreign audiences in to watch their identities traduced in this arrogant manner? I must say that at some level I find this question unfathomable. I don't know how Mexicans, for example, put up with being endlessly portrayed as cowardly and deceitful, or why Japanese audiences cheer on Michael Douglas in *Black Rain*. There is, however, resistance. There is reading against the grain, there are audiences that cheer for the bad guys, or for the birds against Tippi Hedren; and there are genres like the spaghetti Western whose ambiguities clearly represent a rebellion of south against north.

But there are also mechanisms within the Hollywood film which attenuate its normalising, imperial and centralising aspects and which introduce – or reintroduce – plurality, ambivalence, the admissibility of the other, and the possibility of watching films from more than one point of view.

One feature worth noting about imperial discourse is that, precisely in its arrogant slippages – as in Nicholas Ray's *Savage Innocents*, where the characters are Inuit, but the male lead is the part-Irish, part-Mexican Anthony Quinn, while the female lead is Japanese – it departs from literal accuracy not so much into literal mistakes as into metaphor. Sternberg's films set in China do not portray China – well, badly, or at all. They are orientalist fantasies, and the same is true of his *Morocco* and other Foreign Legion films. The setting is a pretext, though the precise choice of setting is conditioned by a century and more of imperial history. Playing fast and loose with history and geography may be offensive if we are literally to believe that the object represented is China or India or wherever, but beyond a certain degree of fastness and looseness the signified – an exotic place, corruption, mystery, romance – takes flight from the referent, if indeed it was ever securely attached to it, and the referent is not perceived as important.

Often, however, the referent is important. The boundary between convenient fantasy and the historically literal is fluid, and can change quite sharply. With the *Anschluss* in 1938, Vienna ceased to be a bordertown on the way to Ruritania and became a place on the real map. It was also the birthplace of some of Hollywood's leading artists, mostly Jewish; if it had been Ruritania before, the pressure of real history meant that it could be so no longer.

After 1945 Europe – that is, western Europe – has a new importance for

America and for Hollywood. It is once again Hollywood's biggest market. It is America's Cold War ally. A million GIs have come back from there, and millions more Americans will go there as tourists with the development of air travel. It also remains a site of fantasy, particularly sexual, and of old-country myths perpetuated by immigrants. The construction of Europe in post-1945 Hollywood movies, for both domestic and foreign consumption, therefore becomes a much more complex affair than before.

For its European representations Hollywood could avail itself of a considerable stock of European-born actors and actresses who had not been assimilated into a purely American typology. For the actors, Hollywood offered good money and the good life in general: in exchange they might be called on to camp it up in various stereotypes.

Gigi, directed by Vincente Minnelli, and produced by Arthur Freed for MGM in 1958, is an interesting example of what Europe could mean for Hollywood. When making *Brigadoon* a couple of years previously, Freed was reportedly asked why he had not shot it in Scotland, where the story is set, and said he'd been there and decided against it, because Scotland did not look Scottish enough and anyway it was too rainy. The Scotland he and Minnelli wanted was a fairy-tale Scotland, distilled from centuries of mythic representation (well, not many centuries, since the myth is no older than Walter Scott). So Gene Kelly and Cyd Charisse could cavort on a gigantic set at MGM amid various kilted dancers of assorted origin, and so what. But *Gigi* posed problems. Minnelli, a Francophile, wanted to shoot the film in France, using locations wherever possible, and doing the studio work at Billancourt. (He had previously used authentic location exteriors, shot by Freddie Young, for *Lust for Life*, but for *Gigi* he wanted location interiors as well.) Even more, however, the film posed problems of representation. The story, by Colette, is about a girl being trained to be a *poule de luxe*, a courtesan, whatever you care to call it: vulgarly, a prostitute. It's not really a nice story, in Production Code terms – nor indeed in any other. The PCA (Production Code Administration) objected strongly to the original outline, in which Gigi carries on a family tradition of being a courtesan, and demanded a cleaned-up proposal in which there is no such tradition and Gigi's only desire was to rescue a rake from perdition and marry him. With these changes, it deemed the story acceptable, given that it takes place in Paris, France. In other words, a displacement: naughty things can be contemplated provided they happen somewhere else. Paris is an ideal somewhere else, because not only is it naughty, it is cultured. The squalid story of a girl's initiation into prostitution is heavily veneered with French culture, which refines and disguises it.

But who should be cast to represent this naughty, cultured Paris. Enter Maurice Chevalier, archetypal naughty Frenchman; and Louis Jourdan, previously cast by Minnelli as the adulterous Rodolphe in *Madame Bovary* and before that chosen by Max Ophuls to play the Viennese pianist and unknowing father of Lisa's child in *Letter from an Unknown Woman* (Vienna, incidentally plays a similar but subtly different role to Paris in Hollywood mytho-topography); also cast was English comedy actress Hermione Gingold, funny, tough, sentimental.

And for the girl? No contest really. Leslie Caron had been an MGM contract artist, she had starred opposite Gene Kelly in *An American in Paris*. She was

French, but with part-American parentage, and was in every sense the obvious mediator to an American public of the ambiguities of the role, which she had performed on the stage, while fitting, alongside Jourdan and Chevalier, the minimal realist criterion that European audiences required. Caron, by then in her late twenties, had just enough of a streetwise quality for the attempts to corrupt her not to seem too shocking.

But there was a complication. For the Broadway production five years earlier, Colette had herself selected an unknown actress of Belgian birth and Anglo-Dutch parentage, Audrey Hepburn, a dancer and a model, wide-eyed and malleable, with just a little steel beneath the gentle surface.

Would Hepburn have been a better choice for the film, had she been available? She had created the part on Broadway, she was now a movie star, hugely popular in Europe as well as in the US. But her suitability for Broadway in the eyes of a Frenchwoman did not guarantee her suitability for Hollywood. In any case her career had taken a new turn following her success at Paramount with *Roman Holiday* and *Sabrina*. Ever virginal (though in real life married to Mel Ferrer), she was the archetypal fairy-tale goose-girl/princess – a role later perfected when she was chosen, ahead of Julie Andrews, for the film version of *My Fair Lady*.

When she was first under contract, Paramount thought, apparently, that they had a new Garbo or Bergman on their hands – a strange but revealing misjudgment. Garbo and Bergman both incarnated the European (specifically northern European, or non-Latin) woman; in Garbo's case 'woman', period. Also neither was virginal; Bergman in particular is always a woman with a past, but a past that was worn lightly, unlike say Dietrich. Dietrich as Joan of Arc is impossible. Bergman played the role twice.

Hepburn, besides being generally limited in her talents, fitted a narrower stereotype, a kind of English innocence (as opposed to continental experience) which could, however, be transferred to the representation of 'East Coast' characters – as in *Sabrina*. This is a curious displacement, whereby New Englanders, and New York society ladies, and also southern belles, could be incarnated through the use of English or English-born actresses, and prompts a small excursus before getting back to the main theme.

The excursus concerns the relation between national stereotypes and the status of immigrant groups in the United States. In American films (excepting a handful set in Britain and France which call for a wide range of social representation), British and French characters – or characters in some way coded as 'British' or 'French' – are almost always aristocratic or quasi, and often cross-coded to dandyism, effeminacy. Irish, German or Italian characters, by contrast, can be coded to a kind of proletarian earthiness. In real life there are plenty of French proletarians (and in the cinema too, since Jean Gabin's career was almost entirely structured around a proletarian image). There are also a number of Irish dandies, beginning with Oscar Wilde. But in Hollywood movies there is a strong tendency to relate national stereotype to the stereotype of the immigrant. Since the English and French are not identified as belonging to the poor, the huddled masses, the stereotype of the English or French man or woman follows suit. You can't have English roughnecks, nor can you have Irish dandies; if Wilde is to remain a dandy, then scrub the Irishness.

An interesting film in this respect is *The Band Wagon*. Again, it's an MGM/Minnelli film, and not necessarily typical. In *The Band Wagon* the entire dramatic dialectic is based on a set of contrasts, almost Lévi-Straussian in its symmetry, between nature and culture, in which culture is Anglo-French European and nature is American, including under American the proletarian ethnicities which make up the white melting pot. When the show fails, for example, the cast do not go to the prepared champagne reception (coded: French, aristocratic) but have an impromptu beer drinking session of their own (coded: German, proletarian, but in its spontaneity also American). The film as a whole is about reconciling traditional European high culture with a sort of hayseed natural Americanness, under the banner of a new urban art represented by Broadway and jazz, and it proceeds towards this goal by invoking a uniquely rich repertory of cultural and national codings.

But enough excursus, and back to the East Coast. Enough too of heroes and heroines. Time to look at a bad guy, George Sanders. George Sanders represents the exact opposite of Audrey Hepburn's youthful English innocence. Sanders was born to British parents in St Petersburg, Russia. Although almost his entire film career was spent in Hollywood, he never lost his British accent. At first he played a variety of roles, but his persona rapidly became that of the cold, calculating, world-weary cynic. Born in 1906, he was only three years older than James Mason, but while in films of the period Mason could move between the cynical villain and the romantic hero, and had a sexual charm in which an aura of experience played a large role, Sanders from the mid-1940s onwards was only ever the middle-aged cynic, the bad guy, the man whose sexual conquests are midway between seduction and rape. He was in fact too cold, too erotically disengaged, to be a villainous seducer in the tradition of Erich von Stroheim or Conrad Veidt; sex for Sanders is solely an expression of power. His was an emotionless sexuality which conforms neither to an American, a Latin, nor even a north European stereotype. It could only be English, though extendable to the playing of Nazis and – for example in *All about Eve* – easterners.

The person who, in the 1950s, best intuited the nature of cultural stereotyping in cinema was Roberto Rossellini. In the course of his abortive attempt to make films for the American market (which existed but was very hard to break into) and for a pan-European market which did not yet exist, Rossellini paired Ingrid Bergman and George Sanders in *Journey to Italy* in 1954. *Journey to Italy* is an attempted mediation of north and south, an attempt to speak to the world public, including the American, about cultural difference. It is an amazingly daring film in many respects, but not least because it constructs a drama around the real-life characteristics of two actors, as much as their screen images. Rossellini knew Bergman well; he had been living with her for four years and their relationship was under strain. He did not know Sanders, but it did not take him long to see that the mask of world-weary cynicism was a real mask, not a stage one. In the film Sanders is an Englishman and Bergman (as often) an undefined north European; they are married, childless, on a visit to Naples. In the course of the film the marriage undergoes a crisis; Bergman goes off alone to discover Naples, Sanders conducts some family business, goes to Capri and has a failed sexual encounter; there is then a dubious reconciliation. In a neat inversion of the imperial touristic

140

film, the narrative adopts the standpoint of the country being visited, not the visitors. But above all the film tries to use the actors, their images as recognisable to both European and American audiences, and their actual selves, as a way of probing the nature of cultural difference, and of returning to Hollywood as it were the realistically corrected version of the script. Italy is not quite what you think it is, nor is Bergman, nor is Sanders. Close, but not the same.

Journey to Italy was not a commercial success. Nor, on the whole, have any films which undo the jigsaw of stereotype without putting it together again in a recognisable way. This has always been a dilemma for European cinema. European audiences are happy with, or can at any rate live with, characterisations of nationality which stereotype without actually descending to caricature. Hollywood in the 1940s and 1950s also became adept at managing the borderline between realism and fantasy, literalness and metaphor, and between properties required by the narrative – good and evil, normality and otherness, innocence and experience – and external referents. European audiences are not troubled by typecasting that has the sort of fluidity that one finds in the images of Bergman or Sanders who may represent Swedishness or Englishness, but are not reducible to it. But European cinema cannot return the compliment. It is uncomfortable with typecasting as a creative way of developing meaning. If one compares *Journey to Italy* with other Italian films of the same period, one finds that actors are often cast to type in comedies and some other genre films – for example, Alberto Sordi as a kind of Mr Average Italian. But in the deployment of foreign actors, at which Hollywood was so adept, there is a positive insensitivity to their signifying properties. Italian directors tend to use American actors for their box-office appeal, their skill and/or their physical appearance, but not for the possibility of linking those properties to the meanings carried over from the actor's other roles or the fine associations that go with their performing style. Fellini's use of Anthony Quinn in a quasi-gypsy role in *La strada* (1954) is perhaps an exception. His use of Richard Basehart in the same film and of Basehart and Broderick Crawford in *Il bidone* (1955) is more typical. Good actors giving good performances, and that's it. In Antonioni's *Il grido* (1957), Steve Cochran is little more than a craggy presence, ingeniously manipulated. One has to wait until 1969, with the superb casting against type of Henry Fonda in Sergio Leone's *Once upon a Time in the West*, to get a sense that European film-makers could turn Hollywood against itself. But *Once upon a Time in the West* was not an Italian film.

11
American friends: Hollywood echoes in the New German Cinema[1]

Thomas Elsaesser

The number of American sons who are tired of daddy Europe, whom they have to feed, while he is showing them nothing but intellectual condescension, is considerable, and their irritation is to nobody's advantage.[2]

I Introduction

What figural place did the American cinema have for the film-makers who eventually came to be known as the New German Cinema, navigating between aiming at an oppositional, avant-garde cinema (and thus prone to condescension) and wanting to revitalise the Weimar legacy (and thus envying the vitality and popularity of Hollywood)? Three paradigms, distinct but mutually interacting in the cultural space we call 'national cinema' can be identified: the colonial paradigm, the elective paternity paradigm and the no-contest paradigm. The evidence could come from many directors' works between the 1960s and the 1980s, though not surprisingly, the Hollywood intertext is most pregnant in films also known outside Germany, prompting the thought that 'Hollywood' not only stands at the heart of the New German Cinema becoming a national cinema, but is likely to be an implicit reference point for any European film successfully addressing an international audience.

The paradigms have, in the case of Germany, to be seen in the context of post-Second World War cinema history. When the Allied Powers in 1945 insisted on dismantling the Ufa conglomerate, the Hollywood majors ensured that they had unrestricted access to the German film market. Against this competition, West Germany nonetheless developed, from about 1948 onwards, a relatively buoyant domestic film industry, staffed mainly by ex-Ufa directors and technicians, and relying on traditional genre films and stars for audience appeal. This domestic industry concentrated on the home market, and calculated its subjects as well as its budgets accordingly.[3] It collapsed, however, when the US majors began to reorganise their European distribution network towards the end of the 1960s, which in turn led to the large-scale decimation of second-run or neighbourhood cinemas.[4] By the mid-1970s, when film production had become mainly state-subsidised or financed by television, German films were either restricted to the art house circuits (where they competed with Hollywood auteur retrospectives) or could be seen in domestic first-run cinemas only if Hollywood had bought them for international distribution and as it were, re-imported them into Germany: this was the case for Wenders and Herzog, as well as for more commercial productions such as Wolfgang Petersen's *Das Boot*, or Volker Schlöndorff's *The Tin Drum* (*Die Blechtrommel*), conceived from the start as an international, big-budget art film.

II 'Colonising our subconscious'

This background, at once economic and film-political, has to be borne in mind especially when looking at the 'colonising' paradigm. Undoubtedly, its best-known instance is a scene from Wenders's *Kings of the Road*, where the two protagonists, after getting drunk in a US patrol post near the East German border, agree that 'the Yanks have colonised our subconscious.' Yet this perhaps over-quoted remark points in several directions, and in the context in which it occurs, it functions both approvingly and critically: one of the two men cannot get the lyrics of a pop song out of his head. It suggests that 'colonisation' is associated with rock 'n' roll, which Wenders had elsewhere called his 'life-saver' as an adolescent, when American popular culture provided the antidote to 'twenty years [of parental amnesia] ...; we filled it with Mickey Mouse and chewing gum.' Furthermore, the site is also important: faced with barbed wire, it seems preferable to have one's subconscious colonised by American rock music than to be an actual colony of the Soviet Union, like the other Germany they can see from the abandoned US Army look-out. Thus, the two men allude to America at a juncture in their journey where they are forcibly reminded of the historical events that had brought the Americans to Germany in the first place, and in what role (as liberators from Nazism, and in order to make Germany 'safe for democracy'). Not unimportant for the structure and ideological texture of the film is the fact that the remark is made also at a point in the two men's wary friendship when a growing intimacy and regression to childhood threaten their sense of separate and (hetero-) sexual identity.

Insisting on the multi-layered and suitably ambiguous context of the 'colonised subconscious' is necessary since, in Wenders at least, it cannot be directly identified with the anti-Americanism with which the paradigm is most commonly associated. The latter surfaced most starkly with the screening on German television of the American series *Holocaust*, a docu-drama which had a huge impact among German viewers but which was highly criticised by film-makers and reviewers for daring to make a soap opera out of Auschwitz. *Holocaust* gave rise to a rash of films made in Germany by German directors about the Nazi period. Among them, the best known became Edgar Reitz's *Heimat*, explicitly conceived as a riposte to *Holocaust*.

How problematic such a 'reply' can be for a film-maker seeking to redefine a national cinema is strikingly apparent in two reactions to *Holocaust*. Elie Wiesel, writing in the *New York Times* in 1978, was shocked:

> The film is an insult to those who perished and to those who survived. In spite of its name, this 'docu-drama' is not about what some of us remember as the Holocaust. . . . I

am appalled by the thought that one day the Holocaust will be measured and judged in part by the NBC tv production bearing its name. ... The Holocaust must be remembered. But not as a show.[5]

A year later, in May 1979, Edgar Reitz also published an article, apropos of *Holocaust*, entitled 'Let's Work on our Memories':

> If we are to come to terms with the Third Reich and the crimes committed in our country, it has to be by the same means we use every day to take stock of the world we live in. ... Authors all over the world are trying to take possession of their history ... but they often find that it is torn out of their hands. The most serious act of expropriation occurs when people are deprived of their history. With *Holocaust*, the Americans have taken away our history.[6]

At first glance, the two statements are identical in judgment and sentiment. They condemn the series' fictionalisation and trivialisation, and fear for the survival of history and authentic memory. But in the case of Reitz, one is bound to ask: who is speaking? How can a German who grew up under Hitler lay claim to this history, appropriate it, and complain that the Americans have 'expropriated' it? One can only speculate about Reitz's sense of rectitude: might it be that the 'colonial' discourse Hollywood/European cinema has surreptitiously usurped another historical discourse, that of Hitler and Auschwitz? If so, then aggressors and vanquished have changed places in the process. Reitz, by claiming 'our history' is claiming victim status: Hollywood ('the victors') makes a film called *Holocaust*, which 'conquers' the world markets, while the Germans (the vanquished) make films called *Our Hitler* and *Heimat*: the intended irony of these titles pales to an unpost-modern white irony, as one blushes to realise the larger irony that cancels it, as 'Hitler' and 'Heimat' connote once more the very causes of the 'Holocaust'. For his part, Reitz might point to an advertisement for *Holocaust*, carried in *Screen International*, which shows jackboots in formation crushing a bleeding Star of David, while the legend proclaims 'The Guild Marches on: Holocaust – Another International Winner?'

The 'mastering of the past' (*Vergangenheitsbewältigung*) which became such a slogan in Germany in the 1970s and 1980s was in no small measure a reaction to and a rejection of Hollywood doing this mastering for German society and its film-makers, while the focus on Fascism as a film subject was also (for Syberberg and Fassbinder) an effective strategy of address, for it allowed the New German Cinema to discover in Nazism a subject and a genre which could rely on audience interest and foreknowledge the world over, making even difficult films like Syberberg's *Hitler: A Film from Germany* accessible to foreign audiences.

A slightly different version of the colonising paradigm can be found in Werner Herzog, who, after a number of tries, finally achieved his international breakthrough with *Aguirre* (1974), quite explicitly about the dialectics of coloniser and colonised, a topic that the director was to pursue also in his subsequent films, such as *Fitzcarraldo*, *Where the Green Ants Dream* and *Cobra Verde*. What is significant for the series is first of all Klaus Kinski, who plays the lead in three of them, and who is himself a figure in whom the Italian spaghetti Western, the international sexploitation film and the European art film jointly and alternatively do battle with Hollywood. To this rich cinematic intertext, Herzog added pastiche echoes of the Brazilian *cinema novo*, and in particular, of Glauber Rocha's magic-realist neo-colonial fable *Black God White Devil*.

Second, however far Herzog travelled to the four corners of the world, he always sought there his native Bavaria, whether in the Australian bush or in the Amazon jungle, in the High Andes or in Railroad Flats, Wisconsin (*Strozek*). It points to the 'colonised' status of Bavaria within Germany itself, where the resentment of the 'hinterland' against the rest extended even to Munich, traditionally seen as the Hollywood on the Isar ('Schwabylon').

Finally, the films that Herzog made with Kinski encapsulate not only his oeuvre, but define a crucial strand of the New German Cinema generally. Yet in what sense is the Kinski/Herzog persona 'typically' German? Herzog relied in no small measure on a number of Hollywood macho heroes, from Douglas Fairbanks to Errol Flynn (especially in the films of Raoul Walsh), from Robert Aldrich's use of Burt Lancaster (in *Vera Cruz*, *Apache* and *Ulzana's Raid*) to Charlton Heston and Jason Robards (who was to have played Fitzcarraldo, until jungle fever got the better of him).

III   Elective paternities or the 'Oedipal' paradigm

The second complex often goes under the name of the 'fatherless society' (Alexander Mitscherlich),[7] and alludes in the first instance to the particularly intense conflicts between fathers and sons among the first post-war generation, who seem to have grown up either without a father altogether (as was the case for Fassbinder and Herzog), or who found their fathers incapable of feeling remorse for, or even admitting to their part in, the Nazi regime (this father-image seemed prominent among writers, but included the son of perhaps the most notorious of film directors under the Nazi regime: Veit Harlan).

Specifically, the phenomenon of urban terrorism during the 1970s is often seen in terms of the Oedipal paradigm, nowhere more clearly than in the omnibus film *Germany in Autumn*. One can speak of a veritable Oedipalisation of history in this film which for the most part is structured around a double drama of father and son, namely that of Hans Martin Schleyer, kidnapped and eventually killed writing a farewell letter to his son, and that of Manfred Rommel, mayor of Stuttgart, and son of 'Desert Fox' Field Marshall Rommel, who after the defeat at El Alamein, was ordered by Hitler to commit suicide, so that he could be given a hero's funeral. *Germany in Autumn* is the attempt to explain via such complex family bonds the relationship between economic affluence and political violence, but also to find in them a model and metaphor for the peculiar continuities within discontinuity that characterise Germany's history, where in less than fifty years four distinct political regimes violently succeeded each other. Yet as Fassbinder's contribution makes clear, neither the narrative closure provided by a double funeral symmetrically inverted (that of the terrorist 'victim' Schleyer, and that of the 'terrorist' Ensslin) nor the double father–son axis between Rommel and Schleyer could contain the paranoid power of the events at Mogadishu airport and Stammheim prison. The confrontations between Fassbinder and his mother, Fassbinder and his homosexual lover, Fassbinder and his former wife are designed to cast doubts on the narrative closure on which a founding myth of West German democracy was built, namely that (masculine) ideals of self-discipline, responsibility and citizenship had done away with the authoritarian personality. Fassbinder, in giving reign to the 'Fascist within', goes further, in that he seems determined to deny to the representation of history the symmetry of the heterosexual lineage so cautiously and perhaps sentimentally imposed by Kluge and his collaborators in the framing events of *Germany in Autumn*: if 'fathers and sons', Fassbinder seems to say, then let it be absent fathers, homosexual sons and masochistic mothers.

Against this 'national' paternity, Fassbinder and other film-makers invoked a quite different lineage of fathers, father-figures and totemic names: thus, Werner Herzog spoke of himself as 'legitimate German culture' in the footsteps of F.W. Murnau, Fritz Lang and Lotte Eisner, while Wim Wenders alluded to John Ford (in *Alice in the Cities*), to Fritz Lang (in *Kings of the Road*), Sam Fuller and Nicholas Ray (in *The American Friend*, *Lightning over Water* and *The State of Things*).

In what sense, however, could the auteurs of the New German Cinema consider themselves as the 'sons' of the Weimar cinema, or even the grandsons? Was there an 'Oedipus complex' to be resolved between the film-makers and the tradition to which they wish to belong? Were the films of Wenders, Herzog, Fassbinder rewriting the Weimar cinema or Nazi cinema? Perhaps there is a splitting of the father image into good Fathers (the Hollywood émigré directors: Fritz Lang, Douglas Sirk); and bad Fathers (Veit Harlan, Arthur Maria Rabenalt, Wolfgang Liebeneiner)? In a very public gesture, Fassbinder 'adopted' Sirk as his father, Wenders did 'mourning work' for Nicholas Ray, and Helma Sanders-Brahms paid fulsome tribute to Defa-director Wolfgang Staudte.[8] Werner Herzog, in an act of calculated homage, remade *Nosferatu*, and undertook a pilgrimage to the Paris home of Lotte Eisner. But another German director, Niklaus Schilling, was happy to admit to his admiration for Harald Reinl, a representative, if ever there was one, of Papa's Kino,[9] while Syberberg paid tribute to equally ambiguous names: in *Karl May*, for instance, to Helmut Käutner and Kristina Söderbaum, wife of Veit Harlan and star of *Opfergang*, *Die Goldene Stadt* and *Kolberg*.

Faced with the discontinuity of German history at one level, but the continuity of the German film industry at another,[10] New German Cinema invented for itself a new kind of history, a genealogy of elective affinities, not only as a way of understanding the overwhelming presence of the American cinema and American popular culture after 1945, but also in order to bridge the gap opened up by Nazism and reappropriate a good Germany: Socialist or *grand bourgeois*, cinephile and professional, international and popular – in short everything that German film-makers (and their films), at least in the 1950s, were deemed not to be. The directors of the 1970s rewrote German history often enough as film history. Reference back to Weimar cinema, for instance, became considerably more frequent under the impact of the New German Cinema's success in America. It was an ambiguous gesture, inasmuch as, in the case of Fassbinder, national history as film history brought him closer to a fundamental reappraisal of, precisely, the much-despised German cinema of the 1950s, and thus to a new understanding of how intensely the national imaginary of cinemagoing (or, rather, TV-watching) Germany was still identifying with the Ufa-style stars and genres of the 1930s and 1940s. Fassbinder's allusions to Ufa movies as a key element for explaining part of Germany's historical and social continuity across all the political breaks since Weimar are negatively confirmed by such ideological-critical studies as Klaus Kreimeier's of the continuities in personnel,[11] genres and stars, but it is also positively affirmed by empirical studies which indicate that well into the mid-1960s German entertainment films were, year in year out, far more successful at the box-office than Hollywood films and that to this day they still enjoy the highest audience ratings when shown on television.

IV Family romance

As a counter-example within the Oedipal paradigm one might refer to some of the films of the New German Cinema made by women directors, who also focused on the experience of adolescence, though emphatically not in relation to either America or popular culture. It was not movies and chewing gum that became the markers of a specifically historical subjectivity, but the mother's reaction to the heroine's first menstruation, or scenes of family strife, intensified by the recall of embarrassing moments, as if only pain and shame could furnish an affectivity adequate to the representation of history in its discontinuous, intermittent presence (*Germany Pale Mother/Deutschland bleiche Mutter*, Helma Sanders-Brahms, 1979; *Hunger Years/Hungerjahre*, Jutta Brückner, 1979; *Something Hurts/Etwas tut weh*, Recha Jungmann, 1980). Dyadic bonds, such as mother–daughter relations (Margarethe von Trotta, Helma Sanders-Brahms) became the privileged metaphors of understanding not only patriarchal society, but the specifically filmic ways of figuring continuity in discontinuity and the authentic as a property of the image.

The conjunction of painful memory and female masochism has in common with the search for continuity through elective paternity the paradigm of identification – identification with the self as other, the other as self: against the male 'I want to be where/who my father once was,' we find 'I want to see myself from where my mother once saw/punished/embarrassed me.' Identification with parental figures in this mode often focused on figures who were themselves tied to the past by guilt, depression and anxiety: ex-Nazis, cowards of conscience, who survived by self-deception and deceiving their children, or alcoholics and drug-dependents, driving themselves to suicide. *The Marriage of Maria Braun, The German Sisters* (*Die bleierne Zeit*, Margarethe von Trotta, 1981), *Sisters or the Balance of Happiness* (*Schwestern, oder die Balance des Glücks*, Trotta, 1979), *Germany Pale Mother, Malou* (Jeanine Meerapfel, 1981) are some of the titles that offer themselves as attempts to enter into a different relationship with national history.

By contrast, one of the most frequently recurring motifs among male directors is that of the 'wild child': the Kaspar Hauser story. Although it would seem to be particularly prominent in Werner Herzog, his *Kaspar Hauser* is only one aspect of the complex, of which the other is the figure of Prometheus, linked biographically

147

by Herzog himself to his trip to the United States as a young man, when he spent six months working night shifts in the steel mills of Pittsburgh. In Herzog, the dialectic of coloniser and colonised, master and slave, is complemented but also rendered more complex by the dialectic of the underdog and the over-reacher, figurations which can be seen as two sides of the revolt against the father.

V   Hollywood, Fascism and the popular

The inner logic of one part of the New German Cinema during the 1970s and early 1980s was thus to engage with Hollywood and its economic supremacy in very indirect ways.

First, by positing an alternative imaginary – that of German Fascism – in order to contrast it as well as compare it with the imaginary of American popular culture. Against both of them – when viewed as imaginaries of the spectacle, of kitsch, narcissism and sentimentality – one could then oppose the notion of mourning work and melancholia, of self-abandonment and self-flagellation as politically and cinematically more 'authentic'. This was Syberberg's strategy in *Hitler: A Film from Germany,* where Hitler's and Goebbels's obsession with cinema emerges as both Germany's 'answer' to Hollywood and American superpower aspirations, and as Germany's fateful attempt to create an indigenous popular mythology for the age of the mass-media and consumer culture which, had it been 'successful', would have saved Europe from, precisely, Mickey Mouse and chewing-gum.[12]

There is something both dangerously naive and historically absurd in this 'what-if' nostalgia for a better and purer Germany, if only it had developed its own popular culture. But one can also recognise in this picture the populist and anti-modernist mirror image of Adorno and Horkheimer's high-modernist equation of the American culture industry with German Fascism. Latterly, Syberberg has radicalised his anti-American position, by suggesting that West Germany after 1945 lost its cultural identity twice over.[13] Not only did the common people embrace American popular culture as an antidote to having been caught out by the mass-deception of Fascist entertainment, but its intellectual establishment also over-identified with the other: this time, with the Jewish émigrés and their view of German culture. By making Walter Benjamin and T.W. Adorno the good conscience by which to assuage their own guilt, and taking over from them a wholly negative view of romanticism, nationalism and popular culture, German intellectuals, according to Syberberg, had missed an authentic coming to terms with the Nazi past just as fatally as had the masses who uncritically and enthusiastically embraced Hollywood and American popular culture after the war.

VI   Wim Wenders and the no-contest paradigm

A more nuanced and differentiated picture of America can be found in the generation ten years younger than Reitz or Syberberg. Apart from Fassbinder and Herzog, it is above all Wim Wenders in whose work the relation to America and Hollywood is central.

Curiously enough, this relation takes the form in which no effort is spared to ensure that conflict and antagonism are avoided and mitigated. In this sense, Wenders's best-buddy or no-contest paradigm is the answer to or sublation of the two previous paradigms, the colonising and the generational. In another sense, however, it stages them, by taking them into a more hallucinatory, but also more specifically cinematic, register.

The paradigm can itself be broken down into three separate complexes – that of nostalgia, or a controlled regression to childhood, where the hero wants to look at himself from the place where he once stood (*Alice in the Cities, Kings of the Road, Paris Texas, Wings of Desire* and *To the End of the World*). Second, that of narrative versus image, history versus the mirror. This is exemplified by the contrast between detectives and angels in *Wings of Desire*, the stories beyond the nuclear flash in *The State of Things*, and the French gangsters against the New York cowboy in *The American Friend*. In each case, it is as if Wenders (or his hero) needs to know he was in paradise (in the desert, in Los Angeles, an 'Angel'?) in order to want to return to history (i.e. Germany, 'Berlin', the Nazi past). Third, the non-conflictual paradigm also needs to articulate itself via standins or representations of the cinematic apparatus, which has to be mastered in order to reassure oneself of access to the maternal, a process whereby Hollywood connotes no longer the father (as in the totem figures John Ford or Fritz Lang), but the ambiguously outlined but nonetheless absolutely necessary presence of the mother.

Wenders seems the only German film-maker who knows the United States well, so much so that he often plays off one America against another. In his early film reviews, for instance, the good America is either that of Nicholas Ray or of San Francisco rock bands like Creedence Clearwater Revival, while the bad America is 1960s Hollywood movies (and spaghetti Westerns, which Wenders detested even though they were Italy's own peculiar homage to America). When he came to make his own films, Wenders did not protest directly against what he perceived as the oppressive dominance of Hollywood; his early shorts dispensed with words altogether and let rock music speak in their place. It was as if for the young film-maker two languages were inadmissible: Hollywood TV dramaturgy and spoken German, so that films like *Same Player Shoots Again* (note the English title, taken from a pinball machine) appear to be anti-narrative films, where long slow pans and a rock music soundtrack point an accusing finger at that to which it refers negatively: suspense, action, dialogue. Only English lyrics could be trusted (besides Creedence Clearwater Revival, it was The Who, Jimmy Hendrix, The Doors) and only a cinema of *temps morts*, of observation could reply to the hectic business of a certain Hollywood cinema of car chases and smash-ups, where action is, according to Wenders 'always a form of pornography, a raping of objects, of people, of feelings, landscapes, and spectators'. The Hollywood of the 1960s became for Wenders both antagonist and mirror, the implied term of a stance adopted intuitively in order to get away from a claustrophobia which in time Wenders would read historically as part of post-war Germany's malaise, but also politically, as colonisation.

VII Wenders and the US: 'The American Friend'

Rather than dramatised as conflict, the latent antagonism towards colonisation by Hollywood is in Wenders most often figured – apart from the elective paternity of Ray or Fuller – in the form of sibling rivalry or an ambiguous friendship: one thinks of the relation between the character played by Patrick Bauchau in *The State of Things* and his Los Angeles producer, who hides from the Mafia by driving round the freeways all night singing 'Hollywood, Hollywood . . . people never had it so good . . . in Hollywood.'

The most subtle and complex example of this antagonism mediated as sibling rivalry and tenuous friendship, however, is undoubtedly *The American Friend*. The story can easily be read metaphorically, as an explicit disquisition about the relationship between Europe and Hollywood: the frame-maker Jonathan who knows that Ripley, the cowboy in Hamburg, is passing off fake paintings at an auction, is bribed into committing a murder in Paris, but then is rescued by Ripley from the consequences of his act. West Germany, in the figure of Jonathan, at first snubs the advances of America, represented by Dennis Hopper's Ripley: Jonathan responds with high-handed moralism to the glad-handed joviality of the *ingénue* cowboy. But soon the relation between these two characters becomes more ambiguous. Not only is Jonathan's aloof inwardness and self-absorption challenged, and eventually cracked open, by Ripley, but Jonathan also seems to need Ripley to tell him who he is by telling him what he is worth.

At another level, the film is about two kinds of Americas, brought into play and played off against each other. The first America – 'violent America' – is that of crime, of exploitation, shady deals, power struggles, pornography, labyrinthine international conspiracies, a cold and hostile, cruel and aggressive America. In Wenders it is associated with plotting, both in the literal and the literary sense, and it is part of the 'imperialist' or colonising side of the United States. Present in that part of *The American Friend* which can be read metaphorically, it is the hold, economic as well as in terms of brute force, that the US has over Europe and over the film industry in particular. Giving, so to speak, the image of superpower America seen from outside, Wenders needs, in order to represent it, a labyrinthine, paranoid plot driven by a complex narration: precisely a thriller story.

Within this world, there is, however, another America, that of Ripley's friendship, whose rhythm and logic do not follow the Chinese-box plot characterising the paranoid subject. Instead, this story progresses by crisscrossing, by paths converging and overlapping and separating again, without ever joining and merging. It is a constellation also to be found in the early Wenders films, notably in *Alice in the Cities*, *Wrong Move* and *Kings of the Road*, where it is the very epitome of narrative progression when structured by man/man or man/child relationships, beautifully and succinctly conveyed by the final sequences of *Kings of the Road* when rail and road, train and truck weave in and out of each other's path. In *The American Friend*, this is the world of equality, of exchange rather than exploitation. Instead of the bribes that Minot (the Paris gangster) makes, the gifts that Ripley and Jonathan make each other (inextricably linking sexuality with visual representation, since these are gadgets showing mainly 'naughty' pictures) connote partnership rather than rivalry, co-operation rather than competition. The two moments – the exploitative and the egalitarian – are carefully interwoven and contrasted in *The American Friend*, because they signify the America of people-oriented behaviour, of an externality and a casualness which do not imply a disregard for life, but on the contrary allow a solitary self to experience the other, learn from the other, tolerate the other in a difference generated from anonymity itself. While both the Mafia's America and Ripley's may ultimately be corrupting, the latter's non-confrontational cool appears as a kind of utopia, where (German) intensity and inwardness can be exchanged for the lightness of touch and easy-going charm, where a mutual identification takes place without creating neurotic dependency. Contact rather than conflict, identity lived and renewed by inter-change rather than by territorial claims seems to be the goal. Yet it clearly is a world that excludes women. In working this out, *The American Friend* plays through all the possibilities that this relationship could take, including its negative connotations, such as the figure of the Double and the vampire – the former as the image of one's own death, the latter as the appropriate figuration of colonisa-tion, one in which the victim seeks out the vampire, to find in him the image of his own desire.

Why does Jonathan (who shares his name with the hero of both Bram Stoker's *Dracula* and Murnau's *Nosferatu*) collude so readily, why is he tempted at all? What has this Hamburg Faust to gain from his New York Mephisto? In the film, the answer once more relates to the problematic status of (German) inwardness to (American) surface: Jonathan's cultural superiority displayed at the auction is defensive, repressing the knowledge of its own precariousness. Hence it is apt that illness should be the central metaphor of Jonathan's condition: what he represses within him makes him vulnerable. The blood disease, inverting the attraction of the vampire's bite, relates to Jonathan's haughty pride in his workmanship, the illusion of thinking himself above the implications of his trade of frame-making, namely his own role in the commodification of painting, and more generally, in the process where art has become a forgery of values. To this disavowal, Ripley holds up a mirror, and tempts Jonathan with the hidden question: what am I really worth, what price can I put on my life, what is the material equivalent of my spiritual pretensions, my rarefied existence: in short, what is my European culture worth? It is the recognition that such culture and refinement as Jonathan displays in his early dealings with Ripley may be a sham, hollow, already decayed, part of a disease, incurable, terminal, which folds the film in upon itself in the final scenes.

Wenders's America is thus characterised by a double signification: as image for the reality of the self, and as the reality of that image. Caught up in the dialectic of subject and object, self and other, inside and outside, subjectivity can only be tolerated as image. But this existence as image is itself doubly coded: Wenders, like Handke and others, categorically refuses the polarity involved in the Oedipal father–son opposition, on which the old inner–outer divide, as well as the sub-ject–object divisions, were modelled. In this sense, it is the two-dimensionality of the image, its function as mirror, which allows for such a perfect elision of the staging of Oedipal conflicts in Wenders's films. At the same time, such elision pro-duces its own reversal: vision and the 'image' are associated, quite logically in a world still dominated by Oedipal relationships, with either pre-Oedipal regression or death. The fascination with the America of Dennis Hopper (as Ripley but also as *Easy Rider*), and the anxiety over 'plotting' as that other side of America, find their common denominator in the reinscription and retranslation of (the image of) 'America' into the means of its mechanical reproduction. Hence the two sides of Hollywood, capitalist hell and life-saving heaven, the latter associated with a newly regained immediacy and primary satisfaction: the innocence which joins, in West Germany's history, GI-America and childhood. America has colonised, even more than the unconscious, the experience of childhood, through Wrigley's chewing-gum and Disney cartoons, through Saturday matinees at the movies and rock 'n' roll from the American Forces Network. These experiences in turn are inseparable from juke-boxes and slot-machines, movie theatres and record-players: gadgets which represent primary pleasure by metonymy.

VIII   America and childhood: in search of the mother

In this respect, America figures in Wenders as neither the son nor the father, but as the image of the maternal. For America is the always re-remembered satisfaction of the image, whose status as memory is safeguarded by access to the means of mechanical reproduction, comparable to the oral satisfaction of the maternal, whose capacity to give pleasure is, however, also associated with the anxiety of separation and loss. In Germany the site of the maternal is inaccessible without encountering the father (cf. in *Kings of the Road* where Hans Zischler's visit to his hometown becomes a settling of scores while his father is asleep), unless the maternal is already identified with Hollywood or the image (as is the case with the character in *Kings of the Road* played by Rüdiger Vogler, who also visits his childhood home in order to find, under the stairs, a rusty movie can full of old comics, a scene which Wenders borrowed from one in Nicholas Ray's *The Lusty Men*). Rüdiger Vogler here puts himself in the place of himself as child in just the same way that Wenders puts himself in the place of Nick Ray, when Nick Ray was young and 'lusty', making a movie with Robert Mitchum. Putting yourself in the place where someone else has once been, and thus constructing an other (a structure of temporal–spatial displacement) in order to come to terms with loss, or with the loss of the Other, this is thus a special, and cinematically charged case, of nostalgia, while it is also an act of mourning for a German childhood that might never have been (seeing how Wenders's autobiographical remarks contradict such an idyll as that of the maternal home in the middle of the Rhine, just beneath the Lorelei): the fantasy of a foundling, like Moses in the bulrushes, or Kaspar Hauser in his privy, which takes us back to the wild child and the prodigal son, associated as we have seen with all three paradigms.

The motif of the man who has to reinvent himself as the little boy lost is both repeated and deconstructed in Wenders's most radical film about America, *Paris Texas*. It is, first of all, far and away Wenders's most complex example of how an entire family turns each other into projections and fantasy figures, de-realising each other until they are no more than products of each other's desires. The father, Travis, has to make himself father by playing through the Oedipal scenario in reverse, retroactively: first by learning to be the double of his son (imitating his son: at school, the swap of boots, the brother motif), then by learning to 'be' a father in front of the mirror and the approving gaze of the Spanish maid, and finally, by initiating a journey and an adventure where both father and son are looking for the mother. When she is finally found – represented as pure product and construct of a number of desiring narratives – the family is not reunited, but the father puts the son in the lover's place, in order to watch himself through the son, returning to the mother: in other words, closure and resolution of the story are attained by elaborate temporal–spatial shifts and displacements, deferrals in time and space through which the Oedipal scenario is not so much lived as reconstructed and re-enacted in the form of an enabling fiction. The film thus dramatises in its very narrative the processes of identification, projection, repression of the Other by doubling the image of the self. It is no longer a matter of the son constructing himself in the image of the father, but the father constructing himself in the image of the son.

From the story that Travis and Jane are telling each other, it is clear that at the core of the film is an unresolved incest fantasy (Travis did not want to be separate from Jane, he refuses the Oedipal order of work, of being responsible and the provider, of being adult, male and father). This fantasy is resolved by being staged, imaged and retold. In the end the family exists purely in the register of the look and specularity: mother and son united under the eye of the father who would like to be in the place where the son is. *Paris Texas*, ostensibly a film about a place, a time and the self (literally the hero's origin, the place where he was conceived) is thus, as all Wenders's movies, a film about remembering, forgetting and repressing, but played out across the image, the photo, the fantasy produced by narrative. Amnesia and ubiquity of images are now tied to the family as impossible unit, which can only survive as an imaginary family.

IX America: Europe's past?

The identity of the New German Cinema, I have been arguing, was, during the brief period it was experienced as such, founded on a series of fantasies, all of which are displaced versions of antagonism and competition, Oedipal rivalry and over-identification with and around Hollywood: perverse in Syberberg, disingenuous in Reitz, geographically dislocated in Herzog, disarmingly devious in Fassbinder, and filial–fraternal in Wenders.

At the same time, these fantasies are eminently readable: first, against a very traditional German history in which America figures as the screen of self-projection and self-alienation ('you have to go away in order to come home' as Luis Trenker's old schoolteacher puts it in *The Prodigal Son*).[14] But they can also be read as an often very precise account of an act of self-creation, by a national cinema that, because it disavows its own popular cinema ('Papa's Kino' of the 1950s and the Ufa genres of the 1940s) has to go to Hollywood to legitimate itself. In the course of this, it stages both a revolt and a submission, thus rewriting dependency into a Kaspar Hauser foundling story and into the return of the prodigal son (cf. the opening scene and repeated motif in Reitz's *Heimat*): both together are Germany's own myth of an 'independent' and 'national' cinema, in a movie business which is global and interdependent or not at all.

This paradox is implicit in Wenders, giving rise not only to a restless wandering career, but to a series of reveries about the destruction of the past as memory and trauma, and its transformation into scenario and spectacle: witness the narrative progress of the hero in *To the End of the World* who steals from the US Navy an imaging device they had stolen from his father, and with which he records for his mother, who is blind, images that can be directly transmitted to her brain. Here, the preconditions for escaping Oedipal subjectivity as conceived from the father are a double Promethean act of defiance, undertaken in order to make way for the reconstruction of a pre-Oedipal state, from the perspective of the son, via fantasies of turning oneself into images and return thus to the mother. Yet because these have become technological fantasies, they are also post-Oedipal, where the past is resurrected as spectacle through the machines of sound and vision: a definition of nostalgia as retrospective narcissism, in which the Other is appropriated not by an act of confrontation or submission to it, but by acts of rewriting, reproduction, simulation. The fiction sets up an endless play of separation and difference, of substitution and deferral, which sustains itself by the simultaneous coexistence of several spaces and time frames: a new geometry of representation by which the old rivalry between Hollywood and Europe might be laid to rest (in Australia ...).

Thus, Wenders can epitomise a typically European attitude, looking to America as the verification or corroboration of his insights into cinema and film-making, and across the movie business, his insights into corporate capitalism or the military-industrial complex, and how a post-industrial 'information' society will shape human relations. At the same time, Americans may want to mirror their own disquiet about US capitalism and its penetration of societies on a global scale, in the image that Europeans like Wenders project of it out of their own cultural and historical situation. To the American experience of American society as at once natural and universal corresponds a European sense of Europe's own difference compared to America's Otherness, a conjunction which in turn allows Americans to experience themselves as different across the markers of European cultural specificity. On the other hand, America as the Other returns to Europeans as their own mirror, in a displacement that is both temporal and geographical, where America is indeed, as Max Frisch has hinted, Europe's future as well as its past.

While Wenders continues a tormented love–hate relationship, binding him to the America within and without, the New German Cinema has transformed its encounter with imaginary America into an increasingly introspective and retrospective look at the old and new Germany within and without; alternatively, it abandoned the figurations altogether in favour of a turn to action, with directors like Wolfgang Petersen (*In the Line of Fire, Outbreak*) and Volker Schlöndorff (*The Handmaiden's Tale, Homo Faber*) making films in North America for global commercial and art house audiences. Although the reasons for these shifts (and the decline of film-making in Germany) are doubtless more complex,[15] it would seem that for much of the 1970s and 1980s it was precisely this multiply figured, projected and introjected 'Hollywood' which gave the New German Cinema its identity, if not to itself, then to its international audiences.

Notes

1 This chapter incorporates passages previously published in T. Elsaesser, 'The New German Cinema's Historical Imaginary', in B. Murray and C. Wickham (eds), *Framing the Past* (Carbondale: Southern Illinois University Press, 1992). A slightly longer version can be found in D. Ellwood and R. Kroes (eds), *Hollywood and Europe* (Amsterdam: VU Amsterdam, 1994).

2 Max Frisch, *Stichworte* (Frankfurt: Suhrkamp, 1975), pp. 80–1.

3 Arthur Brauner, Germany's leading post-war producer, used to point out that the *Heimat* films were so successful for his company because he knew exactly how much each film would make at the box-office. There was thus no point in investing 'even a single penny more' either in the writing and directing, or the locations and production values: he had a product, he knew its market, and that was that. See Claudia Dillmann-Kühn, *Arthur Brauner und die CCC* (Frankfurt-am-Main: Filmmuseum, 1990).

4 An instructive example is the story of the German distribution company Gloria (headed by the legendary Ilse Kubaschewski) which during the 1950s and early 1960s had become prosperous by producing the films it knew it could distribute successfully; Gloria eventually lost out to the Americans in the struggle for the West German distribution and exhibition sector.

5 Elie Wiesel, 'Trivializing the Holocaust: Semi-Fact and Semi-Fiction', *New York Times*, 16 April 1978.

6 Edgar Reitz, 'Arbeiten an unseren Erinnerungen', *medium* vol. 5 no. 79, May 1979, pp. 21–2.

7 See T. Elsaesser, *New German Cinema: A History* (London: Macmillan, 1990), pp. 239–43.

8 See R.W. Fassbinder, 'Six Films by Douglas Sirk', in J. Halliday and L. Mulvey (eds), *Douglas Sirk* (Edinburgh: Edinburgh Film Festival, 1971), pp. 95–107.

9 Quoted in Andreas Meyer, 'Auf dem Weg zum Staatsfilm?', *medium*, November 1977, p. 15.

10 One only needs to recall the notorious fact that virtually the entire film establishment of the Federal Republic in the 1950s and 1960s had played an active role in the Nazi film industry.

11 See Klaus Kreimeier, *Kino und Filmindustrie in der BRD: Ideologieproduktion und Klassenwirklichkeit nach 1945* (Kronberg: Scriptor, 1973), pp. 53–67.

12 See 'The Syberberg Statement: We Live in a Dead Land' (text of a television interview), reprinted in *Framework* no. 6, Autumn 1977, pp. 12–15.

13 See in this context also Eric L. Santner, 'The Trouble with Hitler: Postwar German Aesthetics and the Legacy of Fascism', *New German Critique* no. 44, 1992.

14 For Luis Trenker, see Eric Rentschler, 'How American is It: The US as Image and Imaginary in German Film', p. 609.

15 See Elsaesser, *New German Cinema*, pp. 309–23.

Notes on contributors

Tino Balio is chair of the Department of Communication Arts at the University of Wisconsin-Madison and the acting director of the Wisconsin Center for Film and Theater Research. A specialist in the history of the American film industry, he is the author of numerous articles and books, among them *Hollywood in the Age of Television* (1990) and *Grand Design: Hollywood as a Modern Business Enterprise, 1930–1939* (1993).

Janet Bergstrom teaches film history and theory at UCLA. She was a founding editor of *Camera Obscura*, and she has published many essays on French and German émigré film directors. She is the author of *Like a Road Movie: Chantal Akerman's Nomadic Cinema*, and the editor of *Cinema and Psychoanalysis, Parallel Histories*.

Victoria de Grazia lives in New York City where she is professor of history at Columbia University. In addition to her writing on Italian fascism, *The Organization of Consent* (1981) and *How Fascism Ruled Women* (1992), she recently published *The Sex of Things: Gender and Consumption in Historical Perspective* (1996) and is completing a book called *Market Empire: America in Europe, 1920–1970*.

Thomas Elsaesser is professor of film and television studies at the University of Amsterdam. Among his publications are *New German Cinema* (1989), *Early Cinema: Space Frame Narrative* (1990), *A Second Life* (1996) and *Fassbinder's Germany* (1996).

Ian Jarvie is professor of philosophy at York University, Ontario. His books include *Movies and Society* (1970), *Window on Hong Kong* (1977), *Movies as Social Criticism* (1978), *Philosophy of Film* (1987), *Hollywood's Overseas Campaign* (1992) and *Children and the Movies* (1996). He is working on *Mass Media Pornography*.

Jean-Pierre Jeancolas, a former teacher of history and film history, is a film critic for *Positif* and *Politis*. He is the author of several books about French cinema and one about Hungarian cinema. He was president of the French Association for Research in Film History from 1992 to 1996, and is currently working on the institutions and politics of French cinema in the post-war period.

Richard Maltby is head of screen studies at the Flinders University of South Australia. He is the author of *Hollywood Cinema: An Introduction* and *Harmless*

Entertainment: Hollywood and the Ideology of Consensus. He is currently co-editing a collection of essays on cinematic relations between Europe and America, entitled *'Film Europe' and 'Film America': Cinema, Commerce and Cultural Exchange, 1920–1940.*

Laura Mulvey is postgraduate programme director at the British Film Institute. Her most recent books are *Fetishism and Curiosity* and the BFI Film Classic on *Citizen Kane.*

Geoffrey Nowell-Smith is senior lecturer in film studies at Sheffield Hallam University and the author of the BFI Film Classic on *L'avventura.*

Steven Ricci is head of research for the UCLA Film and Television Archive. He directs the Archive's educational initiatives including conferences, publications and new media applications. Ricci is author and producer of two recent CD-ROMs which deal with the adaptation of rare archival materials: *Executive Order 9066: The Incarceration of Japanese Americans during World War II* and *Tour Historic Los Angeles: Where Hollywood and the City Meet.* As media historian, his work concentrates on Italian cinema history and on the relationship between new technologies and cinematic expression. He is a multiple term member of the executive board of the International Federation of Film Archives.

Christopher Wagstaff is senior lecturer in Italian studies at the University of Reading. He has published articles on Italian cinema and literature and is joint editor, with Christopher Duggan, of *Italy in the Cold War: Politics, Culture and Society 1948–58.*

Peter Wollen is professor of film studies at UCLA. *Signs and Meaning in the Cinema* was reissued in an expanded edition in 1998.

Index

161